Cinema and Machine Vision

Cinema and Machine Vision

Vision

Artificial Intelligence, Aesthetics and Spectatorship

Daniel Chávez Heras

EDINBURGH
University Press

Edinburgh University Press is one of the leading university presses in the UK. We publish academic books and journals in our selected subject areas across the humanities and social sciences, combining cutting-edge scholarship with high editorial and production values to produce academic works of lasting importance. For more information visit our website: edinburghuniversitypress.com

© Daniel Chávez Heras, 2024

Grateful acknowledgement is made to the sources listed in the List of Illustrations for permission to reproduce material previously published elsewhere. Every effort has been made to trace the copyright holders, but if any have been inadvertently overlooked, the publisher will be pleased to make the necessary arrangements at the first opportunity.

Edinburgh University Press Ltd
13 Infirmary Street
Edinburgh EH1 1LT

Cover image: This is a visualisation of a large collection of moving images made by extracting and compressing colour information from television clips from different decades, from the inner ring that corresponds to the black and white 1930s, to the outer ring that is from the 1990s. To learn more about the process for making this image, visit: https://garden.movingpixel.net/public_notes/Tools/Movie-Barcodes/

Typeset in 11/13pt Ehrhardt
by Cheshire Typesetting Ltd, Cuddington, Cheshire and
printed and bound by CPI Group (UK) Ltd, Croydon, CR0 4YY

A CIP record for this book is available from the British Library

ISBN 978 1 3995 1471 2 (hardback)
ISBN 978 1 3995 1473 6 (webready PDF)
ISBN 978 1 3995 1474 3 (epub)

The right of Daniel Chávez Heras to be identified as the author of this work has been asserted in accordance with the Copyright, Designs and Patents Act 1988, and the Copyright and Related Rights Regulations 2003 (SI No. 2498).

Contents

List of Illustrations	vi
Acknowledgements	viii
Introduction	1

Part I Data-Images: Philosophy of Photography and Technologies of Vision

1. Between Archive and Dataset	25
2. Inductive Vision	38
3. Machine Learning and the Philosophy of Photography	60

Part II Pixels in Motion: The Calculation of Cinematic Time

4. Statistical Distance and Emotional Closeness in Film Style	87
5. Computational Analysis of Continuity Editing	99
6. Duration, Motion, and Pixels	114

Part III AI and Criticism: Aesthetics, Formats, and Interactions

7. Algorithmic Films as Data Analysis	131
8. Aesthetic Judgements and Meaningful Dissensus	145
9. AI as Media	161
Conclusion: Machines Made of Images	175
References	183
Index	202

Illustrations

Figures

1.1 'Quantification of human-made products' Excerpt from 'Anatomy of an AI System: The Amazon Echo as an anatomical map of human labor, data and planetary resources' by Kate Crawford and Vladan Joler. https://anatomyof.ai — 31

2.1 Example of object detection on BBC archive footage — 39

2.2 Detected: 'A white shirt on a man' — 40

2.3 Detected: 'The plane is flying' — 40

2.4 Detected: 'Black and silver train' — 41

2.5 Detected: 'A large window' — 41

2.6 Misdetected: 'Man with a hat' — 42

2.7 Misdetected: 'Reflection of a mirror' — 42

2.8 Misdetected: 'Woman holding a cell phone' — 43

2.9 Misdetected: 'Hand holding a banana' — 43

2.10 Misdetected: 'Man wearing a red shirt' — 44

2.11 Variations of 'Man is wearing a shirt' — 47

2.12 One Million geo-tagged photos with Creative Commons licences. CC BY-ND 2.0 David Shamma — 51

2.13 DenseCap detection of 'Elephant with a black and white shirt' — 53

2.14 MS-COCO segmentation and labelling example. Source: http://cocodataset.org/#explore?id=206876 — 54

3.1 Double Gauss lens designs 1978–2010. CC BY-SA 3.0 Paul Chin. — 66

3.2 Polygonal shapes of bokeh are the result of the 8-bladed aperture diaphragm in this 85mm lens at f/1.8. CC BY-SA 3.0 JWCreations. — 68

3.3 6mm lens used in Yorgos Lanthimos, *The Favourite* (2018) — 69

3.4 Camera manufacturers of images in the Visual Genome — 75

3.5 Distribution of apertures in images from the Visual Genome — 76

3.6 Focal length categories in images from the Visual Genome — 76

3.7 Combined aperture, focal length and exposure of images in the Visual Genome — 77

ILLUSTRATIONS vii

3.8 Batch of four samples of inputs and labels 78
3.9 15-layer Convolutional neural network architecture 78
3.10 The photo on the left was taken with a mobile phone (28mm); photo on the right with a DSLR (340mm) 79
3.11 Predicted class of (the whole) image on the left using our focal lens classifier prototype. Predicted label of (a region) of the image on the right in MbM 80
4.1 Shot-reverse shot in *The Silence of the Lambs* (1991) 93
4.2 Demme close-up of Anthony Hopkins in *The Silence of the Lambs* (1991) 94
4.3 Three different aspect ratios in *The Grand Budapest Hotel* (1.37:1, 1.85:1, 2.35:1) 96
5.1 Time continuity visualisation in *The Godfather*'s baptism sequence 108
5.2 Space continuity visualisation in *The Godfather*'s baptism sequence 109
6.1 Complex editing in *Paprika* (2006) 119
6.2 Flying pelican captured in motion by Étienne-Jules Marey c.1882 123
6.3 Top: synthetically generated dolly zoom in *Jaws* (1975). Bottom: mechanically/optically generated dolly zoom 125
9.1 Text and images in shared vector space 169
9.2 Frame from *Blade Runner 2049* (2017) 171
9.3 Image synthesised using the predicted prompt in *Stable Diffusion* v1.5 171

Tables

Table 1.1	*Made by Machine* – project breakdown	35
Table 3.1	Example of EXIF tags extracted	73
Table 3.2	Overview of the extraction results	74
Table 3.3	First five observations of my working data frame, shaped 68,085 rows × 5 columns	74
Table 5.1	Burch's 5 × 3 matrix, as per Frierson	103
Table 5.2	Shot segmentation results	105
Table 5.3	Cinemetrics-like breakdown analysis	105
Table 5.4	'Baptism of Fire' shot by shot fragment from *The Godfather*	106
Table 5.5	'Baptism of Fire' sequence from *The Godfather*, annotated with Burch's continuity matrix	107

Acknowledgements

The following colleagues and friends have supported my work and in one way or another contributed to this book: Tobias Blanke, Catherine Grant, Geoff Cox, Sarah Atkinson, Elisa Oreglia, Mercedes Bunz, Joanna Zylinska, Alasdair Milne, Eva Jäger, Jonathan Gray, Nicolas Malevé, Tim Cowlishaw, George Wright, Mila Oiva, Nanne van Noord, Martin Zeilinger, Stephen McConnachie, Jake Berger, Belén Vidal, Michele Pierson, Richard Dyer, Christian Ulrik Andersen, Lotte Philipsen, Kathrin Maurer, Jakub Fiala, Kate Devlin, James Smithies, Graeme Earl, Mark Coté, Daniel Nemenyi, Nageela Yusuf, Claudia Aradau, Joel McKim, Thomas Scherer, Jasper Stratil, Anne Alexander, Alan Blackwell, Marco Braghieri, Virginia Kuhn.

I would also like to thank the organisers and participants of two events that shaped my thinking for this book: *Ways of Machine Seeing* (University of Cambridge, 2017) and *Aesthetics of Machine Vision* (University of Southern Denmark, 2022). My gratitude goes as well to Gillian Leslie and Sam Johnson from Edinburgh University Press, for all their hard work and professionalism in making this book a reality.

Finally, I owe so much to the love of my partner, Pilar, whose quiet patience and unrelenting faith kept me going when the hours grew long. I learn every day from her courage, intelligence, and kindness. And of course, none of this would have been possible without the support of my family, my sister Anaclara, and my parents, Jesus and Leticia, for a lifetime of honest work, selfless affection, and thoughtful direction.

Introduction

What are films made of? A short answer is that they are made of images; sequences of shots and frames, which in their digital form are made of millions of pixels. A more comprehensive answer would be that they are made of meanings; expressions, representations, and emotions, that are elicited by these images and arise as inter-subjective experiences when films enter into contact with their audiences. Films are moving images that move us; they are in this way moving in two senses: as technical artefacts in and of motion, and as the meanings and affects that these images structure in their viewers. In the artefactual sense, we can easily point to the series of material transformations that film underwent over the past few decades, from celluloid reels to digital video and data streams. In the meaningful sense, we tend to treat films as aesthetic objects; heaps of pixels that when put together in certain ways, can move our minds and spirits beyond what their technical trappings appear to afford.

In a version of the *sorites* paradox, we could ask: at what point and under which conditions does a heap of moving pixels become a moving image, moreover, an image that moves us? Where exactly does this transition occur, and how can we see or understand this transformation? Today we can access every pixel of every frame of *Tokio Story* (1953), manipulate them and analyse these digital moving images as data using a variety of increasingly complex computational techniques. Would this shed light on what makes Ozu's masterpiece aesthetically relevant, and still widely discussed seventy years after it was made? If the answer is no, then we need to ask why – why do we seem to know less and not more about what makes these moving images charged with aesthetic powers when we analyse them as data? If the answer is yes, we need to ask how – how can we teach computers to *watch* films; how can these machines be aesthetically sensitive to human meanings and emotions. Both the apologist and the sceptic need to contend with the vertigo of a gap that such a computational gaze opens before them.

In this book I explore the depths of this gap and find in there a common ground from where to imagine new ways of seeing through machines. My central argument is that machine vision puts pressure on existing epistemic modalities, as it can be at once analytical and generative; a way of apprehending the visual world that lies along a path between creative and scientific computing. To find this trail, we first need a wider view that orients us in a world of images seen for us, but not directly by us, and an understanding of the conditions that enabled the computational analysis and production of moving images under these new technical regimes.

In the last two decades, the flow of digital video has intensified more than any other form of cultural production. According to industry reports, approximately 80 per cent of all internet traffic was digital video in 2023; five million years of it, circulating every month through the capillary structures of the internet. And this trend is expected to continue as we move to faster networks, ultra-high-definition devices, and new data-hungry applications (CISCO, 2020, 2019). Yet, most of these images will never be seen directly by humans. Instead, these flows of digital video are regulated through emerging forms of computation, instantiated as a vast network of interconnected nodes, gateways and devices: the sensory and metabolic organs of new forms of distributed visuality. At the centre of these emerging visual regimes is Artificial Intelligence (AI), a family of technologies now widely deployed in networked societies and already regulating what can be seen, when and by whom. As AI is woven into the fabric of society and becomes a critical part of social and cultural infrastructure, it is internalised as a modality of vision, one that entails a reimagined relation between the seeable and the knowable.

One of the questions that emerges in this context is about the kind of relation we have and can have with images under an algorithmic governance of the visual. As mentioned earlier, films and television are now mostly created and consumed as digital objects. But not only are moving images digital, their whole production-consumption ecosystem has become *datafied* (Schäfer and Es, 2017; van Dijck, 2014). Films are born as data, flow online as data, are consumed as data services, and can be studied as data. As data artefacts, they can also be mobilised computationally, and become the subject and object of emerging types of algorithmic practices, increasingly under the logic of AI systems. In the wake of these technologies, film and media scholars must now confront a new version of an old question: what is cinema (in the age of AI)? What is the future of the cinematic image under the gaze of machine vision? And more tantalising still, what is to become of its past?

INTRODUCTION

Initially, it might seem counter-intuitive that we would want to out-source some of our most pleasurable watching to machines. Films, and more recently also television, occupy a privileged position in contemporary popular culture and are one of the most sophisticated forms of human expression; they are reified, have their own exhibition buildings, festivals, and award circuits; they can inspire rapturous acclaim or hostile vitriol. Not all of this can be said of footage from a dashboard camera, CCTV, or a Zoom call. Yet, the membranes between all these images are more and more porous, and the styles and convention of broader computational culture are feeding back into cinematic culture, just as cinematic culture continues to exert its influence in digital culture, online platforms, and gaming worlds. Computing already mediates our relationship with visual culture in significant ways, films and television included; what is rapidly changing under the aegis of AI is the nature of this mediation.

Many of us know, for example, that what we watch on screen and call a film comes to us as a digital video file. We might not often think about it or get to witness it directly, but intuitively we are aware that the vehicle for this video file is some form of digital storage and transport. Except for a few diehard celluloid fans, it is safe to say that most filmmakers and their audiences have embraced digital storage and transmission of moving images. What is far less apparent however is that these video files and data streams can also be, and indeed are being, activated as computational artefacts, and that our relation with the images we love so dearly and so direly is a fundamental part of this activation: our collective viewing is now a key part of the machinery; the hopes, fears, and desires elicited by these moving images are instrumental to the larger socio-technical assemblages of AI because they can be quantified, extracted, and mobilised as data.

Cinema and Machine Vision explores the ways in which humans and machines are imbricated in this radical re-imagination of the visual through the paradigmatic case of films and television that are said to be 'seen by machine'. The notion of teaching computers to watch films opens a series of useful aesthetic problems in film and media scholarship. On the one hand, films are highly structured, they are made of patterns of light in motion produced according to well established norms and conventions; the vast majority are now 'born digital', they are digitally manipulated and distributed through digital networks. In principle, this ought to make films and television prime candidates to be studied using computational methods. Yet, as I noted earlier, these moving images and the complex relations they hold with their audiences have so far proven to be surprisingly resistant to quantitative approaches and computational analyses. Compared to other areas in the arts and sciences, film and media scholarship has been quick in recognising the ontological displacements in digital imagery, but relatively slow in embracing computational epistemologies and their methods, some of which are now quite common even in the study of other types of cultural production such as literature and even art history.

Several reasons can be offered to explain the slow adoption of these methods in film scholarship, including the complexities of a medium that combines sound, images and language in sophisticated ways, and the data-intensive qualities of digital video as the vehicle for these multi-modal cultural media objects. Although there is some truth in these reasons, my contention is that the resistance to computing in film scholarship is symptomatic of a deeper epistemic mistrust in quantifying moving images in isolation of how they are viewed, interpreted, and discussed. It is this omission that I believe has kept moving images from being studied computationally more widely. But this is changing rapidly: the hard distinction between numbers and images that was initially eroded through mass adoption of digital video is now being completely dismantled through the flattening effects of AI and its associational powers. Not only is it possible to capture at least some of this viewing and interpretation of images computationally, but it is also possible to store it and deploy it elsewhere, as if it was a disembodied computational gaze.

This ability to summon a computational gaze in ways that are seemingly independent from any individual viewer is empowering when patterns can be found across large collections of digital objects, much in the vein of Lev Manovich's *Cultural Analytics* (2009, 2020) or Franco Moretti's *Distant Reading* (2013). Just like natural language processing allowed for the distant reading of texts, so too is computer vision being said to enable distant viewing of films, allowing critics a way to step back from the piecemeal analysis of individual films, and to gain new perspectives at the level of large archives and collections. However, these approaches often conflate ontology with history, inheriting many of the intellectual assumptions of industrial big data analytics and its rational illusions of distance and objectivity. In the case of using computer vision methods for the distant viewing of films, a key question that haunts these practices is where does this computational gaze comes from, whose vision is being encoded, and how; who are the subjects of machine vision, and where can we locate exactly their new subjectivities?

To engage the cinematic image not only with, but *through* computers, we must ask not only how to use computers to find patterns in films, but how to interrogate the regimes of visibility brought about by computational technologies; what can and cannot become visible and knowable

INTRODUCTION 5

through AI technologies. As some of the most mystifying moving images in visual culture today, films and television, their history, theory, and criticism, remain key referents in this research programme: their conceptual tools are necessary to understand how (and why) teach computers to watch films and television, and to locate what exactly machines are said to be 'seeing' for us. The approach I present in this book is not in opposition to cultural analytics or distant reading of images, but complementary to them, hopefully lending epistemic depth to these practices by informing the way they construct moving images as an object of study and its critics as computational subjects.

While it is often remarked that there is unprecedented access to the overflow of moving images circulating online and an increasing availability of ever-improving algorithmic methods with which to process them, my contention in this book is that the contemporary study of moving images needs an as yet incomplete computational theory of spectatorship. Vast as this project is, my aim in what follows is to make progress towards such a theory. Through a series of case studies and computational experiments, I identify key aesthetic and epistemic assumptions embodied in the practice of machine-seeing films and television, map these assumptions onto the wider historical context of technologies of vision, and propose novel critical computational practices for moving image research under a modified division of labour between critics and machines. My goal with this is to go beyond questions of pattern-finding and ask what *ought* to be seen in the age of AI; what concepts are needed in order to cast in a computational space a sense of the aesthetic, alethic, and the political dimensions of imagery, and what are the critical practices required to re-create these concepts and these meanings under an algorithmic governance of vision. These are the hard questions posed in *Machine Vision*, questions that beg for a form of radical reciprocity between aesthetics and computation and the forms of knowledge and pleasure they can jointly enable.

Applied Visionics

The form of reciprocity described above requires an interdisciplinary outlook, which often means standing at a junction where several bodies of knowledge, theories, and methods converge, but without necessarily following them to their originally intended destinations. This is an increasingly busy junction, and to get our bearings one of the most obvious entry points is Paul Virilio's *Vision Machine* (1994). Writing in the mid-1990s, Virilio glimpses the contours of machine vision as a technology deployed in society at large. In the near future, he argues, there are going to be machines capable of 'completely interpreting the visual field', cameras connected to computers that will pave the way for 'the automation of perception, for the innovation of artificial vision, delegating the analysis of objective reality to a machine' (p. 59). More importantly, he also anticipated some of the vexing consequences of 'splitting the viewpoint' with and among machines, and of the possible effects of this disembodied 'sightless vision'. The statistical optics of the computer, he claimed, would render 'rational illusions' that distort knowledge and power relations (p. 75).

> If seeing is in fact foreseeing, no wonder forecasting has recently become an industry in its own right, with the rapid rise of professional simulation and company projections, and ultimately, hypothetically, the advent of 'vision machines' designed to see and foresee in our place (p. 61)

Although Virilio briefly mentions the *perceptron* (Rosenblatt, 1957), which was an early type of computing system designed to recognise images automatically, he does not elaborate further on what its possible distortions of knowledge might be, nor does he give any more details or technical specifications on what he calls 'the visual thought of the computer'. For him, these vision machines were still very much hypothetical, useful as thought experiments to speculate about a probable future.

In parallel to his speculations, the groundwork for what he called *visionics* had in fact been in development since the 1960s as a sub-field of AI known simply as 'computer vision'. Among some of the early technical work in this area was Lawrence G. Roberts' PhD thesis entitled 'Machine Perception of Three-Dimensional Solids" (1963), and the Summer of Vision Project at MIT, in which Seymour Papert tasked students to create a computer system that described what it saw. The project started in July 1966 with simple objects like balls, bricks, and cylinders, and was meant to progressively move onto more complex objects and configurations by the end of August (Papert, 1966). This is now often used as an amusing anecdote in computer vision courses to illustrate the naïve early understanding of vision as a narrow technical task that could be 'solved' by students in a lab over the course of a month.

Computer vision became in this way a sub-field of AI, albeit a peripheral one. In 1980, influenced by the neurophysiology experiments of Hubel and Wiesel (1959), Kunihiko Fukushima proposed the *neocognitron* (1980), now seen as the first 'deep' convolutional neural network. Broadly described, an artificial neural network is a computer system based on interconnected nodes – or 'neurons' – which process and transmit signals (numbers) to each other depending on certain initial conditions.

Convolutions are a type of mathematical operation that enables this processing, and 'depth' in this context refers to the number of layers of neurons in a given system.

Today, artificial neural networks are much more diverse and sophisticated, and they underpin many of the systems that have come to be commonly called AI. But this was not always the case, and there was nothing inevitable about the rise of this new AI paradigm. Neural nets were largely abandoned in favour of other approaches in AI for almost a decade, until Fukushima's *neocognitron* was recovered and fitted with a mathematical technique to minimise error known as back-propagation (LeCun et al, 1989). The back propagation algorithm had been known for decades, but became relevant in this context because it is an effective way of connecting multiple layers in a neural network, allowing it to be deeper and more complex. Together, these are the key technical developments that underlie what eventually became widely known as 'Deep Learning' (LeCun et al, 2015).

Yet, despite having all the technical pieces in place since the late 1980s, neural networks were once again largely ignored for the next twenty years. What changed the most in that time was not the principles of neural computing, but the processing power of computers and, most significantly, the datafication of visual culture at a large scale. Deep Learning succeeded as an AI approach only after visual cultural production was datafied, specifically, when there were enough images publicly available online so as to assemble the large datasets that these systems required to outperform other competing approaches in AI. The history of Deep Learning, which eventually came to be the dominant paradigm in machine learning and allowed for many of the systems we recognise today as AI, is intimately linked to online visual culture, its history and practices, as well as its social and technical sub-cultures.

This large reorganisation of visual culture brought about by the mass adoption of digital technologies has influenced and is reflected in humanities scholarship. In a converging track, the disciplinary melange now known as digital humanities has charted these changes in social and technical life. Three major moments in its recent history can be distinguished here: an early phase, close still to humanities computing (McCarty, 2014 [205]), with an emphasis on creating research infrastructures, the digitisation of large corpora of artefacts and their organisation in databases, as well as the explicit desire to rebrand these activities from a support service to a fully-fledged academic discipline (Hayles, 2012). This was followed by a shift of emphasis and diversification towards what Schnapp and Presner called Digital Humanities 2.0 (2009), a second wave that aimed to be 'qualitative, interpretive, experiential, emotive, generative in character', in which 'print is no longer the exclusive or the normative medium in which knowledge is produced and/or disseminated'. The third moment is described by Jones (2016) as 'the eversion cyberspace', which he maps to the mass adoption of social media platforms, the emergence of tech giants and the introduction of new gaming interfaces.

According to Jones, sometime between 2004 and 2008 cyberspace was 'turned inside out', and our understanding of it changed from a virtual space removed from our quotidian experience to our everyday becoming digital in essence: 'from a world apart to a part of the world' (p. 19). This last phase posed a whole new set of questions for humanities disciplines and a significant challenge in the opposite direction from the first moment: not only to digitise, curate, archive, and preserve culture, but to deal with the deluge of born-digital cultural data created every day. This is what Schäfer and van Es call 'the datafied society' (2017) – the same phenomenon that made Deep Learning possible.

Shortly after this process of datafication intensified in the late 2000s, the idea of studying culture through data started to gain currency. Earlier I alluded to Manovich, and he too places his *cultural analytics* in this timeline, drawing a distinction between digital humanities, which he argues is mostly concerned with smaller collections of cultural artefacts created by professionals, and social computing, which tends to work with larger datasets of 'non-professional, vernacular culture' circulated after 2004 (2016, p. 3). This distinction is less relevant now than what it was only a few years ago, but it is telling of how films sit awkwardly in this classification: they are 'too new' for traditional humanities, whose scholars, Manovich claims, are 'shut out from studying the present' on account of copyright restrictions on professionally made cultural products, but are 'too old' for social computing, since most of the history of the medium occurs before 2004. Furthermore, films are fewer in number, when compared to, for example, books or tweets, but are significantly more capital and data intensive, which contributes to explain why they are latecomer artefacts in the study of culture as data.

Computational approaches in film studies, meanwhile, predate digital computing and datafication. In yet another converging track at the machine vision juncture, we find a niche group of film scholars working on this area since the mid-1970s. The most identifiable figure in the early days of quantitative methods is Barry Salt and his measurements of average shot lengths (ASL).[1] Originally a physicist, and taking inspiration from similar attempts in literary studies, Salt wanted to determine stylistic differences between film directors 'based on more objective facts than have ever been

INTRODUCTION 9

used in the field of style comment before' (Salt, 1974, p. 22). He continued to work in this vein of science-inflected methodology in the following decades and produced a substantial volume of work on the history of film style (1992, 2006).

Based on Salt's work, Yuri Tsivian and Gunars Civjans released *Cinemetrics* in 2005, which Tsivian describes as an online application 'designed to collect, store, and process scholarly data about films' (2009). The application consists of a simple web interface through which users can input cutting patterns and calculate ASLs by watching a film on a separate screen and clicking every time there is a cut. In line with the first wave in digital humanities, *Cinemetrics* focused on digitisation and retrieval using a database: the time-consuming part of the calculation of ASLs, which is to measure and count the shots, is performed manually by humans. When I first encountered the *Cinemetrics* in 2011 its database had close to 7,500 entries; at the time of writing it had over 22,000, including trailers, short films, television series, and music videos (Civjans, 2011). This is a modest dataset by today's data science standards; these annotations are in fact accessed as a set of tables and used through a website interface rather than distributed and analysed using computational methods.

And there are digital and computational tools that predate *Cinemetrics*, some of which include more advanced technologies. For example, the MoCA project (1994), which back then purported to have computer vision libraries designed to 'extract structural and semantic content of videos automatically', including scene segmentation and shot-boundary detection (Pfeiffer et al, 1998, p. 329) – the very same task that *Cinemetrics* crowdsourced to humans. And similarly, several digital tools for annotation and statistical analysis of film emerged after, for example AKIRA III (2007), a general annotation tool, or VIDEANA, a program that allegedly supported camera motion estimation, detection and recognition of text and faces, and audio segmentation (Ewerth et al, 2009). Notably, these and similar projects faded and were abandoned towards the end of the decade, in what we could call the first winter of computational moving images studies.[2]

Cinemetrics survived this winter and remains a relevant referent in quantitative approaches to film, partly because it successfully managed to crowdsource its data acquisition to scholars who understood ASL and purchased into its value as a proxy signal for film style. Tsivian references this epistemic ambition when he notes that '[Cinemetrics] helps to generate questions that are of use not only to the history, but also the theory of film' (2009, p. 99). And this sentiment is echoed by scholars who coalesced around the platform, such as James Cutting (2011), Nick

Redfern (2012, 2013), Ji-Hyun Shon (2014), and Mike Baxter (2014a, 2014b). Quantitative methods, as Redfern puts it:

> [lead] us to reflect on the nature of what we do as film scholars – to think about the questions we can ask and the range of methodologies available to answer those questions. [. . .] I argue that we should abandon Film Studies as a subject or discipline and focus on the study of film as a complex object of inquiry that demands an ecumenical methodological perspective. (2014, p. 3)

This call for diversification in methods came on the back of an earlier ontological displacement, at a time when films were leaving their celluloid bodies behind. David Rodowick's *Virtual Life of Film* (2007) is exemplary of this earlier moment. Analogue media, he argues, are recordings, isomorphic traces of a pro-filmic event, while digital media produce tokens of numbers. Digital films might initially appear indistinguishable from their analogue counterparts, but the former are *transcriptions* while the latter are *calculations* (p. 116, emphasis in the original). And this strand of critical work focused on the history and theory of digital images has been continuously updated since, for example in Denson's *Discorrelated Images* (2020), Gaboury's *Image Objects* (2021), or Ray Smith's *Biography of The Pixel* (2021).

Simultaneously, a new wave of methodological and epistemic displacements enacted this pluralisation in practice, for example the 'creative and performative critical approaches to moving image research' of Grant's *videographic criticism* (2014, 2015, 2016), or Atkinson's participant observer approach to digital film production (2018), that pioneered an emerging ecosystem for practice-based research in film with and about the digital, its technologies and infrastructures such as *Media Commons*, the *VAT project*, or the *Film Colors project*. There are also specialised journals such as *[in]Transition*, conferences, like *Besides the Screen*, and online resources like *The Videographic Essay* or *Audiovisualcy*, which regularly host and promote moving image scholarship carried out *through* digital methods. And this outward orientation in objects and methods finds familiar echoes in digital humanities scholarship, for example in the work of Heftberger (2018), Mittell (2019), and the computational approaches of Arnold and Tilton (2019), and Bhargav et al (2019).

These various disciplinary tracks intersect in machine vision: the epistemic diversification of film and media studies, its objects, and methods; the *datafication* of visual culture during the second part of the 2000s; the adoption of scientific computing and data science techniques in the study of culture; and the emergence of new computing paradigms that leveraged this abundance of data. We now come back full circle to Virilio, and

INTRODUCTION

to the issue of splitting our viewing with and among machines, which returns in full force, not as a hypothetical thought experiment, but in the form of fully realised technical systems which feed from and at the same time reshape visual culture. From a critical perspective, the question at this multidisciplinary junction is how to imagine a form of *applied visionics* – a type of technical practice that embraces and incorporates new AI technologies, as it simultaneously lays their technical mechanisms and intellectual assumptions bare and open to criticism and redesign; a form of self-reflective machine vision able to recognise and *show* the rational illusions it creates.

Critical technical practice

The *applied visionics* I imagine entails a concerted effort to disassemble machine vision into its various technical and conceptual constituents *through* technical practice, in this case informed by the intellectual frameworks of moving image studies. However, this emphasis on computational practice should not be confused with so-called 'data-driven' approaches, nor with a commitment to 'solve' any established tasks in computer vision. This is not a computer science book. Similarly, although I draw from film and media studies, cultural analytics, and distant reading in the humanities tradition, this is not a digital methods book or media philosophy book. As hinted at earlier, I am keenly aware that film scholarship has a rich history of engaging with digital imagery and algorithmic thought, and while I draw from some of these debates, a reader looking for the latest update on digital film theory might find the emphasis on machine learning and its technical details frustrating. Meanwhile, a technologist seeking out-of-the-box implementations of computer vision for processing digital video might be equally discouraged by the denser passages on film and media history and theory. Both readers might feel that these debates are in disarray with their respective disciplines, and I am sure I will lose some of these readers as a result.

But I am also certain that for other readers the payoff of engaging in *applied visionics* will outweigh this initial disorientation, and hopefully suggest new routes of exploration and discovery. Those who make it through *Machine Vision and Cinema* can expect a detailed account of how certain questions about our relationship with moving images can be instantiated computationally, the technical aspects of this process, and the various intellectual trade-offs of such a move. In other words, more than digital methods applied to films, this book offers a cross-disciplinary deep dive into the computational aesthetics and epistemics of the moving image. I suspect this approach might be more appealing to 'undisciplined' scholars and practitioners, and to those that are more used to the joys and difficulties of working between arts and sciences. As any serious inter-disciplinarian knows, one thing is to borrow and repurpose concepts from other disciplines, and a quite different proposition is to also borrow methods, practices, funding, and lab equipment.

This additional kind of technical reciprocity is at the heart of *Cinema and Machine Vision*, and it takes from the recognition that although there are numerous strands of film scholarship concerned with digital technologies, there are fewer that are overtly computational in scope, and fewer still where concepts of film theory can be recognisably instantiated as realised computational systems. In other words, although film studies as a discipline engages with digital and algorithmic images, and more recently also through digital methods, film theory does not (yet) have a computational body. And conversely, while contemporary computer vision is heavily dependent on digital imagery, and sometimes moving imagery specifically, many researchers and engineers in this field remain unaware of the history, theory and criticism of film, and its associated intellectual frameworks and traditions. This makes collaboration challenging, while film scholars are accustomed to dealing in shots, plots, and meanings, these terms are foreign to most computer scientists and machine learning engineers, who are used to pixels, vectors, and data projections.

To enact their mutual interest in computational images and machine vision at the technical level, the type of *applied visionics* I have in mind is closely aligned with what Philip Agre calls *critical technical practice*: 'a technical practice for which critical reflection upon the practice is part of the practice itself' (1997a, xii), and which he argues requires 'one foot planted in the craft work of design and the other foot planted in the reflexive work of critique' (2014). This is akin to other critical approaches in practice-based research and material thinking such as *speculative design* (Auger, 2013) or *critical making* (Bogers and Chiappini, 2019), but with an emphasis on computational systems and concerned specifically with the discursive practices of AI:

> . . . the whole point of a critical technical practice is to work from the inside, driving the customary premises and procedures of technical work toward their logical conclusions. Some of those conclusions will be problematic, and the whole complex process of reaching them will then provide the horizon against which critical reflection can identify fallacies and motivate alternatives. (Agre, 1997a, p. 107)

A critical technical approach, according to Agre, implies a commitment to design, computer craft, and an analysis of AI as a set of both technical and

INTRODUCTION 13

discursive systems. Ideally, such practice allows to identify both the intellectual impasses as well the horizons of possibilities opened by specific technical configurations. I take this to mean thinking through some of the problems posed by machines that are said to watch films on our behalf by building or intervening in such machines myself, and by producing a record of the technical decisions that were made along the way and the horizons of error these interventions produced.

To guide these interventions, I also draw from computational aesthetics, a family of approaches that ostensibly use quantification and calculation as methods for assessing the merits of works of art and cultural productions more generally. In its modern form, computational approaches to aesthetics are often attributed to Birkoff's mathematical theory of aesthetics (1932), as subsequently elaborated by Bense's information aesthetics (1965). But the idea of measuring taste empirically is much older and can be considered a fundamental problem of modern western aesthetics that arose hand in hand with modern technologies of measurement and calculation in the early eighteenth century. I return to this earlier history in Chapter 8.

The research agenda of computational aesthetics has since been absorbed by AI, with its purpose rephrased accordingly as 'the research of computational methods that can make applicable aesthetic decisions in a similar fashion as humans can' (Hoening, 2005). This shift towards AI and the imitation of human behaviours recasts computational aesthetics from its ambitions of a mathematical science of taste and towards human–computer interaction, design, and engineering. Under the current paradigm of AI technologies that feeds from visual culture, the problem of designing aesthetically sensitive engines becomes entangled with many layers of human activity, mirroring the shift of emphasis in philosophy from the evaluation of aesthetic objects to the qualification of aesthetic experiences. This does not make computational aesthetics any less concerned with quantification or calculation, but it does radically change its perspective on what exactly is being counted, how, and by whom, which creates the need for a form of critical self-awareness in computational aesthetics.

The approach I suggest is therefore not experimental in a scientific sense, but rather in a creative sense, as a set of computational thought experiments informed by philosophy, specifically by the philosophy of photography, moving images, and art more generally. And because *Cinema and Machine Vision* depends on establishing strong lines of correspondence between film scholarship and contemporary AI research, my focus is on the design and critical evaluation of systems that *are said* to be aesthetically sensitive towards images. This defines a field of action and a set of limits in the research presented in this book, which deliberately excludes many systems and industrial applications where machine vision technologies use images for other purposes. The focus on systems that are said to be aesthetic also highlights the dual logic of analytic and creative practice: designing computational systems that attempt to measure and assign aesthetic value to moving images, while showing how claims to aesthetic sensitivity in machinery arise in discourse; how they are formulated by the designers of the systems and how these formulations enact assumptions about both computer users and moving images.

This dual logic requires taking computational work seriously as a matter of craft, this is to say, to be willing to fully embrace the technical nature of the work with computers; the methods, processes and constraints of this type of work, including the explicit desire to create systems that *work*, meaning that they do what they are supposed to do; that can be used, built upon, combined, and improved by others. At the same time, it also requires questioning where this desire for working systems comes from, noticing the conditions of failure and success embedded in such systems, who sets these conditions, how they are formalised and encoded; what alternatives there are and what are their trade-offs. Actualised systems, as Agre points out, do not simply work, or fail to work, there is always a rich gamut of qualifiers and assumptions that go with these assertions:

> Every method has its strengths and weaknesses, its elegance and its clumsiness, its subtle patterns of success and failure. These things ought to be the subject of intellectual discussion and dispute, both in particular cases and as general matters of methodology – and not as a separate category of research but as something continuous with the presentation of technical projects. (Agre, 1997a, p. 14)

Following this approach, in *Cinema and Machine Vision* I investigate the types of questions that can and cannot be asked computationally about moving images: when do we say computers succeed or fail to 'watch' films, and under what circumstances that might change. This process of flexible feedback between system building and theory building is a distinctive aspect of this book, but it does place additional demands on the reader. And this type of critical technical engagement comes with limitations too. In practice not every idea can be actualised into a system and not every actualisation yields critical insight. One can afford to be more agile the further one gets from a discipline's centre, but the lack of gravitational pull also leaves one exposed to contradiction, miscommunication, and operational dead ends. These caveats notwithstanding, and because I am also interested in how machines fail to watch films, how we critically assess

INTRODUCTION   15

these failures, and how we can reimagine our relation with these machines and these images, I feel confident in asking the reader to forgo some of the structure of their disciplines to venture with me in a heterogeneous discussion that spans old and new technologies, popular and avant-garde cinema, and that goes from concrete existing systems to possible ones; from working with large audiovisual archives to modelling computational moving images; and from institutional infrastructures to the development of a personal critical technical practice.

Made by Machine

An excerpt from a practical manual of experimental television from the 1930s reads as follows: 'Now, while television is here, I would not have you believe that the received images are perfect; nay, they are not even good, but it is this very fact that gives the television experiment a thrill' (Collins, *c.* 1932). The manual consists of a series of experiments designed to be followed by the 'amateur experimenter' so that they could produce their very own televised images. It was aimed at a small and short-lived community of hobbyists and mechanical TV aficionados and included detailed step-by-step instructions and plenty of diagrams showing how to build a photoelectric cell, an amplifier tube, and fit them with a perforated rotating disk. This system for recording and transmitting moving images had been developed a decade earlier by Scottish inventor John Logie Baird. The same year the manual was published, the BBC broadcast its first experimental television programme using this technology:

> The BBC's involvement with John Logie Baird's broadcasts on the 30-line mechanical system was an acknowledgement that the medium had a future. It also aimed to discover whether or not it was possible to make programmes that were entertaining beyond their novelty value. (BBC, 2020)

Mechanical TV remained experimental only for a brief time; it was soon displaced by a newer technology, the cathode ray tube, and over the next decades television went from a thrilling experiment to become global mass media.

Ninety years later, there is scope again for the BBC to call television 'experimental', this time in the wake of AI technologies. In 2018, the British broadcaster commissioned *Made by Machine: When AI Met the Archive*, an experimental television programme in which 'Computers trawl through more than quarter of a million shows using a variety of machine learning techniques, then let loose to create short programmes-within-a-programme in the style of BBC Four' (*Made by Machine*, 2018).

The programme aired in September as part of a joint initiative between BBC Four and the broadcaster's research and development unit, BBC Research & Development (BBC R&D), with the objective of using AI 'to help create two nights of experimental programming' (Cowlishaw, 2018). The resulting programming block was called *BBC4.1 AI-TV*, and included the commissioning *The Joy of AI* – a documentary that traces the history and relevance of artificial intelligence – and the rebroadcast of programmes using an automated scheduling tool developed internally at BBC R&D.

I will be using MbM as a go-to case-study in several sections of *Cinema and Machine Vision* to ground the technical and theoretical discussions on a concrete example of a computer system specifically designed to watch moving images on our behalf. The idea is to give the reader a tangible existing system as a point of departure and to launch the discussions in the book from common ground. As these discussions move from data to criticism and from existing systems to possible ones in later chapters, MbM will figure less prominently. Still, despite MbM not being the only case-study presented, nor equally relevant for every chapter, it is exemplary of a moment where AI technologies are seen as experimental and full of potential to reshape the media landscape; a moment that is reminiscent of the thrills of mechanical television and the possibilities imagined by amateur technologists before the broadcasting of images became an industry. The images of MbM are similarly far from perfect, but the program shares its experimental ambition to explore technology beyond its novelty value, and a sincere, if not always accomplished attempt at self-reflexive machine vision.

As such, *Made by Machine* deserves a brief introduction of its own. The project was developed in-house at BBC R&D by a small team comprised of a technologist, a developer, a user experience designer, and me. We had additional support from a producer, who commissioned the packaging of the programme, including the presenter and the treatment of a script based on our notes. We all worked under the leadership of the head of Internet Research and Future Services division of the broadcaster's R&D division. I was first approached about joining the project in early February 2018, when the initial idea was to design a small-scale machine learning experiment using material from the BBC television archive. In April, this idea was picked up by the editor of BBC Four, who informally commissioned it to BBC R&D as a full-length television programme. The project in this new form started in May; it was designed, produced, and delivered by early August, and the resulting program broadcast for the first time on

INTRODUCTION   17

5 September 2018 at 9 in the evening on BBC Four, where it was seen by under half a million people in the UK.

MbM is experimental in several ways: although it is furnished and presented officially as an experimental documentary, the best way to describe it is as a demonstration of a family of technologies. The programme is comprised of four sections, each corresponding to one computational technique used to traverse the BBC Television Archive and automatically concatenate clips of video. These sequences constitute the main content of the programme and were themselves not edited together 'by hand', by a director, producer, or scriptwriter, but *generated* through a system designed by technologists, developers, and researchers, who made the machines that made *Made by Machine*. In this book I touch on the design of the project and focus on the first section of the program, which frames the chapter about archives and datasets, and serves to launch everything that follows. To a lesser extent, I also discuss sections three and four of the television program, which come into play in later chapters about generative models and multimodal systems.

Finally, a word about my role in this project. I was the only academic researcher involved in MbM, and the only participant external to the BBC. This gave me, on the one hand, an insider's perspective, and a distinct conceptual influence in the project, but on the other it kept me a step removed from its institutional context and the many practical decisions needed to make the results of our experiments fit for national broadcast. I want to stress that whatever was accomplished in this process is the result of genuine collaboration and a shared desire for experimentation, with both computing technologies and media formats. We worked together with the ambition and unbound enthusiasm of those experimenting with a medium that was yet to be established, and with the conviction that AI was something that could be intervened critically and technically, as well as shared with a broader audience.

The team behind MbM dispersed shortly after the project concluded, and the technologies we used have since been developed at speeds that back then were difficult to imagine, and even today are vertigo-inducing. Meanwhile, public perception and social attitudes about both AI and public broadcasting have evolved too, making this experimental documentary somewhat of an oddity in public media. Yet my intention of making AI a matter of public record, and the idea of showing the limits of what it can and cannot do as a medium remain, and although I will not commit something as detailed as a manual for amateur *AI TV* aficionados, and I will not engage with every aspect of MbM at the same level of detail, my hope is that the reader will find in its experimental form something refreshing against a media backdrop increasingly dominated by big tech.

Concentric layers

I have introduced the notion of watching films and television with/ through computers, the kinds of questions that arise from this practice, and a methodological approach to tackle these questions. I have also introduced *Made by Machine* as a case-study to open the discussion and given a general indication of what to expect from this book. To close this introduction, I will now turn to the structure of *Cinema and Machine Vision*.

The book has three main parts, each corresponding to a specific coupling of theory and practice:

I. DATA-IMAGES: PHILOSOPHY OF PHOTOGRAPHY AND TECHNOLOGIES OF VISION
II. PIXELS IN MOTION: THE CALCULATION OF CINEMATIC TIME
III. AI AND CRITICISM: AESTHETICS, FORMATS, AND INTERACTIONS

Part I places computer vision in the wider context of technologies of vision by tracing its connection to photography and photographic practices. The reader is shown how to disassemble contemporary computer vision systems by tracing the images used to train them and is prompted to consider whose vision is encoded in these systems and how. The goal is to start with images as data, but then broaden the scope to consider the automation of perception more generally, as a set of historically situated practices that involve several layers of human labour and are designed on top of an extensive material and technical milieu of agents, tools and devices, that both predate and are remediated by digital computing.

In Chapter 1, I examine the conceptual and technical differences between the archive and the dataset, and the types of value they create from their constituent images. This distinction is used to frame a discussion about how contemporary AI techniques work by abstracting computational models from large datasets, how large media conglomerates extract value from audiovisual archives using these techniques, and to identify several hidden layers of human labour that are involved in this process.

Informed by literature in digital platform studies and journalism, the reader is shown how global digital networks and social media enabled the automation of visual labour. This argument is illustrated through the example of a niche community of amateur photogra-

INTRODUCTION 19

phers who unwittingly played a key role in the configuration of deep machine learning through their participation in the website Flickr. I complement this with an example of how to disassemble a computer vision system.

Having identified the historical becoming of computer vision, Chapter 2 takes a deeper look into it through the literal and metaphorical lens of photography. Through a technical genealogy of photographic practice, including its lenses, the types of images they produce and how these are used over time, the reader is shown how the aesthetic and epistemic value of such practices underpins the claims of accuracy and effectiveness of computer vision. The discussion makes explicit a connection between the claims to knowledge of machine learning processes and the epistemic advantages of photographic images, by drawing from the 'New Theory' in the philosophy of photography of Dominic McIver Lopes and Diarmuid Costello. By focusing on the social and technical practices whose norms govern the photographic process, a distinction is made between counter-factually-dependent and belief-independent informational processes, thereby demystifying notions about non-human machine vision and machinery that is said to think by itself.

Chapter 3 further develops the link between computing, optical devices, and the regimes of visibility they create. The reader is presented with a model of vision that distributes information processing, storage, and recall, between 'hardware and wetware'. Through this division of labour, the situated individual perceptions of many can become one large perceiving machine. The design of such cognitive assemblage and its potential reorganisation is explored through a practical experiment to repurpose a typical computer vision classifier using focal length data. The result is a system re-designed to be blind to what images depict and be sensitive instead only to how they depict. This discussion about the computation of space closes the chapter and the section by hinting at the complementary aspect of photographic imaging: the mechanical calculation of time.

PART II focuses on the temporal dimension of machine vision. It takes the previous discussion about inductive vision and 'unrolls' it in time: from the computational analysis of time-based media to the computational production of new temporalities and moving image formats. Through a critical analysis of *distant viewing* as an intellectual practice, the reader is encouraged to question the effectiveness of 'state of the art' AI tools in film and media studies, and to challenge the widely held assumption inherited from big data analytics that computer vision increasingly outperforms human vision. Simultaneously, the reader is asked to consider the role of such tools in a less obvious but much more consequential transformation in the production-consumption of audiovisual media: from sequences of discrete still images and the creation of cinematic time, to their atomisation into free-flowing pixels and continuous streams of what I call *datamatic time*.

In Chapter 4 I critically examine *distant viewing* – an emerging scholarly practice that extends Franco Moretti's *distant reading* from the study of literary texts to the analysis of film and television style. The discussion draws from and contrasts two approaches to the analysis of film form: the *stylometrics* of Barry Salt, Yuri Tsivian, Mike Baxter, and others, who quantify formal film features to perform statistical probes and identify style patterns over large corpora of films, and the decidedly qualitative aesthetic approach of Mary Ann Doane and Béla Balázs, who emphasise how specific style choices and embodied spectatorship of films communicate ideas, emotions, and themes. Through an experiment in automated shot-type detection in *The Silence of the Lambs* (1991) and other 1990s films by Jonathan Demme, the reader is invited to question the limits and possibilities of analysing films at a distance and is prompted to reassess the claims that computers outperform humans, which are often found in popular discourse about AI and big data analytics.

Extending the probe from individual shots to their sequential arrangement, Chapter 5 focuses on editing and its computational analysis, specifically on continuity editing in popular Hollywood cinema. Drawing from the works of Noël Burch, David Bordwell, and Kristin Thompson, the reader is guided through an experiment in identifying and encoding units of meaning inferred not from the shots themselves but from their sequential organisation. The dynamics over time of these invisible relational units are then analysed through sonification – an auditory analogue to visualisation where data and information are represented and conveyed through non-speech sound. Case studies discussed in this chapter include computational analysis of popular films such as *The Godfather* (1972) and *Dunkirk* (2017).

Chapter 6 returns to the work of Mary Ann Doane, this time in her reading of Henry Bergson and her arguments about the production of cinematic time. An experiment in reverse cinematography (neural in-painting) is presented to show how duration and motion can be 'released' from any still image using generative machine learning techniques. The reader is asked to consider how techniques such as these erode cinematic time by weakening frames, shots, and scenes as logical temporal units in film spectatorship, and how 'neurally hallucinated' moving images, in which motion is algorithmically generated instead of captured and repro-

INTRODUCTION

duced, point to a shift towards what I call datamatic time – a temporal form that dissociates motion from duration. Examples discussed in this chapter range from the time-sculpting of Russian film director and theorist Andrei Tarkovsky, to the experiments of early pioneer of photography and cinematography Étienne-Jules Marey, to the dolly-zoom technique in *Jaws* (1975), to net-art projects like *r/place* (2017).

Part III shifts the focus from using computer vision to analyse films to rethinking film criticism and scholarship computationally. Critics, their methods, and their role in the social construction of meanings about moving images are analysed through the algorithmic lens of computational technologies. This discussion primes the reader to imagine an alternative division of labour between critics and computers, as well as the novel types of media interfaces that this redesign entails.

Starting with Chapter 7, I address the encounter between interpretative intellectual traditions in film scholarship and inductive methods in scientific computing. This chapter explores the fantasies and anxieties that arise when critics confront cinematic worlds that have already been seen *for* them, but not directly *by* them. The reader is drawn into this discussion through the algorithmic films of Hollis Frampton in the 1970s and an in-depth analysis of latent space projection techniques.

Chapter 8 centres on film and moving image criticism, specifically in how aesthetic judgements are made with/through computer systems. By bringing together the work of Noël Carroll in the philosophy of art, with the interactionist critique of Philip Agre in the field of AI, the reader is invited to consider how computers are used to pass algorithmic judgements about films and television, the new roles critics might play in the production of and interaction with inferred visual worlds, and the new kinds of questions that can be asked from moving imagery as a result. The discussion includes examples of film reviews, recommender systems, and a proof of concept for a 'computational film critic'.

And to close this third part, Chapter 9 considers the idea of inductive computing as a medium of inscription for film criticism and scholarship. It examines the epistemic split between creative and analytic practices, the pressure put on this division by generative AI, and the emergence of a novel kind of technical imagination that assumes radical reciprocities between aesthetics and computation. The discussion returns to Agre's critical-technical approach and connects it with the enduring appeal of 'practical theorists' like Dziga Vertov. Through examples of large language models and the concept of *computational ekphrasis*, the reader is invited to redefine the technical dimensions of theory-building through AI.

These three parts and their chapters cut orthogonally across methods, techniques, and levels of analysis, with each chapter adding a new layer that builds up from technique to theory; from counting pixels to calculating meanings; from video analytics to computational criticism. And accordingly, as one goes up these layers and the discussion moves from existing systems to possible ones, the accompanying examples and experiments become more speculative – more design than implementation. The path I carve through these layers is not meant as a definitive framework, but more of a cross section that lays bare the components of machine vision, articulating for the reader what is aesthetically and epistemically at stake in these contingent assemblages.

Notes

1. Salt initially measured shot lengths in feet of celluloid. He is often cited as the initial proponent of the average shot length as an analytical metric for film, but there are undoubtedly earlier versions of the idea. For example, Kristin Thompson mentions a German writer of the name Georg Otto Stindt, who compared the number of shots per reel in German and American films in the early 1920s. See: Thompson, 2005, p. 117.

2. AKIRA III is still technically usable but is no longer supported beyond its original Windows 2000 environment. VIDEANA on the other hand is not being distributed as far as I can surmise; it has no official website, and I could find no other traces of its development beyond the couple of articles cited in this work – I suspect it is abandoned. MoCA libraries are now outdated and unavailable.

Part I

Data-Images: Philosophy of Photography and Technologies of Vision

CHAPTER 1

Between Archive and Dataset

Archives are assembled for humans to keep and explore while datasets are intended for machines to process and produce. Arguably, archives are created under a historical impulse; they are organised according to the record-keeping needs of the cultures that build them. This historical impulse requires a high degree of structuring, usually in the form of hierarchical ontologies that facilitate cataloguing and retrieval, and that aspire to a certain degree of historical accuracy, integrity, and permanence. These are some of the characteristics that we tend to expect from archives. Datasets also respond to the sense-making needs of the cultures that build them, however they come together under a different impulse; they tend to be contingent assemblages, made in response to specific *a priori* needs and questions relevant to engineering and the sciences. In data science and machine learning engineering, for example, datasets tend to be granular, flattened to matrix-like structures whose individual items are not meant to be publicly accessible or even individually meaningful to human observers. Instead, data in these systems is much more mercurial, flowing from one repository to another through interconnected networks, and constantly changing shape depending on the specific applications for which it is intended. And because contemporary AI applications rely on vast amounts of data, datasets made for machine processing can be significantly larger and are usually not limited to canonical artefacts, or a small collection of pieces deemed significant enough to go 'on the record'.

From this it follows that archives and datasets produce value in almost opposite ways: while archives endow their constituent artefacts and records with additional symbolic layers, making them stable and tractable, datasets that feed contemporary AI systems atomise these artefacts, stripping them from context in order to make patterns visible through computational processing. In the first case value is produced by stability and addressability, in the second by aggregation and mutability.

Moving images are of particular interest to these definitions because they illustrate and further problematise the above distinctions. Film archives, for instance, are organised collections of individual films whose records include directors, years, countries of origin, performers, producers, et cetera. However, each of these films can also be thought of as a collection of frames and a dataset of images. And through computing, these individual frames can relate much more freely, not only to other frames in the same film, but to a multitude of other frames in a multitude of other films. Film archives can in this way be reconceptualised as datasets, enabling in the process different modalities for the production of meanings and value, from description to prediction, and from analysis to generation. To elaborate on this idea, let us consider in detail the case of *Made by Machine* (henceforth MbM).

First, I will situate the project in the context of a political economy of datafied films and television; the value of audiovisual production as computational artefacts, how they are exploited by media corporations, and where does the BBC television archive sit in this ecosystem. I will then give a general overview of the project, its objectives, constraints, and design, including an account of how the archive became a dataset.

MbM was commissioned under the deceptively simple premise of creating a TV programme from archive material using machine learning. There were only three qualifiers in this brief: 1) the one-hour programme had to be 'watchable' as a finished product that could be broadcast on national television; 2) it had to show how machine learning could be used to machine-see the television archive; and 3) it had to somehow condense and re-create the style of BBC Four, the commissioning channel (Harrison, 2018). These were, in principle, the only editorial constraints of the project. But to put this brief into context, some basic background on the media corporation, its archive, and its transit towards digital and computational technologies is in order.

The BBC is one of the largest public media organisations in the world; it was created in 1927 and started broadcasting television in 1937. BBC Films was founded in 1990 as the film production branch of the corporation; and, after a number of iterations, *iPlayer* was launched in 2007 as the corporation's video-on-demand streaming service. Today the corporation offers a wide portfolio of services, including news, entertainment, and educational content in multiple media formats and channels. It is a staple of British cultural life, as well as internationally known for its news coverage and high-production value programming. In terms of moving images, the corporation's television archive is one of the largest in the world, with over 700,000 hours of television distributed in about 400,000 programmes in various formats: from film to magnetic tapes to digital storage (BFI, 2018; Lee, 2014). And since the 1980s, these thousands of hours of material have undergone overlapping phases of digitisation, first to CD, DVD, and DAT, and later directly to files. This is a process of datafication of moving images that accelerated after 2010, 'from a trickle to a flood' (Wright, 2010), when television production migrated entirely to digital formats and was ever since 'born digital'.

Concurrent with this flood of digital video came the need for infrastructures of access and retrieval, which led to the creation of the *Redux* system. This was originally a rather obscure technical solution for a tapeless archive, but its importance grew in parallel to the transformation of moving imagery into digital content, and it eventually became 'the mother of all VoD systems [. . .] a video-on-demand test bed where we can try out the systems that acquire, store, search and deliver content' (Butterworth, 2008). And this was in turn one of the most significant ancestors of today's *iPlayer*, the BBC's public-facing video-on-demand platform.

According to OFCOM, the UK's broadcast regulatory body, in 2018 a significant portion of British audiences still watched broadcast television – a modality in which the BBC channels dominate viewing habits (OFCOM, 2018, p. 20). However, most of this viewership of 'linear' broadcast television was comprised of people aged 54 or older, while younger audiences (16–34) were getting most of their audiovisual content elsewhere, including about one hour per day of YouTube, and half an hour of subscription video-on-demand (SVoD) services. In this 'non-linear' modality, Netflix, Amazon, and NowTV (owned by Sky) increasingly dominate viewing habits, with more than twice the audience of the BBC's *iPlayer*. This daily half-hour of non-linear watching by younger audiences is particularly significant because it corresponds to 'scripted content' such as film and television (OFCOM, 2018, p. 21). For this type of cultural audiovisual products, the decline in traditional TV watching is commensurate with the sustained growth of dedicated SVoD services, which in the UK had over ten million subscribers at the time of writing. The Broadcasters' Audience Research Board (BARB) has called this phenomena 'SVoD Nation': no longer a niche viewing modality, but 'an established part of the television ecosystem' (BARB, 2018, p. 28). According to OFCOM, this downward trend of broadcast television viewing and the sharp change in the viewing habits of younger audiences is expected to continue (2023, p. 3).

The archive became in this way not only a collection of digital files, but a crucial part of infrastructure at the back end of a digital service, in a model similar to other streaming companies, and indeed increasingly competing in this arena with the likes of Netflix, Amazon, and more recently Warner Media and Disney. Like the BBC, these companies hold their own audiovisual archives, which they commercialise and exploit in terms of films and television programmes, but increasingly also as computational artefacts. One of the most significant shifts in this transition to digital moving images is the way value is produced along the production chain, not only by selling audiovisual products to audiences, but by extracting value from these audiences through their interactions with audiovisual products. In other words, moving images under the streaming economy are both products bought and sold in the entertainment market, and computational resources in the data market.

Netflix was one of the first companies to understand the value of this turn towards data, and a major actor in today's media and technology landscape. And its success can be explained, at least in part, by how the company treats its audiovisual archive as a dataset. When large media companies licensed many of their titles to Netflix in the late 1990s and early 2000s, they saw streaming as just another ancillary market in the broader cycle of audiovisual distribution and exhibition – one more 'window' of exhibition, to use industry lingo. Media conglomerates sold Netflix distribution rights for their films and TV, but the streaming company got much more than they bargained for; besides audiovisual products to sell to audiences, they also bought a different type of computational resource altogether, something equally if not more valuable: the ability to extract and encode aesthetic preferences at global scale by exploiting these moving images as computational artefacts.

Netflix still routinely acquires the rights for individual films and TV series; moreover, it is today one of the largest commissioners of original content. But as a digital platform, the company exploits not only films or shows individually, but its catalogue as a whole. The value they place on treating moving images as data is clearly exemplified by the Netflix Prize, which in 2007 awarded one million US dollars in a public contest to whomever could improve their recommendation algorithm by 10 per cent, based on a large dataset that the company made available *ex professo* (see: Buskirk, 2009; Lohr, 2009).

At the time, Netflix subscribers could review films and rate them on a five-star scale; the company kept these ratings, part of which it made publicly available for the contest. The dataset was collected from 1999 to 2005, and it consisted of over 100 million anonymised ratings from almost half a million viewers. The Netflix Prize ran for nearly three years and the winner team, BellKor's Pragmatic Chaos,[1] managed to increase the platform's prediction accuracy by identifying specific statistical properties in the data that they could model into blended predictors.

These blended models allowed for a more accurate prediction of future viewer behaviour, which in turn developed into a subfield of machine learning research into recommender systems. To give an example, Toscher and Jahrer from the Big Chaos part of the winning team identified 'Small long term effects and stronger short term effects', which account for significant variance in rating patterns, and were possibly produced by users sharing their Netflix accounts.[2] Meanwhile, Piotte and Chabbert from the Pragmatic Theory part of the team identified other useful features, like the number of ratings a user made in a single day, and the elapsed time between watching and rating, and between ratings. The statistical significance of these features as predictors suggested to them that 'ratings provided immediately after having seen the movie and ratings provided months or years afterwards have different characteristics' (Piotte and Chabbert, 2009, 4). In other words, when users rate many items at once they are likely rating films they have seen in the past; they are rating based on distant memory rather than fresh experience.

These examples show how seemingly weak individual signals, like ratings, can be exploited when aggregated by the millions and analysed computationally. Moreover, it gives us a peek into the early days of an industry, how it produced new forms of economic value, but also the emerging issues that came along with it. In 2006 researchers managed to de-anonymise the competition's dataset (Narayanan and Shmatikov, 2006), and some of the users of the streaming service filed a class action lawsuit against the platform (Singel, 2009). Netflix cancelled the second edition of the prize short thereafter and has not released another dataset as significant since. The streaming company now conducts most of its research in-house and it rarely reveals viewing figures, let alone datasets. In 2017 the streaming company removed the five-star rating system and replaced it with a thumbs up/down button, and in 2018 it shut down the user review feature. Titles in the platform now show a personalised 'match score' as a percentage.[3] And although the company maintains a public dedicated research website, focused almost exclusively on machine learning and advanced analytics, most of the methods discussed in this site are not replicable without the data. Over the span of a decade, data extraction became more sophisticated and simultaneously fenced off from public view.

In hindsight, the Netflix Prize is now seen as a one-off case of public access to corporate data, but for our purposes here it clearly illustrates how treating films and television as data has been a key aspect of the company's financial success. In an interview, a senior executive at Netflix described their business as 'putting the right content in front of the right person at the right time, using the big data that we have available' and he went on to describe how treating their content as data had allowed the company to engineer 'taste communities' (Yellin, 2017). Community detection is a well-known task in network analysis, used for example to identify specific groups within larger social media networks (see Girvan and Newman, 2002). And by employing different types of machine learning techniques this idea can be extended, not only to map existing communities of viewers, but to predict future audiences. This can in turn be used to inform the commissioning of new films and shows, which in effect brings into existence the predicted audience.

In this way, moving images are leveraged as data to facilitate the extraction and aggregation of digital traces, what we could call 'micro affective resonances' produced by users as they watch moving images through the platform. These are minimal, passive, and even implicit expressions of aesthetic preference, like the seemingly trivial thumbs up/down, or even less overt viewing habits, recorded by simply using the platform. These traces can be processed into signals and in turn be transformed through computation into intangible data infrastructures. And from this perspective, the streaming giant trades in films and television no less than in computational models and digital services. Like many of its big tech siblings, it is both a media company and a technology company.

The ability to extract this type of value from their users is a key aspect of the platform's access to finance. In 2019, Netflix spent USD 15 billion in content; to put this figure into context, this is more than the cost of China's Beijing Daxing International Airport, one of the largest in the world. Such an investment can only be achieved through a sizeable claim on the future: the extraction of rents from future air passengers in the case of the airport, or of subscribers and advertisers in the case of Netflix. But unlike the airport's eight runways and 70,000 square meter terminal, for the streaming platform a significant portion of its claims on the future relies on aesthetic infrastructures, vast inter-subjective webs of meaning that might not be as tangible as concrete but can be just as lasting. In other words, much of the trust placed in Netflix by its investors is built under the assumption that there are meaningful statistical properties observable in large datasets, like the ones found by Pragmatic Chaos, and that these properties or effects can be used to calculate meanings, and predict taste and future patterns of consumption.

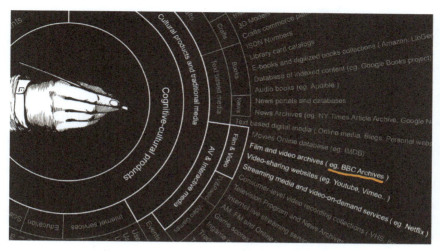

Figure 1.1 'Quantification of human-made products' Excerpt from 'Anatomy of an AI System: The Amazon Echo as an anatomical map of human labor, data and planetary resources' by Kate Crawford and Vladan Joler. https://anatomyof.ai

But even though it shares the market for on-demand content, the BBC differs in a key aspect with other streaming companies in that it is a public service corporation, financed for the most part through a licence fee which is officially classified as a tax levied on UK residents. This is an important distinction: Netflix and Amazon are beholden only to their shareholders, while the BBC has a legal obligation, as per its charter, to 'promote Public Purposes' and 'act in the public interest' ('BBC Charter', 2016, secs 4, 5). These public purposes include quality and creativity – arguably also pursued by commercial competitors – but also freedom of information and the promotion of learning and education, which are seen as matters of public interest, and are thus financed through taxation. By treating information and entertainment as a public service, in many ways the purposes of the BBC are meant to reflect the declared values of modern liberal democracies: individual freedoms and democratic governance; notions of impartiality, fairness, transparency, and accurate representation ('BBC Charter', 2016, secs 6, 12, 14).

From this perspective, and as per the public corporation's agreement with the UK government (BBC Agreement, 2016), there are two aspects that differentiate and complicate the data practices of the BBC with respect to its commercial counterparts. First, the explicit goal to strike a balance between the commercial exploitation of content (s65 4a) and the public value of making technological development openly available (s65 4b). This requires the BBC to share its technological developments, which in the case of data is interpreted as a commitment to open standards: 'technologies where opportunities to participate in their creation are made widely available, free of charge or on terms that are fair, reasonable and non-discriminatory' (s65 2). And second, the corporation's commitment to keeping and providing public access to its archive (s69). This obligation was introduced for the first time in the 2006 Framework Agreement (BBC Agreement, 2006, p. 47 sec86), and is now fulfilled in partnership with the British Library in the case of radio, and with the British Film Institute in the case of television.

This makes the television archive a particularly elusive source of data. On the one hand, the British broadcaster does not have to lease its content like Netflix originally did; it has its own archive to exploit, at least in principle. On the other, as a public broadcaster, the BBC needs to extract value from its archive in a way that is in the public interest. Part of the corporation's answers to these questions is expected to come from its R&D branch, which has been experimenting with machine learning techniques in various forms over the past few years, initially with a view to create operational efficiencies in TV production; in other words to automate 'repetitive' or 'formulaic' processes in the TV production pipeline:

> ... editing programmes is a deeply creative role, but an editor's first task when putting a show together involves finding good shots from a huge number of video assets [. . .] Sorting through those assets to find good shots isn't the best use of the editor's time – or the fun, creative part of their job. We think that AI could help to automate this for them. (BBC R&D, 2017a)

However, this was soon understood to be a narrow framing, and in 2017 BBC R&D signed a five-year partnership with eight UK universities to 'unlock the potential of data in the media' by creating a framework to make BBC data available for research (BBC R&D, 2017b). This framework focused on data science, but extended to the arts and humanities, and to creative domains: 'It's not just about physical sciences and engineering, it's about using data to be more creative' (Samantha Chadwick in BBC R&D, 2017b).

This is the broader context under which MbM was commissioned, at this juncture between the dwindling viewership of linear broadcast television, fierce competition from big tech and media companies with their proprietary data and tools, and the then vague promise of so-called creative AI. In this sense, MbM is at once a cultural product – a television programme; a technical ensemble – a computational system; and an intellectual data practice – a form of machine-seeing moving images.

As a television programme, the commission had three explicit goals, all aligned to the BBC's declared public purposes and mission to 'inform, educate and entertain', these were a) to show some of the limits and possibilities of the family of computational technologies popularly referred to as 'artificial intelligence' as applied to moving imagery; b) to activate and give public access to the BBC television archive through these technologies, and c) to create an entertaining television programme out of archive footage using these technologies.

As a computational system, our objective as a technical team was to see if, and to what extent, a computational model abstracted from the television archive could be used to produce a TV programme. The intuition behind this is that television is a highly conventional and structured medium, which suggests it ought to be possible to find patterns and learn meaningful computational representations of it through machine learning by analysing a large corpus from the archive. The idea was to test this hypothesis by: 1) applying different computational techniques to analyse and automatically annotate archive material; 2) cast these annotations as the dimensions of a multi-variate time series problem using machine learning; 3) use the learned representations as a 'television generator' that could compose new sequences of archive material automatically and produce television.

Finally, from a critical perspective, my own scholarly objectives going into the project were: a) to understand what kinds of knowledge are enabled through this type of computational analysis of moving imagery; b) to situate this knowledge in the wider traditions of film and media scholarship; and c) to aim towards a critical-technical framework for machine-seeing moving images. A fundamental condition for this last dimension of the project as well as the substance in this book is to shed some light on the human and computational processes involved in designing machine vision systems, the theories, assumptions, and choices that go into the making of these technical assemblages. Following this logic, and given the context presented above, we can take MbM as an example of how audiovisual archives morph into datasets, and how moving images become computational artefacts.

As mentioned earlier, MbM is comprised of four sections, each corresponding to a computational technique. Using the metadata generated through these techniques, new short sequences of clips are automatically edited together into the twelve-minute segments that are presented in the programme. The underlying assumptions for selecting these techniques were that: 1) films and TV can be construed as an organised combination of visual, linguistic and plastic representations; 2) that this organisation

34   CINEMA AND MACHINE VISION

is purposefully designed by the programme-makers; and 3) that these dimensions are entangled and often correlated with each other in ways audiences can decode and process upon viewing.

With the first three techniques the goal was to analyse and encode how these dimensions are organised as a coherent discursive stream of self-contained units purposefully designed by programme makers, namely by directors, scriptwriters, and editors, whom it was assumed would have the most creative control over what is said on screen, and what is shown and how. The last technique was designed to model the relations between these three dimensions across time to learn a basic computational representation audiovisual structure, assuming programmes are encoded by their makers and decoded by their audiences in a more or less stable manner. It was thought that the model abstracted through this last technique could then be used as a generator to automatically create new sequences of archive material: 'television by the meter' – as we once referred to it.

These basic assumptions are some of the instrumental *a prioris* to which I referred earlier, which are expected in the configurations of datasets but not necessarily in archives. The structure of the television archive is in this case completely ignored; categories that are important to archivists such as genres, years, producers, performers, et cetera, are subsumed into the functional purpose of the dataset, which semantically and structurally absorbs and reshapes any other organisational logic to facilitate computability. A categorical reorganisation and structural reversal are at play here, and interestingly, this reversal is also enacted in the narrative structure of the television programme, where technique structures content. Each of the techniques was called an 'AI mode' and is demonstrated through a sequence of archive material created by concatenating clips annotated with 1) similar objects, 2) similar topics in the subtitles, and 3) similar patterns of motion in the video footage. The outputs of these three techniques were then fed as input features to a machine learning algorithm in the hope of 4) learning their correlations across time. This last section was called 'AI mode: mixed' (Table 1.1).

Each of these four sections is bookended by a human presenter who provides an extra layer of context by explaining the logic of these techniques, and by a CGI talking head, an 'artificial host' who represents 'the voice of the machine' and describes its own functioning through anthropomorphisation, through lines like 'watch and learn, like me!"

In terms of data, the corpus was the result of a long and fraught process that stretched beyond the remit BBC R&D. Constraints in this regard were twofold: technical and legal. On the technical side, from the pro-

Table 1.1 *Made by Machine* – project breakdown

Section name in TV programme	High-level concept	Formal element	Method	Tool
Object detection	Visual	Visual representation	Computer vision	DenseCap
Subtitle analysis	Linguistic	Speech	Text analysis	TF-IDF
Visual energy	Plastic	Motion	Motion estimation	Vector subtraction
Mixed mode	Relational	Time	Time series modelling	Deep Learning

grammes available in digital form only a portion is directly accessible through the aforementioned internal Redux subsystem, which allows programmatic on-demand access to digital files. This reduced the scope to a subset of about 270,000 individual programmes, dating back from 1953 to the present day.

These programmes were automatically segmented using the internal scene detection algorithm of BBC R&D's Content Analysis Toolkit. This algorithm initially detects shot boundaries in edited video content by calculating the Euclidean distance between pixel colour values from one frame to the next. Above a certain threshold, an abrupt change in pixel colour values can indicate a change in shot. The algorithm then tries to identify scenes as clusters of these detected shots by comparing their colour histograms and calculating boundaries for these clusters. The idea is to automatically identify scenes as self-contained semantic units whose constituent shots tend to involve a distinct group of people, places, or actions – to separate a panel of specialists in a studio from a field reporter, for example. I return to automatic segmentation in Chapter 5.

Using this algorithm, the programmes were segmented into scenes, and further filtered to exclude short scenes (under ~10") or long scenes (over 1'55"). Although not very common, the shorter scenes were discarded on account of 'breaking the flow' of the sequence, while the threshold at the long end was decided under legal advice, since anything under two minutes allows these clips to be more comfortably protected for broadcast under the Fair Dealing provision of the UK's legislation on copyright (*Copyright, Designs and Patents Act*, 1988). And in fact, as the project evolved to not only accessing and sorting archive material but to actually (re)using it for broadcast, a much more stringent set of legal constraints became apparent: the BBC does not own the all the rights to many of the holdings of its archive (BFI, 2018) and therefore many programmes had to be manually discarded.

This issue was further complicated because in some cases, particularly in natural history and music, specific sections within programmes were unusable on account of copyright, even when the rest of the programme was, in principle, cleared for rebroadcast. Whether specific clips of archive material could be used depended on a number of factors, from music copyright to specific production companies, directors, and even cinematographers, holding some or all the rights for particular sections of the programmes and for different time periods. There was no straightforward way to automatically filter machine-generated clips for copyright, so to fully clear archive material for broadcast was a cumbersome time-consuming process that involved manually pre-selecting programmes that posed a low risk, and then showing the generated sequences to the BBC's specialised legal counsel, which meant several of the generated sequences had to be manually discarded and re-rendered several times over until a 'clean' sequence was achieved.

Another type of clip that was manually discarded was brand packaging. In particular, channel credits, 'idents', and trailers, which were in many cases part of the archived video streams. Trailers are comprised of clips from the programmes they trail, and because these programmes could also be part of the dataset, not filtering trailers could have resulted in clip duplication. Credits and idents on the other hand were deemed to be too confusing to leave in as part of the generated sequences; they included, for example, continuity announcements and other contextual information that made no sense outside of their original schedule, so these were removed at the request of the commissioning editor. Like with copyright, there was no simple or automated way of blacklisting any of these sections of the video-streams; their content, duration and occurrence within the programmes was somewhat haphazard, and like for copyright, several renders were also needed to manually filter out sequences that included these branding elements.

After all these constraints and interventions, the BBC television archive was reduced to a dataset of 15,572 clips. In terms of viewing time, this amounts to approximately 150 hours, or about a month's worth of TV watching for an average UK viewer,[4] which is arguably more than it is usually analysed in traditional media scholarship but still quite a possible corpus for a single researcher to tackle. This dataset is a small fraction of the archive, which as a whole accounts for ~150 years' worth of material – more than anyone would be able to watch in a lifetime.

This overview of the context and technical specification of MbM illustrates some of the key conceptual and material transformations that need to be enacted for archives to be cast as datasets that are amenable for computing, including the various choices, assumptions, and negotiations with existing ways to store and organise moving images. It should be apparent from this example that some of the most significant choices in this process are made at an early stage, when deciding the shape of the data; the features, sampling strategy, granularity, and desired output of the system. In other words, datasets are shaped after the systems for which they are intended, and in this sense, they are machine oriented. And this orientation is given; it is a layer of subjectivity that constraints automated vision even before any more complex computational processes are performed.

As machine vision relies on images, it inherits their technicity and some of their artefactual properties, but also the inter-subjective features, such as issues of perceived value, legal ownership, and social and cultural functions. The horizons of possible operations, purposes, and types of machine vision imaginable are therefore largely constrained by cultural assumptions about images, and how these assumptions lend themselves or resist being modelled computationally under the inductive logic of contemporary machine learning technologies. In short, the transition from archives to datasets enacts a particular kind of techno–aesthetics.

Notes

1. The name is a portmanteau of three different teams that merged during the competition: BellKor (Robert Bell, Yehuda Koren and Chris Volinsky), Pragmatic Theory (Martin Piotte and Martin Chabbert), and BigChaos (Andreas Töscher and Michael Jahrer).
2. The key insight Toscher and Jahrer had was to devise a way to incorporate time as a dimension into their restricted Boltzmann machine and k-nearest neighbour models (see: Töscher et al, 2009, p. 23, and Jahrer et al, 2010).
3. According to my viewing habits on Netflix, I am a 98 per cent match with *Apostle* (2018), but only 89 per cent with *The Devil Wears Prada* (2006), which to me sounds unreasonable, but now prompts me to consider that the algorithm 'knows' something about my taste in films that I do not.
4. Assuming the average of five hours a day given by BARB (2018).

CHAPTER 2

Inductive Vision

Data repeats itself, the first time as training, the second as prediction. Datasets bear upon datasets in the recursive and nested logic to machine learning systems, and in the types of vision these systems afford. Keeping with the example of MbM, let us turn to how machine vision works by induction, and the division of labour this design entails.

Let us start with one of the most common tasks in computer vision: object detection. This was the first technique applied to the BBC television dataset in conjunction with automated captioning. We used an implementation of DenseCap (short for 'dense captioning'), which is a method designed to 'localize and describe salient regions in images in natural language' (Johnson et al, 2015, p. 1). It consists of an integrated architecture of artificial neural networks specialised in both object detection and image captioning. The aim of DenseCap is to integrate these tasks into a unified system that could describe the objects of a scene and their relations.

For any given image passed as an input, DenseCap outputs several regions corresponding to detected objects (that can be visualised through the familiar coloured bounding boxes overlays), a confidence score of these detections, and a list of descriptions in natural language. The result is an annotation not just of objects in an image, but of relations between objects, actions, and places, such as 'a parked motorcycle', 'a man on a bicycle', 'a window on the building', and so on. Each clip in the BBC television dataset was annotated using the descriptions generated by DenseCap, at a three second sample rate and only including instances detected above a high threshold of confidence.

The annotations in natural language were then cast in vector space and cosine distance was calculated between them. Finally, using a similarity matrix of these distances, clips were concatenated into sequences by recurrently calling similar clips one after the other, a type of 'walk' through latent space. For the television programme, the annotations in natural language and their corresponding bounding boxes were shown fading one

INDUCTIVE VISION 39

Figure 2.1 Example of object detection on BBC archive footage

after another so that viewers could follow what was being detected and the degree of confidence in this detection: the thicker the bounding box, the more confidence on the predicted label (Figure 2.1).

The idea of using DenseCap in this way was to design a machine-led 'walk' of the television archive, this is, to generate sequences whose constituent clips followed a thread of similar depictions: a type of automated associational editing that identifies and juxtaposes similar visual tableaux belonging to different programmes of the archive.

One of the better-known examples of this type of algorithmic walk is Christian Marclay's 'The Clock' (2010), an art project that collates thousands of film-clips with depictions of clocks and people telling the time, all carefully edited so that the times represented on screen correspond to a real time duration of twenty-four hours. For his long-format montage, Marclay enlisted the help of a team of assistants who watched thousands of hours of films painstakingly searching for clocks, watches, and characters telling the time. In other words, he used human computers to perform his ambitious algorithmic walk through many hours of cinematic material.

The guiding intuition was that we could replace human computers with digital ones, and perform a similar type of associational montage, less ambitious in terms of accuracy, but perhaps richer in terms of complexity, given that our system would not be restricted to detecting simple objects like clocks, or Marclay's previous piece 'Telephones' (1995), but could, in principle, output more complex captions of the scenes.

Figure 2.2 Detected: 'A white shirt on a man'

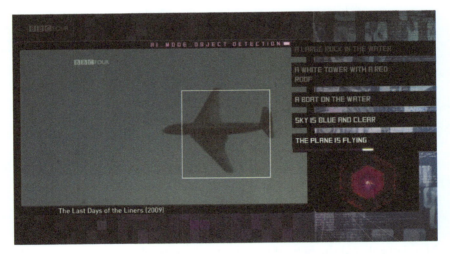

Figure 2.3 Detected: 'The plane is flying'

The results, however, did not match our expectations. Object detection through DenseCap was able to correctly identify some objects, and to an extent also some of their attributes, in particular men and the colour of their shirts, crowds, architectural features, transportation, and cows in fields (Figures 2.2–2.5).

But it proved quite limited at other basic detections: it consistently misgendered women (Figure 2.6) and outputted these and other misdetections with high confidence scores, for example describing a blurry background

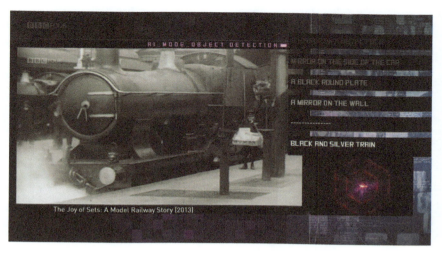

Figure 2.4 Detected: 'Black and silver train'

Figure 2.5 Detected: 'A large window'

painting as 'a reflection of a mirror' as the most salient detection instead of the woman in close-up directly addressing the camera in the foreground (Figure 2.7). These inaccuracies were particularly pronounced in shallow focus shots and/or grainy footage (Figure 2.8) and further compounded in shots with camera motion and/or complex framing (Figures 2.9–2.10).

Selective focusing, framing conventions, and camera motion are all basic staples of cinematic discourse, but instead of being encoded and accounted for in the computational representation, they had a detrimental

Figure 2.6 Misdetected: 'Man with a hat'

Figure 2.7 Misdetected: 'Reflection of a mirror'

effect on the expected performance of the system. How do object detection systems like this fail to 'see' these seemingly simple scenes?

From a technical perspective, there are several reasons that can be conjectured for the system's mediocre performance. For example, a low sampling rate at fixed intervals in video streams is likely to include frames with motion blur, which adds noise to the signal and makes accurate detection more difficult. Perhaps this effect can be attenuated by increasing the sampling rate or fine tuning the sampling strategy, for example

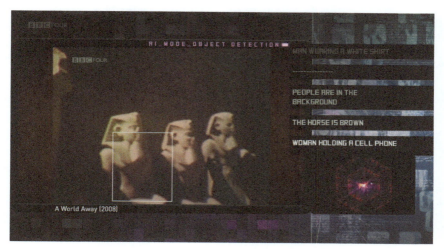

Figure 2.8 Misdetected: 'Woman holding a cell phone'

Figure 2.9 Misdetected: 'Hand holding a banana'

by extracting intra-coded frames only.[1] It is also likely that our embeddings make for a poor representation of image semantics on account of the density and/or diversity of the vocabulary used to describe them, meaning that DenseCap annotations were simply too similar and sparse to form a robust model in vector space. This too could be technically addressed in several ways.

But alongside these technical issues, a broader set of questions arises with these failings, notably how do we *know* that the system has failed?

Figure 2.10 Misdetected: 'Man wearing a red shirt'

And under what conditions do we expect it to be successful? In other words, what does it mean to say the predicted captions or the generated sequences can be improved or optimised? What is the benchmark for this?

In most computer vision literature, the answer tends to be that the baseline for comparison is human performance at the same or a similar task, but when it comes to vision this only complicates matters further: whose vision, exactly, is the system trying to replicate? And what does vision mean in this context? Perception, cognition, hermeneutics? All of the above? None of the above? Where does the *vision* part of machine vision come from?

These questions cannot be answered in terms of system optimisation but invite us instead to turn our attention to how these systems are organised and regulated through human activity. As stated earlier, MbM was made by people, but this is true in a broader sense; the computational representations leveraged in this project are contingent on an intricate web of relations – a socio-technical milieu that is purposefully configured and mobilised when these systems are deployed.

In the case of contemporary computer vision, this milieu can be traced back to ImageNet (2009), and further still to the rise of social media platforms during the second half of the 2000s, and specifically to the photography platform Flickr (2005).

Let us consider ImageNet first, a foundational dataset for computer vision and machine learning more generally, and the result of a collaborative effort, largely orchestrated by its designer and co-creator Fei-Fei Li. The project began in earnest in 2007 when Li met with Christiane Fellbaum, one of the co-creators of WordNet, which is a hierarchical lexical database for the English language. Using WordNet's lexical structure, Li and her colleagues conceived of a large dataset of labelled images which eventually became ImageNet (Li, 2019).

These images were sourced from the internet, initially via simple web queries and eventually upscaled to a process of massive parallel downloading. Soon thereafter, however, the labelling of millions of images proved to be a bottleneck in this production process. By Li's own estimations the project would have taken nearly twenty years, had it not been for crowdsourcing (Li, 2010). On the back of labels sourced through Amazon Mechanical Turk (AMT), ImageNet took off. By December 2008 her team had gathered about 3 million images and over 6,000 synsets;[2] by April 2010, 11 million images and over 15,000 synsets (Li, 2010). The project was officially presented in 2009 by Deng et al, and was set up shortly after as an open competition called the Large Scale Visual Recognition Challenge (ILSVRC), in which researchers used ImageNet as a benchmark to compare and improve their recognition and classification algorithms. Sometime after, Krizhevsky et al (2012) outperformed all other competitors by a significant margin, initiating the turn to neural networks and so-called 'Deep Learning' in AI research.[3]

More than a decade after its creation, ImageNet remains a widely used benchmark and a key referent in AI research. Many datasets for computer vision are subsets of the original 14 million images scraped off the web and labelled using 20,000 categories, and even those that are not directly taken from ImageNet are still conceptually indebted to Li's key intuition of crowdsourcing imagery and labels from the internet.

Besides its sheer scale, ImageNet is culturally significant because it provided a viable blueprint to reorganise productive forces, specifically labour and knowledge, by designing a system with which to muster thousands of hours of visual labour and compress them into a more or less stable computational artefact. Once captured, the potentialities of such labour can be stored and released at a later time, which in turn means this compressed latent visual labour can also be exchanged in a new marketplace, as an array of novel services of disembodied general vision: object detection, face recognition, image classification, and more recently style transfer and image synthesis. The conditions of success or failure of these systems hinge on their capacity to simulate the human process of inter-semiotic translation between natural language and images; describing, categorising, and synthesising visual worlds using language. Li's key insight from this

46   CINEMA AND MACHINE VISION

perspective was to find traces of this process online and extract a usable signal out of them.

And herein lies the significance of Flickr. The photo platform served as an infrastructure for the systematic sourcing of imagery. From its creation in 2004, Flickr cultivated and indeed grew around the Creative Commons initiative, its ethos and its communities (Lessig, 2003). This included several communities of amateur photographers who released their images under a Creative Commons licence. By 2009, the platform hosted about 100 million images licensed in this manner, making it the largest Creative Commons photo library assembled to date (Metawelle, 2009). This rapid growth came hand in hand with the wide adoption of social media and the mass adoption of consumer-grade digital cameras. The combination of amateur photography and licencing made Flickr's collection ideal for the large-scale harvesting of imagery needed for ImageNet.[4]

Similar to the foundational bargain of other social media platforms, the taking and tagging of images was undertaken voluntarily by users as a way to negotiate their participation into the social dimension of Flickr. By carefully tagging their own images, photographers inadvertently became the first in a long chain of labellers of what later became large datasets. It is precisely this initial layer of free labour that made the growing collection searchable programmatically through the platform's API (Application Programming Interface), which in turn allowed for the large-scale harvesting of images by their tags. And this mode of access befitted ImageNet lexical ontology very well, as researchers could filter down their hierarchical categories by adding or removing tags from their queries.[5]

In 2007, just at the time ImageNet was being assembled, the slogan of the photography platform was 'Share your photos. Watch the world.' In hindsight, this statement is very revealing: it prefigures the idea of a globalising gaze that one could cast upon 'the world' in exchange for one's own relatively small contribution of localised photographic practice. Today Flickr is somewhat of a relic of the heyday of blogging and the infancy of social media, but the platform played a significant role as a techno-aesthetic infrastructure in the rise of a machine learning paradigm that came to dominate AI research for the next two decades.[6]

With this knowledge, we are in a better position to disaggregate machine vision into its constituent elements and to reverse-engineer its nested logic, whenever and to the extent that these operations are in fact possible. Let us return to MbM and object detection and captioning to seek whose vision is encoded in it, by disassembling a specific recurrent detection: the system's obsession with men in shirts. This label and its variants,

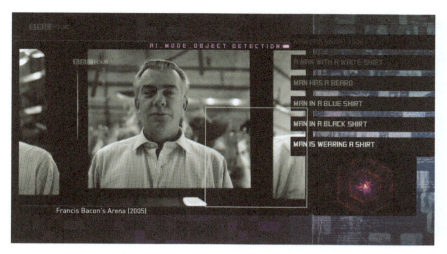

Figure 2.11 Variations of 'Man is wearing a shirt'

sometimes including colour attributes (Figure 2.11), are the most commonly predicted objects in the final generated sequence, and also noticeably prevalent in many other rendered sequences that did not make it into the final programme.

Taking these captions at face value, it is tempting to infer that the frequency of detection is somewhat representative of the BBC's television output in terms of gender representation on screen, a well-documented issue in film and television. According to a content analysis report, for example, the gender difference of on-screen people in BBC channels still favours men (62 per cent) over women (38 per cent) (Cumberbatch et al, 2018, p. 8).[7] Considering that our dataset includes programming spanning several decades prior to gender representation being an explicit concern for the British broadcaster,[8] it seems highly likely that there are many more instances of on-screen men than there are of women in the television archive. I could not find any reliable data on shirt-usage in the BBC, but again, given the timespan of the sampled programmes, it is reasonable to assume shirts might correlate with men who wear them.

There are, however, other possible sources of bias intrinsic to computer vision. The abundance of detected men in shirts could also be attributed to the underlying data used by DenseCap, which was trained on the Visual Genome dataset, a crowd-sourced collection of densely annotated images. This dataset is specifically designed to map representations of detected objects to language graphs (Krishna et al, 2017, p. 2). Compared to other large datasets, the Visual Genome is smaller in number of images but much denser in total descriptions per image.[9] Every image is annotated with an average of fifty region descriptions ('cycling elephant', 'city street'), thirty-five objects ('bicycle', 'wheel'), twenty-six attributes ('grey', 'large'), twenty-one relationships ('rides on', 'is with'), and a set of questions and answers ('who is riding the bicycle', 'where is the elephant?'). This allows for localised graph representations of each region in the image, as well as an integrated scene graph representation that describes relations for the whole image (p. 8–9).

In the Visual Genome dataset, 'man' is the most frequently occurring labelled object at almost 140,000 images, for only about 60,000 instances of 'woman'. And similarly, 'shirt' is in the top ten most frequently labelled objects, while 'white' is the most frequently used attribute in region description (Krishna et al, 2017, pp. 47–62). It is also possible, then, that given this training data, DenseCap learned a more robust internal representation of these labels and is therefore particularly sensitive to predicting captions like 'men in white shirt'. This issue has been in fact observed and acknowledged by researchers when crowdsourcing the labelling for the Visual Genome: 'collecting scene graphs directly from an image leads to workers annotating easy, frequently occurring relationships like wearing (man, shirt) instead of focusing on salient parts of the image' (Krishna et al, 2017, p. 43).

Although according to researchers several strategies were put in place to mitigate for these effects, it is still likely that some of the properties of the original data distributions were passed on to the models trained on these datasets.[10] What is more, one level deeper in the disassemblage, we find those who produce the annotations of these datasets. Like ImageNet, to annotate the Visual Genome dataset, over 30,000 unique labellers were employed through Amazon Mechanical Turk (AMT). According to their website at the time of writing, AMT enables organisations to 'harness the collective intelligence, skills, and insights from a global workforce to streamline business processes, augment data collection and analysis, and accelerate machine learning development' by breaking down 'manual, time-consuming project[s] into smaller, more manageable tasks to be completed by distributed workers over the Internet (also known as "microtasks")'.

The labour of these AMT workers, or 'turkers' as they are sometimes called online, is an often-overlooked human component of computer vision systems. In aggregate, these labellers constitute a distributed workforce used to build the datasets that were later used to train computer vision models. The distributed nature of their labour makes them difficult to pin down in terms of their specific and embodied ways of seeing, but it is clear that they are not, as is suggested by Amazon, 'a global workforce' or a generic 'collective intelligence', but rather a particular group of workers whose interpretive faculties cannot be dissociated from their culture; where they come from, their gender, their age, the language they speak, et cetera.[11]

In the case of the turkers employed to label the Visual Genome, these collective cultural characteristics are significant: over 90 per cent were from the USA, and over 60 per cent were under 34 years of age (Krishna et al, 2017, p. 44). These are not the traits of 'global' or 'general' demographics, but of a much more homogeneous group whose collective interpretations of imagery are mobilised when DenseCap detects objects and describes a scene. This layer of human labour should give us pause to consider how computer vision embodies, quite literally, the worldviews of a particular group of people; it is their perception and understanding of imagery – what they consider 'easy' or 'salient' – that is being encoded in their labelling, and then learned and abstracted into the computational model used to machine-see the BBC archive.

In contrast, over 90 per cent of BBC Four viewership is aged over 35 (OFCOM, 2017), which means that in a sense there are at least three layers of viewing nested across several decades: the older British audience of BBC Four saw how the younger US ATM workers saw the even older BBC TV archive. On the other hand, in terms of gender, the male to female ratio of the labellers appears to be more balanced at 54 per cent to 46 per cent (Krishna et al, 2017, p. 44), and corresponds better with the audience of BBC Four, which is approximately 53 per cent to 47 per cent (OFCOM, 2017).

These visual palimpsests are quite common in machine vision assemblages. In his typology of technical objects, Simondon argues that the assemblage is the least stable configuration, as they can be 'temporary or even occasional', and he names the construction site of buildings or shipyards as examples of contingent assemblages (2017, pp. 76–77). AMT can be thought along these lines, as a type of hyper-contingent factory: a large construction site set up in the cloud (in Amazon's cloud),[12] where tens of thousands of workers coalesce to build a massive dataset one 'micro-visual task' at a time, thereby compressing millions of hours of regular human vision into a computational artefact.

Given the distributed and fragmentary nature of this production process, which summons an *ad-hoc* labelling group from an ever-changing pool of workers, it is particularly difficult to know more about who exactly is doing the viewing for/behind/in the machine. One reference to their ethnicity in the literature, Huff and Tingley (2015, p. 4) suggest that although AMT workers are mostly white, compared to other instruments for demographic measurement in the USA, the crowdsourcing platform attracts in proportion younger Hispanic and Asian respondents and fewer older African Americans. But this is only a snapshot view of the platform in 2015, and it has also been shown that the AMT workforce is highly volatile and has changed significantly over the years (Difallah et al, 2018; Ipeirotis, 2010). This makes the vision part of machine vision systems rather intractable in terms of those doing the viewing, yet what is clear is that designers and labellers play a significant role and bring with them the worldviews and biases that will later be reproduced and amplified through automation.

Buolamwini and Gebru (2018), Noble (2018), and Klare et al (2012), among others, have shown how datasets consistently under-sample groups already under-represented in many other social arenas; particularly women, black, Asian, and non-white people, and have pointed to the consequences of these and other sources of bias in the resulting computational systems. To be clear, these biases are widely documented, and critics are correct in pointing them out. Yet, in my view the call to address issues of power and injustice in AI should not be reduced to better or more representative datasets. Underlying data is critical, but being better represented in a dataset does not *de facto* change people's actual social standing and political agency. Or on the contrary, one could argue that by 'fixing' uneven datasets we could in fact be contributing to the erasure of difference and unwittingly assisting with the concealing of structural inequalities in more sophisticated ways.

In other words, the question of whether machine vision ought to accurately reflect the collective judgements of its underlying human seers or attempt instead to correct these judgements after the fact is not trivial and cannot be answered at the level of 'better data', meaning more representative or ethically sourced, although such data might be desirable anyway. Even when we admit there is a lot to be done to improve datasets, and even if we conceded there was such thing as a perfectly balanced dataset, we must be careful not to make the inferential leap to fairer or more just forms of AI from more and cleaner data.

To address the issues of representation from a broader perspective, a moral subject needs to be conjured as an externality to data, not as an abstract ideal of what is socially desirable and the impact machine vision has or could have in this ideal, but as a concrete effort to identify the people involved in the organisation and enactment of these desires. Locating power dynamics in machine vision systems will inevitably involve the people whose views are encoded in them, and our focus therefore must shift from data to those involved in the constitution of machine vision; how they enact their desires through technical means and what are their conditions of participation and exclusion in these assemblages.

This task is much more difficult in Deep Learning systems due to their inductive logic. As we saw with ImageNet, many collections of annotated imagery used in computer vision are subsets or variations that can be traced back to a handful of these large datasets created by academic researchers, and more recently also sponsored by large corporations. The Visual Genome is no exception, it is comprised of images from the intersection between two other datasets: YFCC100M (Thomee et al, 2016)[13] and MS-COCO (Lin et al, 2014), both of which use images from Flickr. And like in the case of AMT workers, the community of Flickr photographers whose pictures were siphoned from the web to assemble the Visual Genome are from specific communities, with their own identities, interests, and indeed biases. In the case of YFCC100M, for instance, most photographs were taken in London, Paris, Tokyo, New York, San Francisco, and Hong Kong.[14]

Figure 2.12 shows a map of one million geo-tagged photos with Creative Commons licences, the kind of images used to train computer vision systems post-ImageNet.

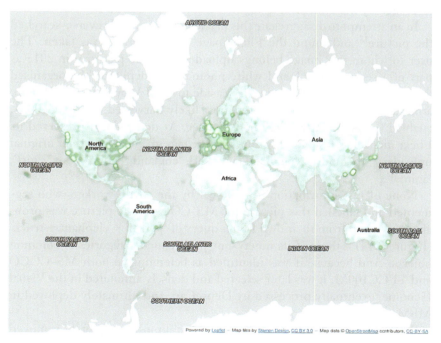

Figure 2.12 One Million geo-tagged photos with Creative Commons licences. CC BY-ND 2.0 David Shamma

MS-COCO, on the other hand, also collects some of the same Flickr pictures but further refines their annotation by segmenting regions of the image into pre-defined common object categories. These common objects were identified partly by a small group of children aged 4–8, but are also inherited categories from yet another dataset, PASCAL VOC (Everingham et al, 2010). And these categories were finally narrowed down by the researchers themselves, who removed difficult-to-find objects and privileged object categories according to 'their usefulness for practical applications' (Lin et al, 2014, pp. 744–745). Because there are probably few practical applications to detecting ancient Egyptian kings or puppets, these labels did not make it to the final 91 categories in MS-COCO and were thus never available as captions in MbM.

To complicate things further, even in datasets created from scratch, researchers very often rely on retrieval systems that use their own machine learning systems and pipelines of AMT workers, so here we find another nested layer of people whose points of view are being abstracted and generalised, but of whom we know almost nothing. By the time the DenseCap detects an 'elephant with a black and white shirt' (Figure 2.13), it has become exceedingly difficult to disaggregate the many layers of vision leveraged by the system.

In an attempt to disaggregate this particular example, I reverse-searched the picture[15] and found the Flickr page from where it was taken. The user to whom this image belongs uploaded it to the platform in 2013 as part of a series of black and white photographs depicting the organised washing of circus elephants in the seaside town of Weymouth, in Britain, around 1987, and the picture was most likely harvested in YFCC100M, enabled by the Creative Commons licence. At that point it preserved its Flickr identifier, title, description, and the tags given to it by their original uploader: 'weymouth', 'elephant', 'dorset', 'england', 'child', 'boy', 'girl', 'animal'.

None of this information was known by the AMT workers who segmented and labelled this picture for MS-COCO. The picture was probably picked up from their own Flickr query of 'person + elephant + truck' (Figure 2.14) – three of its ninety-one pre-defined categories of common objects. And because it was identified as belonging to both MS-COCO and YFCC100M, it was later selected and densely annotated in the Visual Genome, eventually processed by DenseCap, and ultimately deployed in MbM.

The captions produced at this point are almost completely removed from the uploader's original descriptions, as are their reasons for keeping this particular image and any context of the depicted scene itself. Through

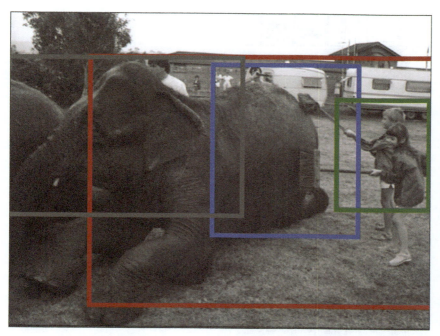

Figure 2.13 DenseCap detection of 'Elephant with a black and white shirt'

this disassemblage exercise, we can then sketch a more accurate picture of how machine vision is constituted, and where the vision in it comes from, at least for this one example:

1. In 1987, a man saw some circus elephants being washed in the southern coast of England. He found this scene interesting enough to photograph, so he did: he captured some light through a lens which made an impression in photosensitive emulsion affixed to some strip of celluloid.
2. Sometime after the elephants were washed, this negative was used to print the captured scene onto photographic paper, where it remained, slowly degrading, for the next couple of decades.
3. As the photographer grew old, he probably remembered this scene, found the piece of paper and scanned it, at which point a decade's old record in photosensitive paper became bitmap x on a computer.

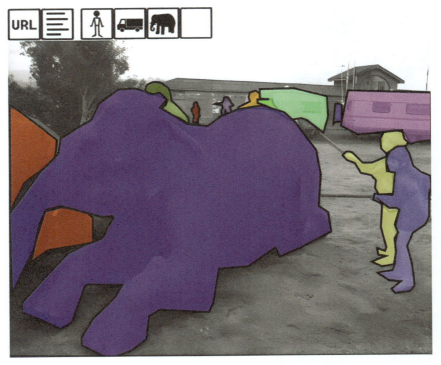

Figure 2.14 MS-COCO segmentation and labelling example.
Source: http://cocodataset.org/#explore?id=206876

4. Sometime after, he uploaded this bitmap x to Flickr, probably as a way to share the picture with others.
5. A couple of years later, and unbeknownst to him, his picture, among hundreds of thousands of others, was extracted from the platform through a script engineered by machine learning scientists and engineers. The picture of the elephant was then seen entirely out of context by a group of workers distributed throughout various parts of the world, although likely in the US, who in all likelihood never met the photographer, but who, for a few cents, encoded and attached their own annotations y to his bitmap x.
6. Shortly after, another group of scientists and engineers put millions of these x, y digital pairs through a computational engine designed to identify non-linear relations between x and y, and used this model to predict potentially similar interpretations y^n in other bitmaps x^n.
7. A few years later, a group of technologists and a researcher in the UK, who have met neither the photographer nor the paid annotators, nor

the other scientists, used this computational model to make predictions on a sample of pictures taken from a set of television programmes.

8. These predictions were then recirculated as yet another television programme, whose audience saw the seeing of others as if they were the visual interpretations of a disembodied machine.

By tracing the technical lineage of a single picture in the pipeline, it becomes clear that when the computer is said to be 'seeing' on our behalf, a vast and intricate network of visual, para-visual, and post-visual events, scattered in time and space, is being mobilised.

This underlying logic of machine vision can thus be understood primarily as a type of inductive vision, in which millions of small traces of human perception and cognition are abstracted into computational models. As a result of this process, much of the image's ontological density is stripped away – its provenance, context, and social interpretations are collapsed, obscured, or otherwise lost to the viewer at the end of the induction pipeline. Images lose in this way their symbolic density, as their traditional representational powers, which come from their concrete historical orientation, are gradually eroded in favour of computability and subsumed into broader, newer, powers of automated vision.

That these photos are what in technical literature is referred to as 'non-canonical images' – pictures of everyday people in their everyday circumstances, including mundane scenes, places, and objects – points to a significant departure and reorganisation of visual knowledge. Even if, as we have seen, these photos are not representative of global visual culture, they are still a much wider slice of it than pre-ImageNet datasets, which had been mostly designed and sourced in the context of scientific laboratories.[16]

That these images are taken *en mass* from 'the wilderness' of the internet, marks an important turn to culture in computer vision and AI more generally, which had hitherto been more preoccupied with logic and mathematics than with everyday people, their desires, and certainly their collective aesthetic inclinations.[17] This move is a conceptual departure from the laboratory as a controlled environment in which to conduct experiments, and towards what Italian autonomists called 'the social factory', a construct by which 'the whole of society lives as a function of the factory and the factory extends its exclusive domination to the whole of society' (Tronti, 1962). According to the *operaistas*, to extend such domination, labour had to be redefined to encompass not only the material transformations workers performed at the factory, but also to include the surplus value created through collective social and cultural production.

In his reading of Romano Alquati, one of the lesser known *operaistas* who interviewed workers at the Olivetti computer factory in northern Italy, Matteo Pasquinelli reframes this question of labour in the digital economy as a cleavage between flows of energy and information:

> At the beginning of the industrial age capitalism started to exploit human bodies for their mechanical energy, but soon it became clear, Alquati notes, that the most important value was originated by the series of creative acts, measurements and decisions that workers constantly had to perform. Alquati calls *information* precisely all the innovative micro-decisions that workers have to take along the production process, that give *form* to the product, but also that give form to the machinic apparatus itself [. . .] With Alquati we visit the belly of an abstract machine that is a concretion of capital no longer made of steel. For the first time the cybernetic apparatus made palpable and visible the transformation and sedimentation of information into fixed capital. (Pasquinelli, 2015, pp .6–8, emphasis in the original)

Pasquinelli's re-framing of the productive process certainly echoes Fei-Fei Li's efforts to configure computer vision towards popular culture. Today, images cannot be easily understood to stand by themselves, not even as products. Their valorisation, to keep with Marxist terminology, largely depends on their added informational and computational dimensions, which in practice are very often given as metadata. As Harvey and LaPlace note: 'A photo is no longer just a photo when it can also be surveillance training data, and datasets can no longer be separated from the development of software when software is now built with data' (2019).

The value of an image is in this way increasingly a function of how easily it can be handled as a data object and computed into computer vision systems. However, we must also remember that these images and their metadata are traces of visual culture as much as increasingly a part of it. That these images are circulated and reproduced as digital files through the internet does not fully account for their existence, on the contrary, as we have seen, by treating images *cua* data their origins are very often obfuscated, and their ontologies displaced. We must take care not to let their ubiquity nor their datafied modes of circulation confuse us; these are photographic images; they embody technical ways of seeing that contemporary machine vision inherits and selectively reproduces.

In this way, our inquiry into machine vision unfolds into a deeper layer of technical regimes on which it is built and which it remediates. And it follows from this that photographers too need to be recognised as key historical subjects in the constitution of what we might call, following

INDUCTIVE VISION

57

the operaistas: a social factory of vision, which enlists the powers of photographic and para-photographic practices. In the next chapter we take a closer look at these powers and how they co-constitute machine vision *beneath* data.

Notes

1. In video compression, an intra-coded frame (I-frame) is a complete still image encoded without reference to any other frame. At decoding time, these key-frames are used to decode other frames and for random access, which in digital television are encoded at $+-0.5$ seconds to provide a fairly accurate refresh period when users scrub through the progress bars during playback in video streams. Our *DenseCap* sampling is considerably lower resolution than the encoder's number of I-frames. I did run some experiments extracting I-frames using FFMPEG, expecting these to be 'cleaner' than fixed-rate samples frames, and while they were indeed larger data-wise, perceptually I found there was no difference in terms of motion blur.

2. A *synset* or a synonym set is a technical concept widely used in information retrieval and computational linguistics. WordNet, which is the lexical database on which ImageNet is based, defines it as a set of one or more synonyms that are interchangeable in some context without changing the truth value of the proposition in which they are embedded.

3. Before convolutional neural networks became popular again, computer vision was dominated by other approaches with an emphasis on algorithms, for example restricted Boltzmann machines, first proposed by Smolensky (1986) but rediscovered along with other forms of neural networks in the mid-2000s (see: Hinton and Salakhutdinov, 2006). Fei-Fei Li's own earlier work on Caltech 101 is also exemplary of this transition (see: Fei-Fei Li et al, 2004; compare with: Griffin et al, 2007). For more on the Neocognitron see: Fukushima (1980) and for more on Deep Learning see: LeCun et al (2015).

4. As elaborated on in the previous chapter, images can be protected by copyright in different territories and under different legal systems. Copyright issues can result in contrived legal cases; for example, David Slater's 'Monkey Selfies'. In 2014 a US court had to rule on whether Indonesian macaques could own copyrights of the selfies, and in 2015 PETA filed a lawsuit against Slater on behalf of Naruto, the macaque (Wong, 2017). Newer datasets are more careful to advertise their use of Creative Commons imagery, and to issue accompanying privacy statements. Flickr 1024 (2019), for example, very publicly states that the images are 'not the property of our laboratory' and are 'available for non-commercial use only. Therefore, you agree NOT to reproduce, duplicate, copy, sell, trade, or resell any portion of the images and any portion of derived data'. And Flickr Faces HQ even offers a web interface to find if any of your photos are in their dataset, as well as a process to remove them if that is the case.

58   CINEMA AND MACHINE VISION

5. At the time of writing, approximately half of all ImageNet images (~7 million) corresponded to Flickr URLs.

6. As computer vision spreads to other domains, so too do its constituent datasets. For example, with an influx of industry investment in the various projects for autonomous vehicles, the sources for images have expanded in the last few years from everyday pictures of amateur photographers to roads and cars, and imagery for these new set of applications is being sourced from dashboard cameras and street video feeds (Caesar et al, 2019; Yu et al, 2018; Cordts et al, 2016).

   But the interest in popular photography has not diminished. Instead, shifts like these are assimilated and built on top of previous layers of research, and so these new datasets are added to the existing ecology that drives the general programme of computer vision both as scientific and an industrial pursuit. In this extended ecology, and certainly for most general applications and academic AI research, the use of Flickr images is still pervasive: from 'historical' general datasets such as PASCAL VOC (Everingham et al, 2010) and Microsoft's COCO (Lin et al, 2014), to more recent and specific ones like Flickr Faces HQ (Karras et al, 2019) developed to train generative adversarial networks; Flickr 1024 (Wang et al, 2019), which is designed to create super resolution images, and of course the Visual Genome, which we used in MbM for dense captioning.

7. This report did not include observations from BBC Four, only the larger BBC One and BBC Two were analysed, but very little variance was found between them.

8. To the extent that comedy panels in UK television are any indication of gender representation on screen, significant change starts to occur in 2008, see: https://www.strudel.org.uk/panelshows/byyear.html

9. ImageNet (Deng et al, 2009) has over 14 million images, one object per image; Tiny Images (Torralba et al, 2008) has 80 million images, one object per image.

10. See: Section 4.1 'Crowd Workers' in Krishna et al. 2017.

11. This also makes them a particularly vulnerable workforce, as the conditions of their employment are under-regulated and the nature of their 'micro-tasks' completely alienates them from the ubiquitous products and services they are contributing to create. This means they do not have good ways of assessing the worth of their collective labour, which in turn makes it very hard for them to unionise or otherwise organise to gain leverage in the many labour markets where they participate. In this, they are a symptom of the larger political economy of AI, to which I return later. See: 'Turking for a Living' (http://video.newyorker.com/watch/annals-of-ideas-turking-for-respect).

12. I am referring to Amazon Web Services (AWS), arguably the largest and most profitable provider of cloud services in the world.

13. Yahoo Flickr Creative Commons 100 Million.

14. These are the only cities with more than 10,000 unique entries in the dataset.

15. I used the 'search by image' feature in Google.
16. Caltech 101 and 256 are examples of this kind of dataset.
17. Contrast, for example, contemporary AI research, with its focus on mining for datasets online, with Shannon's Information Theory of the 1950s.

CHAPTER 3

Machine Learning and the Philosophy of Photography

In 2019, Fei-Fei Li was asked about the choice of using photographs for ImageNet during an event celebrating the tenth anniversary of the dataset: 'That's a great question,' she replied, 'We didn't really stop to think much about it [. . .] I suppose we wanted as realistic a representation of the world as possible' (Li, 2019).

Li is not alone in her assumption about realism and photography. A widely shared intuition about photographic images is that 'the camera does not lie' or that in any case it lies less than other methods of depiction. In an often-cited passage of his influential *Ontology of the Photographic Image*, André Bazin (1960 [1958]) wrote that the invention of photography and cinema:

> satisf[ies], once and for all and in its very essence, our obsession with realism. No matter how skillful the painter, his work was always in fee to an inescapable subjectivity. The fact that a human hand intervened cast a shadow of doubt over the image. (p. 7)

What he meant exactly by 'realism' has been the subject of much debate since, but this view of photographs as trusted visual renderings of the world due to their alleged automatic mode of production has proved remarkably enduring.

Li's response earnestly voices just such a view, which assumes that drawings or paintings are inextricably bound to the mental states and technical abilities of their authors (as well as the embodied command of these states and abilities), while photographs appear to be pictures produced through mind-independent processes, which is to say, they capture whatever is in front of the camera regardless of what the photographer believes about what is in front of the camera. For example, I might firmly believe that I look exactly like the actor Danny Trejo, but this belief will play no role in how my selfie actually appears to others, which is to say, my subjective understanding of my appearance has no bearing on the appear-

MACHINE VISION AND THE PHILOSOPHY OF PHOTOGRAPHY 61

ance captured by my camera. Under this logic, were I to include many photos of me in a dataset used to train a Trejo classifier, it simply would not work as intended.

This idea of mind-independence is at the centre of many popular intuitions about the photographic image and informs some of its forensic uses. Very few of us would be likely to admit animation (a sequence of drawings) in lieu of video surveillance footage (a sequence of photographs) as evidence of an event having taken place or proof of the identity of those involved, especially when the stakes of credibility are high, as they are when such images are used to secure a conviction or deny a person entry to a country, for example. It is clear from the type of relationship we have with photographic images that they hold a privileged epistemic position compared to other forms of visual representation, and that this position is commonly explained as an intrinsic recording feature of the photographic process, which amounts to saying that cameras can only show what is there to be seen.

This popular notion of mind-independence mechanical process has also informed philosophical explanations about the epistemic advantage photographs seem to hold over other types of images in, for example, the works of Cavell (1979); Cohen and Meskin (2004); Walden (2005); Abell (2010) among others. One formulation of this argument proposed by Gregory Currie (1999) is that we treat photographs as traces as opposed to testimonies. The former are counter-factually dependant on nature, like a footprint, in a way that the latter are not, like the tale of how I once took a step in the mud. For the footprint to be any different, Currie would argue, the sole of my shoe would have had to differ accordingly, while a description of the step I took, however rich or detailed, necessarily implicates the intentions of the describer and belongs therefore to a different epistemic register altogether. According to this view, the social credibility lent to photographs makes them more akin to light detections captured as a result of a mind-independent mechanical processes, while paintings and other pictures made by hand tend to be seen as someone's depiction of a scene; this is, as the result of an embodied cognitive and creative process.

This is the dominant logic that underwrites computer vision too, at least in its current form and so far as it is powered by photographic images, from which it inherits, exploits, and amplifies their epistemic advantage founded on this mind-independent conjecture about the photographic process. When millions of photographs are aggregated into large datasets and used to train machine learning systems, the representational powers of photography and computation compound, to the point where predicted labels are also seen as traces, for instance 'face detection' and not 'face depiction'. The predictive tokens produced by computers are thereby presented as the counter-factually-dependent *and* mind-independent detections of something or someone. This person or this object was seen automatically and therefore *had* to be there to be seen.

But to what extent is this view really warranted? Does it hold in a world of CGI, deepfakes, and other forms of synthetic imagery?

As commonly encountered as it is, this explanation about the epistemic advantage of photography is far from accepted in arts and humanities scholarship. In philosophy in particular, the mind-independent thesis has been put under mounting pressure by the so-called New Theory of photography, whose proponents argue for an expanded view of the photographic event as a multi-staged process of which only some parts can be said to occur automatically (Maynard, 1997; Phillips, 2009; Lopes, 2016; Costello, 2017). Costello, for example, identifies a contradiction in ascribing epistemic value to photographs on the basis of their supposed mind–independence processes while simultaneously characterising these processes as automatic. A process cannot be both natural and automatic, he argues, without radically separating humans from nature (2017, p. 42). Automatic processes are causally-dependant but not spontaneous according to Costello. For a process to be called automatic it should be possible to specify it in terms of the labour that is being delegated to a mechanism, one that serves human ends and therefore necessarily involves human minds. Costello asks:

> just what is it exactly that is supposed to 'happen by itself'? [. . .] In photography, almost everything that expresses comparable choices [to painting] happens *off* the support – the choice of lens, distance, lighting, moment of exposure, point of view, etc. [. . .] This can give those who have no idea where to look the impression that the photographer has done very little, or that the mechanism is responsible. But this is plain ignorance. The fact that so many of the acts take place prior to the image appearing 'all at once' does not negate the photographer's responsibility for what then appears. Merely noting depth of field markers in an image already tells us much about what the photographer was after. One needs to be a competent judge in photography as in any other domain; and this requires a basic grasp of the internal relations between focus, depth of field, and exposure that most Orthodox theorists fail to evince. (2017, p. 45, emphasis in the original)

From this perspective, photographs are seen as faithful visual representations by virtue of their mechanisms no less than by the ways in which such mechanisms are controlled and regulated by photographers. A closer inspection of photographic processes requires us to consider that our intuition of what is a 'realistic' image rests as much on what a photograph shows than on how it shows it. In other words, that the photographic

MACHINE VISION AND THE PHILOSOPHY OF PHOTOGRAPHY 63

image is granted its privileged epistemic position in society by adding, not subtracting layers of subjectivity; not 'without the creative intervention of man' (p. 7), as Bazin would have it, but precisely because of it.

A critical view of computer vision is therefore incomplete without considering photography as a creative practice as well as a technology comprised by its own family of technical devices and internal relations, governed by norms that are very often imposed by the social functions it serves and that are carefully policed by its various communities. But to include creativity and subjectivity as an explanation of photography's epistemic advantage requires a different type of work, one that involves locating the technical cultures and institutional contexts where these layers of subjectivity form and sediment in order to understand just how photographers make depictions that appear more realistic than others under specific contexts. If the depicted is indeed epistemically bound to the process of depiction, why should we not care about this process when it comes to computer vision?

One of the reasons photographic cameras appear to record the world automatically is that many of the calculations needed to render space visible are pre-programmed in the photographic devices themselves, most significantly in photographic lenses. When photographers 'pull' an image into focus by adjusting the focus ring, the lens is doing some of the heavy lifting in terms of the calculations necessary to harness light convergence and render a slice of space visible in a specific manner. This is not to say the lens itself 'knows' or 'thinks', but rather that thought has been put 'into' the lens as information that is, quite literally, crystallised in its design, and that the photographer is able to interface with this latent space of calculation through the camera controls. Let us expand on how this coupled system of photographer and lenses works through an example.

A camera system differs in many ways from human vision, one notable example being that the human eye auto-focuses light unconsciously. The opposite is true in a photographic system, where focusing is carefully controlled through lenses and lens mechanisms. At its most basic, a lens consists of one or more pieces of transparent glass arranged so as to bend light, usually with the purpose of making it converge at a point in space, which in optics is called a focal point. The distance between this focal point and the lens is known as focal length, and it is calculated using the lens maker's equation. For an image of an object to form and be in focus, the light it reflects would have to go through the lens and be projected onto an image plane (a surface or a screen) placed exactly at its focal point and perpendicular to the lens axis. The distances between object, lens, and image plane are calculated using the thin lens formula.

'Focusing' has in this way a double meaning: we use it to describe the appearance of an image – as its edges are rendered sharp and its shapes are well-defined – but also to describe an algorithmic process of convergence, where a distinct signal has been made differentiable through calculation. Appearance and process are both contingent on each other and on the signal field they operate in, such that to focus means to maximally condense a signal that we wish to observe in all its possible definition; in its concentrated (convergent) form, and to the expense of the rest of the field. Photographers pull focus by adjusting the focus ring in their lenses, in a manner not dissimilar to how machine learning scientists and engineers experiment and fine-tune their algorithmic hyper-parameters. Both can be seen as algorithmic processes, only in one case the gradual minimisation of error to achieve convergence is performed by the photographer who looks at the changing appearance of the image and progressively adjusts their lens, while in machine learning minimisation of error is performed mathematically through a loss function defined by the system designer. In both cases an error space has been defined and an algorithmic process designed to minimise error in this space.

That we have not traditionally thought of photographic lenses as machinery with which to calculate is perhaps because their inputs and outputs are presented as images and not numbers or letters. We do not know, for example, whether an image is in focus if presented as a matrix of pixel values, or a sequence of tokens; the photographer needs to see it 'all at once' in order to evaluate it. However, the intermediate steps of interaction involved in producing photographic images are in fact heavily mediated by algorithmic processes and standardised metrics: focal length, exposure, aperture, and ISO, among others. These can and often are expressed as numbers that describe the internal relations of the photographic mechanism, and their different permutations for a variety of lenses constitute the palette of choices available to photographers at any given time. That photographers need not perform optic calculations themselves in order to mobilise their effects is one of the most salient affordances of photography as a technology, and connects it to computer vision in their shared overarching project to automate visual perception through calculation, with the obvious difference that in the case of photographic lenses such calculation is performed by an analogue machine: a computer made of glass.

Like with machine learning techniques, frameworks, and conventions, it took time for photographic practices and the images produced by them to sediment as visual and technical standards in culture. In the early days of photography, to achieve the convergence of light required to produce images in focus was far from a solved problem, and still very much an experimental endeavour. Consider, for example, that not all colours will converge at a single or precise focal point when projected through a single piece of glass because light from distinct colours will have different refracting indexes. In optics, this phenomenon is called chromatic aberration. Photographic lenses thus developed into arrangements of several glass elements of different shapes and materials to correct for these and other undesired effects of such optical aberrations. For example, the Chevalier Meniscus of 1839, famously used by Louis Daguerre, was a lens composed of two elements (layers) made of several types of glass that in combination compensate with each other to reduce chromatic aberration, or in other words to minimise this particular kind of error.[1]

One year later, an Austrian mathematician named Joseph Petzval employed several human computers to aid in the design a new four-element lens capable of under-one-minute exposures: the Petzval Portrait. His design produced photographs that were centrally sharp but that softened out of focus around the edges, creating a vignetting effect. This effect proved to be extremely popular, as this trade-off between speed and focus was well suited for portraits, where faces occupied a central space in the picture and longer exposure times were a limitation. 'The lens was not without flaws, but the qualities of the image that it produced were so distinctive and well-appreciated that it defined expectations for photographic portraiture for the next six decades' (Peres, 2007, p. 159). Now consider this in opposition to landscape photography, where regions of interest were often less consistently centred in the frame and photographed objects were often inanimate.

With the development of faster photosensitive emulsions in the 1850s,[2] photographic lenses and cameras began to incorporate other mechanical elements such as aperture stops[3] and eventually camera shutters, which allowed greater control over the intake of light (Kingslake, 1989, pp. 10–12). As these elements gained popularity, the combination of lens, aperture, and exposure settled into a well-defined palette of technical choices – the hyper-parameters, so to speak, that came to regulate and structure photographic practice thereafter. Conversely, as photography became more accessible and diverse as a practice, lens manufacturing grew into an industry and lens design specialised. Take as an example the famous Double-Gauss family of lenses, of which there are hundreds of branching variants commercialised by different manufacturers, several of which are still in use today (Figure 3.1).

From a technical perspective, the design of photographic lenses can be thought of as the trade-offs negotiated between the physical and material

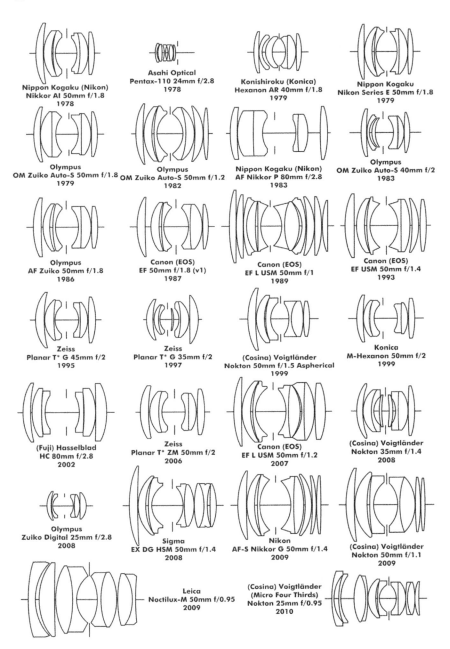

Figure 3.1 Double Gauss lens designs 1978–2010. CC BY-SA 3.0 Paul Chin.

constraints of optics and the social functions given to the images these mechanisms afford, for instance some lenses were better suited for portraits, others for landscapes. Gradually, and under the evolving norms of different social contexts, some of the undesired optical effects and their proposed technical corrections got thematised into aesthetic forms, some of which endured, like the vignetting effect produced by the Petzval Portrait, which is now available as a filter option in mobile phone applications like Instagram.

Take focal length as an example of these techno-aesthetic developments. Today focal length is widely used as a standard measure for lens classification, since it correlates with the size of the image plane and the aperture of the camera to define, among other things, the field of view (how much of a given scene fits into the frame) and the depth of field (how much of it is in focus at any given time). For a full-frame format, a wide-angle lens (for instance 28mm) will cover a wider field of view and have a deeper focus range, while a telephoto (for instance 300mm) will magnify to a narrower area and have a shallower focus range. In between we find a 50mm, often called a 'normal' lens.

Over time, the effects produced by different focal distances become attached to specific social narratives. Long telephotos tend to be used in sports and nature photography, where subjects are often moving at a distance and backgrounds can be out of focus. Wide lenses, on the other hand, privilege field of view and deep-focused scenes instead of magnification. Depicted through a different lens the same subject can be made to look *in fraganti* in a leaked mobile phone picture (28mm), or like a posing model for the cover of a fashion magazine (175mm) (Wieczorek, 2019).

And as photographic practices transform, for example by fitting mobile phones with cameras, lens aesthetics are remediated digitally, sometimes weighing even more heavily in popular expectations and assumptions about images. Large phone manufacturers like Huawei and Nokia, for instance, partnered with camera and lens manufacturers Leica and Zeiss respectively, to produce multi-camera devices with lenses of different focal lengths. In the case of the Huawei P series, such partnership was overtly marketed with the slogan 'rewrite the rules of photography' in direct reference to its capacity to reproduce and control lens effects such as shallow depth of field and *bokeh*, which occur at longer focal distances and narrower apertures (Figure 3.2).

Recent high-end mobile phones by Nokia and Apple are also both fitted with several cameras of varying focal lengths, including telephoto, macro, wide, and ultra-wide: 'Capture the entire scene with the 118° wide-angle lens and ZEISS Optics', reads the Nokia advertisement, and

Figure 3.2 Polygonal shapes of bokeh are the result of the 8-bladed aperture diaphragm in this 85mm lens at f/1.8. CC BY-SA 3.0 JWCreations.

Apple includes focal length, aperture, and even the number of lens elements per camera in its advertisements.

References to traditional photography made sense as marketing copy, because up to that point some of the effects available on these phones had only been available to professional and semi-professional SLRs users. Notably, however, lens effects very often began their technical lives as an attempt to address a specific problem of knowledge rather than a style. The type of ultra-wide lens now touted by mobile phone manufacturers was first conceived in 1924 as a scientific instrument to survey clouds in the sky – the Hill Skye lens. Its creator, Robin Hill, argued that this type of imaging of the sky could 'not be accomplished without distortion' (Hill, 1924, p. 999), and thus designed a lens and a stereoscopic process that enabled the necessary reshaping of light so as to project a whole hemisphere of sky onto a flat rectangular surface. Hill saw his lens as a measuring instrument and the heavily distorted images it produced as matters of scientific record, but over time this type of lens and the depictions it afforded were assimilated in the wider photographic canon, for their aesthetic qualities no less than their epistemic ones.

Nearly 100 years later and in a very different social context, the effect produced by the ultra-wide, meaning the trade-off that allows a massive field of view to the expense of barrel distortion, reappears thematised as a

Figure 3.3 6mm lens used in Yorgos Lanthimos, *The Favourite* (2018)

style of cinematography, for example in a costume drama about the troubled reign of Queen Anne of England in the critically celebrated film *The Favourite* (Lanthimos, 2018). 'The wide lens is twofold. By showing you the whole room and also isolating the character in a small space – like, a small character in a big space – you get a feeling of no escape', comments cinematographer Robbie Ryan (in Grobar, 2018) about the narrative use given to the somewhat forgotten 6mm fisheye lens, with which he shot the Lanthimos' royal fable (Figure 3.3).

And in yet another very different context, the aesthetics of the ultrawide returns to technology design with the popularisation of virtual simulations, for example in 360° and 180° videography, where several images are computationally 'stitched' together to produce an all-encompassing field of view in the former, or a stereoscopic, hemispheric view in the latter – much like what Hill had originally envisioned (See: Amadeo, 2017).

We can see through these examples how the effects produced by ultrawide lenses gain their cultural content historically. In common parlance we say these lenses produce heavy distorted images, but this implies an idealised notion of an undistorted 'natural' vision, an ideal made explicit by calling the 50mm a 'normal lens', often under the common misconception that it is the focal length that most closely reproduces the human field of view.

Unsurprisingly, calling the 50mm 'normal' is as common a practice among photographers as it is debated in aesthetics. By looking at its history and technical design, it quickly becomes apparent there is nothing inherently 'normal' about the 'nifty fifty', on the contrary, as Allain Daigle

(2018) shows, calling this lens normal has little to do with human vision and is instead the result of adopting 35mm celluloid as a standard support in cinematography. According to Daigle, had it not been for the industrial organisation of the Hollywood studio system in the early twentieth century, and in particular the standardising efforts of the US Motion Picture Patents Company (Belton, 1990, p. 659), what we today call a normal lens in still photography would have been probably twice as wide (25mm). To some, wider lenses such as these feel in fact more natural: '[a 28mm] simply matches the way I instinctively happen to see, and it also is fairly close to the natural field of view of human eyes when not focused on anything in particular' (Thein, 2013), while others would instead put the case forward for a 35mm or 43mm to be counted as 'normal' (Wieczorek, 2019).

Comparisons such as these are always fraught, and even assuming there was in fact a lens that was demonstrably the closest to standard human visual perception, on what grounds would it be reasonable to assume this so-called normal human vision would free from distortion, or that this alignment to human vision would in itself produce an epistemic advantage? If, instead, we allow that optical distortion comes with its own set of epistemic affordances, the case for mechanical vision as a simulation of human vision weakens considerably. From this point of view, we ought to at least extend these simulation endeavours to the visual regimes of non-human animals. For instance, some of the earliest types of creatures of which there are fossil records, like the pelagic trilobite *Opipeuter*, have been found to 'have [had] enormous eyes, subtending a panoramic field of view' (Clarkson et al, 2006). These were free-swimming trilobites, and so their near 360° field of view, as distorted and disorienting as it might seem to us now, afforded them a distinct advantage to sense their surroundings and detect possible predators stalking them from any direction.[4] Our human field of view is in comparison quite limited, but by reshaping light through optical and computational processes we are able to replicate this wider field of view, and gain in the process the type of distorted perspective Hill sought to leverage with his sky lens, or that 180°/360° videography now affords. We appear to know more, not less, by eschewing standard human visual perception in favour of other ways of seeing, often modelled after the seeing ways of others, even or especially when this otherness includes non-humans.

Joanna Zylinska touches on this in her *Nonhuman Photography* (2017) in which she explores how non-human entities, such as machines, animals, and even plants, participate in photography as a broader field of activity. From a post-humanist and media ecology perspective, she argues that all photography is to an extent 'nonhuman', with cameras, sensors, algorithms, and infrastructures all actively shaping the images we produce and consume. An elaboration of this reaction to anthropocentric frameworks in media studies finds new echoes in the wake of computer vision technologies. Andrew Dewdney, for example, suggests we *Forget Photography* (2021) altogether to break free from the dominant discourse of visual representation, which he argues is deeply implicated in the configuration of systems of power and control. To me, what comes across strongest in both cases is not so much a radical opposition to our photographic condition, but a powerful desire to dismantle a specific photographic regime, whether through a critique of anthropocentrism or a programmed erasure of its referents and signifiers in capitalist societies.

Although I share many of the political dimensions of these arguments, philosophically I find myself more in tune with the New Theorists, whose aesthetic critique does not require the reconfiguration of the medium but is instead articulated from within photography and its institutions – humans and their linguistic signifiers included. When I reference trilobites and their visual systems above, I am less interested in them as nonhuman animals, than in how their visual perception differs from what we call normal vision in ordinary language, and how that difference is again enfolded, through technical means, in human vision and the language, old and new, that we attach to it.

From this perspective, and to go back to the wide lens example, we can see that as new forms of VR simulation gain ground over previous forms of visual representation, it is likely that the notion of what is a normal lens is refashioned towards smaller focal lengths and wider viewing angles. And conversely, that the images produced by these lenses are progressively seen as less distorted and more 'realistic' from a human perspective. If mobile phone cameras and popular films are any indication, this is happening already, and will accelerate as we spend more time 'immersed' in virtual worlds swimming freely like trilobites in a primordial digital soup made of computationally stitched up images.

Through this techno aesthetics of the wide angle, we can now *see* how lens effects and aberrations are not incidental to photography but rather a fundamental dimension of its epistemic advantage, since they enable distinct relations between the seeable and the knowable; between knowledge and the appearance of knowledge. That images are seen to be *about* something inasmuch as *of* something suggests that we put our faith in photography not because it offers faithful images of the world around us, but because we believe that photographic distortions can help us access truth values not available to us through human perception alone. Computer vision, I argue, does not gain its powers by treating images as non-human detections of the world, but rather by measuring the human beliefs that are instantiated in these images; by building a thin but broadly spread layer of inductive computing on top of a technically robust and socially mature optical regime.

From this point of view, the ideological triumph of computer vision is not that it enables novel ways of seeing, but that it managed to lodge itself in photography by effectively erasing from view the technical seams of such coupling. Here I want to suggest that we might give post-ImageNet computer vision a different name: inductive photography. Hence, even when there is nothing unnatural about an ultra-wide field of view in the same way that there is nothing intrinsically natural about the 50mm lens, the ideal of a standard human perspective, coupled with the strong belief that it can be somehow reproduced through photographic means, remains an enduring fantasy across optical and computational domains in the techno-genesis of machine vision. And it is enduring because, as with any strong ideological construct, it promises to reconcile what appear to be mutually exclusive ideas: that machine vision can accurately simulate human and non-human vision; that computers are incrementally approximating our ways of seeing while simultaneously diverging from it.

One way of investigating inductive photography and the rational illusions it creates is through technique itself. If we admit that images obtained through optical means derive their powers from the meanings they are given over time, and these meanings are largely how images become *about* something, it ought to be possible to point the inductive logic of machine vision to what images are about and not only what they are of.[5] From a critical technical perspective, the question becomes if and how we can use machine vision to look at itself: are there self-referential forms of machine vision that can reveal the joints and seams of its own techno aesthetic constitution? In other words, is there a critical variety of inductive photography?

As a response to these questions, let us return to MbM as a case-study and ask: is it possible to identify the optical perspective in MbM? What lens or lenses are encoded in the computational gaze we set upon the BBC Television archive?

Based on the discussion above, we might start by finding traces of the photographic processes that went into the machine vision system we used. We know that the Visual Genome uses images originally sourced from Flickr, and that the photo platform hosts many of its images along with their EXIF data, which is an international metadata standard for

MACHINE VISION AND THE PHILOSOPHY OF PHOTOGRAPHY 73

digital images and sound that includes tags for camera settings and lens information.[6]

EXIF metadata is far from perfect. Its structure is borrowed from TIFF files and is now over thirty years old. Digital cameras changed dramatically over the last decades and there are many differences in how the standard has been used over time, even among cameras from the same manufacturer. So, one of the first challenges of working with EXIF is inconsistency. For instance, some manufacturers such as Nikon use custom format fields not common to other brands and encrypt the metadata contained in them. This makes it difficult to extract, disaggregate, and process EXIF data across camera types and manufacturers. Moreover, this metadata is not generally available for not-born-digital photographs, like those taken with analogue cameras or pictures that were scanned. These caveats notwithstanding, EXIF is still the most widely used metadata standard for photography and a key resource to research the equipment and technical practice that underlies the creation of photographic images in the digital age. And precisely because of its longevity and pervasive use, it is one of the few signals available to trace at scale a genealogical lineage from lenses to computers.

In this line of thought, I extracted EXIF metadata from all the images whose Flickr IDs matched the ones present in the Visual Genome. The metadata standard is comprised of over twenty thousand tags, but I only selected tags that were general enough so as to be reported by most cameras. From this selection, I only focused on the tags containing data about the parameters over which photographers tend to have more choice and control, namely their choice of camera and lens, as well as the aperture, exposure and focal length settings. Table 3.1 shows a list of the tags that were queried, and an example of the values extracted. Table 3.2 shows an overview of the extraction results.

The extraction process yielded a relatively dense distribution, with over 83% of accessible images returning metadata in at least one of the five of the queried tags. The one exception was <Lens info>, for which only

Table 3.1 Example of EXIF tags extracted

Tag	Value
Camera manufacturer	Canon
Camera model	Canon EOS 7D
Exposure	1/1600
Aperture (F-number)	2.8
Focal length	145.0 mm
Lens info	0EF70-200mm f/2.8L IS II USM

CINEMA AND MACHINE VISION

Table 3.2 Overview of the extraction results

Category	Count	Percentage
Total number of IDs processed	103,077	100.00%
Unavailable URL request (500 error)	18,521	18.00%
Available image but with no data in any of the queried tags	443	0.40%
Available images with data in at least one queried tag	84,113	81.60%

Table 3.3 First five observations of my working data frame, shaped 68,085 rows × 5 columns

Camera manufacturer	Camera model	Exposure	Aperture	Focal Length
Canon	Canon PowerShot S2 IS	1/640	4.0	72.0 mm
Panasonic	DMC-FX9	1/13	3.6	9.9 mm
Canon	Canon EOS 20D	1/250	11.0	560.0 mm
Nikon	NIKON D50	1/250	5.0	125.0 mm
Canon	Canon PowerShot SD600	1/320	2.8	5.8 mm
. . .	. . .	. . .	. . .	. . .

10% of accessible images returned values. Considering this, I decided to exclude <Lens info> from the initial analysis and use it instead as a control group to verify results from the other group of tags. I also parsed over apertures and focal lengths to bin them into categories: twelve bins corresponding to full f-stops for apertures —from $f1$ to $f45$, and seven focal distance bins corresponding to a commonly used classification:[7]

- Ultra-wide (<24mm)
- Wide (24–35mm)
- Normal (35–85mm)
- Short telephoto (85–135mm)
- Medium telephoto (135–300mm)
- Super telephoto (+300mm)

I parsed over exposures to remove faux entries (a small number of older mobile phones reported infinite or zero values for exposure), and I also standardised values such as 'NIKON' and 'Nikon Corporation'. The consolidated dataset includes all values in all remaining tags for a total of 68,085 entries, which is 66 per cent of all images that comprise the Visual Genome (v2.1). A sample of this working data frame is shown in Table 3.3.

My analysis of EXIF data shows the clear dominance of Digital Single Lens Reflex (DSLR)[8] over other types of equipment, with Canon and Nikon being the two major manufacturers, combining for over 64 per cent

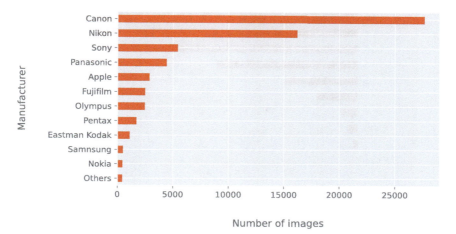

Figure 3.4 Camera manufacturers of images in the Visual Genome

of all cameras; more than eight times the share of the third largest manufacturer, Sony, at 8 per cent (Figure 3.4).

From these, the ten most popular camera models all correspond to Canon EOS and Nikon DX systems, with the only exception of the Apple iPhone 4, at number nine. The most common camera in the dataset is Nikon's D90, an entry-level DSLR released in 2008, and the first model with video-recording capabilities. The second most popular is the semi-professional Canon 5D Mark II, released the same year, closely followed by the 7D also from Canon, released in 2009.

In terms of how these cameras were used, I identified large apertures f 2.8, 4, and 5.6 as the most popular, accounting together for 74 per cent of photographs (Figure 3.5).

For focal length, lenses between 35–85mm are the most common, accounting for 50.7 per cent of the images, with the least popular being the super telephoto, only used to take 1.6 per cent of the photos in the dataset (Figure 3.6).

Exposure, finally, was more evenly distributed between the extremes with the notable exception of 1/60, identified as significantly more popular than all other shutter speeds. This is possibly due to the common belief that this is the slowest shutter speed one can use without needing a tripod. Figure 3.7 shows the ten most common combinations of aperture, focal length, and exposure parameters in images in the Visual Genome, all of which are under direct control of their photographers.[9]

These findings point to the practices of a 'proficient consumer' community of photo enthusiasts working with DSLR equipment. These are

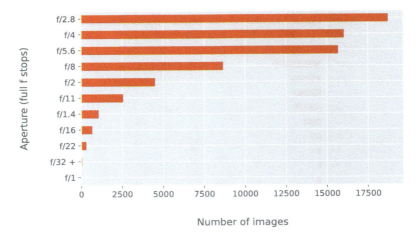

Figure 3.5 Distribution of apertures in images from the Visual Genome

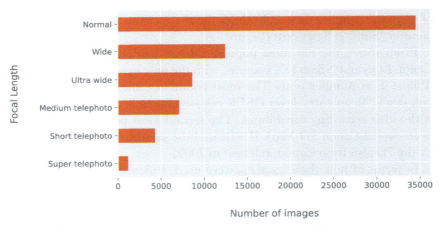

Figure 3.6 Focal length categories in images from the Visual Genome

generally non-professional photographers who nevertheless were willing to invest in a bulkier and more expensive camera and take the time to learn how to operate it manually. Users of the Nikon D90, for example, who were recent converts migrating upwards from point-and-shoot photography. Or more established and committed users of a Canon 7D, who probably own a few lenses already and are aficionados, semi-professional, or close to going professional. This grouping is also supported by the smaller control group sample of lens data from the <Lens Info> tag, which shows inexpensive lenses that come bundled with cameras to be very popular, for example the 18–55mm *f*/3.5–5.6 included in both Nikon and Canon

MACHINE VISION AND THE PHILOSOPHY OF PHOTOGRAPHY 77

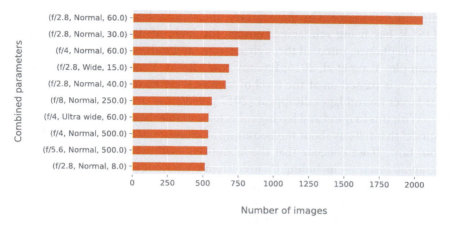

Figure 3.7 Combined aperture, focal length and exposure of images in the Visual Genome

starter kits (camera body + lens), but also includes a few more expensive lenses (particularly on longer focal lengths, such as the 100–400mm $f/4.5$–5.6L or the EF70-200mm $f/2.8$L, both by Canon). These lenses overlap with professional practice and were probably acquired as second or third lenses for purpose-specific photography, such as wildlife or sports, both of which featured heavily in a manual sampling I conducted over images taken with these two camera models.

Based on this, we are in a position to show that the dominant perspective encoded in the photographs that comprise the Visual Genome, and that by extension are mobilised in MbM, is closely aligned to the photographic practices of this community of DSLR enthusiasts. If one were to ask not about the accuracy in detecting what is depicted, but about the implied optical perspective of this particular computer vision system, we could now reply with some degree of confidence that this perspective falls within the focal range of an 18–55mm lens on an APS-C or APS-H camera; apertures between $f3.5$ and $f5.6$, and a likely exposure 1/60s. Setting aside some of the other complexities of MbM for a moment, we could say that this was the dominant lens through which the BBC archive was seen: 'the preferred lens of the machine'.

Today, DSLR photography of this kind is somewhat of a dying practice. Sales of this type of camera have been steadily declining over the past decade (CIPA, 2019), as photographs of everyday life are now routinely taken with mobile phones and circulated through social media (Herrman, 2018). However, while the equipment and the communities that supported the DSLR visual regime recede into history, lens aesthetics are anything but gone. On the contrary, the standard of photography set by DSLR has being reimagined under the logic of digital computing and mobile phones, pursued through software and indeed through AI (See for example: Yang et al, 2016; Ignatov et al, 2017). Technicity, as Simondon claims, is passed on at the level of technical elements, even when objects or larger assemblages disappear (2017 [1958]).

With this in mind and having collected a usable dataset, I set out to train a model that tells us about the becoming of images; not only what they depict but how. If we concede that the 'aboutness' with which we invest photographic images – including their epistemic advantage – is a function of the depicted no less than of the depiction modality, such an aesthetic machine is as justified as one that distinguishes cats from dogs, or hot-dogs from other sandwiches. Could we not train machines to learn about optical perspectives as well as what these perspectives are used for at given times in history?

To close this section, I present a prototype along these lines as a proof-of-concept. A system designed to be purposefully blind to what photographs are *of* and a resulting type of vision that cares nothing about recognising objects, people, or scenes, and is instead trained to learn only about how its images were made and the optical perspectives they embody, in this example the focal distance of the lenses with which they were taken.

Using my EXIF dataset and the images from the Visual Genome, I trained a focal length classifier to distinguish between photographs taken with a wide-angle lens from those taken with a telephoto. The class boundaries are drawn at under 24mm for the former and over 135mm for the latter. Each class was given little over 12,000 training samples (Figure 3.8). The model was trained from scratch using a VGG-based deep convolutional neural network architecture (Figure 3.9).

Figure 3.8 Batch of four samples of inputs and labels

Figure 3.9 15-layer Convolutional neural network architecture

MACHINE VISION AND THE PHILOSOPHY OF PHOTOGRAPHY 79

class: 'wide angle'   class: 'telephoto'

Figure 3.10 The photo on the left was taken with a mobile phone (28mm); photo on the right with a DSLR (340mm)

Results show test accuracy of 83 per cent after fourteen epochs of training. I manually sampled the model at this checkpoint by running inference on several out of sample photographs. The results of this testing suggest that, with some exceptions, such as irregularly shaped images from elongated panoramas, grainy images, or images captured with digital zoom, the predictions of this classifier were reasonably accurate for photographs taken with either very long or very wide lenses. Figure 3.10 shows a comparison of two successfully classified images using this method. For the casual observer who sees these images all at once rather than pixel by pixel, there are many apparent differences: one is the Shard in London, the other a baby orangutan in Borneo; one is a night scene, the other was taken in broad daylight. However, when it comes to the type of lens used to render these scenes visible, *a posteriori* knowledge might in fact be a task for which computer vision is much better suited. In particular deep convolutional networks can help with their progressive and content-agnostic abstraction of local pixel relations.

Going back to MbM, I used this focal length classifier on frames from one of the mislabelled sections mentioned in Chapter 2. Figure 3.11 shows a comparison between the predictions outputted by the two systems. Which classification can be said to be more accurate? Which prediction

class:'telephoto'   label:'reflection of a mirror'

Figure 3.11 Predicted class of (the whole) image on the left using our focal lens classifier prototype. Predicted label of (a region) of the image on the right in MbM

tells us more about the image? What kind of knowledge is at play in each classification, and when or why would we prefer one kind over the other? This is perhaps an extreme example, but it clearly illustrates the possibility of self-referential inductive photography, and a glimpse at the many other possible forms of machine vision that remain unrealised.

With additional data, extended training and fine-tuning, and systematic testing, a much more sophisticated lens classifier is possible. But more than as a fully-fledged method, I present this example here as a way to address the questions raised earlier through technical means. There are of course many other possibilities, even within the framework of a classifier and even with this relatively modest dataset. Knowing, for example, that photographers not only manipulate the shape of light but also its speed, we could analyse exposure as a signal of the immanent temporalities of computer vision systems or remove the classification layer and use the model as a generator to evaluate similarities between images without resorting to pre-defined classes.

Furthermore, just like this analysis of focal length gives insight into the spatial relations between photographers and their subjects, and an indication of how these relations are thematised, it is reasonable to expect an analysis of exposure times would also show correlations; initially of light source, of style, and ultimately of usage. And these need not be treated as isolated dimensions, nor indeed separated from existing approaches aimed at detecting objects or people. On the contrary, through this experiment I show that incorporating photographic features to the scientific apparatus of computer vision complements it and can potentially make it more robust for some of its existing tasks or contribute to designing new tasks altogether.

If I am correct about this, machine vision can evolve from systems designed to name what is in the picture, to systems that approximate what

MACHINE VISION AND THE PHILOSOPHY OF PHOTOGRAPHY 81

specific people see in the picture. In this section I have shown how our relationship with the photographic image underwrites our relationship with computer vision more generally and have given an example of how to explore this relation computationally. From this perspective, a critical programme of machine vision requires a techno-aesthetics of photography in order to explain why we believe we know something when we look at it through a computational gaze, whether this belief is warranted, and the epistemic advantages and disadvantages of the images produced in this process. Photography is an imaging no less than an imagining technology, and it is in these terms that I suggest we need to understand the layer of inductive computing now wrapped around it.

Notes

1. The daguerreotype process was black and white (or more precisely black and silver), however chromatic aberration was still a problem as images would appear misaligned even when rendered in monochrome..
2. Specifically, the wet collodion process, introduced by F. Scott Archer in 1851.
3. The first aperture stop device was introduced by John Waterhouse in 1858.
4. According to Clarkson, other trilobite species, like the Cryptolithus or the Conocryphe who were bottom-dwellers, had very little need for eyes (them living in the dark most of the time) and in time eventually lost them in favour of other sensory organs. See: https://www.trilobites.info/eyes.htm
5. For a discussion on this distinction, see Maynard (1997).
6. Developed in 1998 by the Japan Electronic Industries Development Association (JEIDA), eventually absorbed by the Japan Electronics IT industries association (JEITA) and the Camera & Imaging products association (CIPA) (See: JEITA Standards).
7. These categories are not policed or enforced by any particular institution, as the boundaries are seen as irrelevant in most areas of photographic practice. They are, rather, more of a tacit agreement among photographers, lens and camera manufacturers. Of the tags queried, focal distance was the most challenging because, as I noted earlier, these values are relative to the size of the sensor. The standard "full frame" sensor was adopted as an equivalent of 35mm film stock, but as digital cameras shrunk in size so too did their sensors. The effect is particularly stark in mobile phones, whose sensors are increasingly small, so in order to compare their focal length to that of larger cameras one needs to multiply their reported EXIF value by a crop factor so as to obtain a 35mm equivalent. This crop factor is different across models and manufacturers, for example many Apple iPhone models have a sensor crop factor of 7.6, if the focal length in their EXIF metadata is 4.3, the 35mm equivalent is a little over 30mm. If one were to accurately measure focal length one would need to extract the size of the sensor from EXiF (assuming this is not given

as the 35mm equivalent), calculate the crop factor for each individual camera model, and then match it to the corresponding entry in the dataset. I did not have the time resources to do this. However, through controlled manual sampling I identified entries that reported focal lengths consistent with two types of cameras widely available at the time these pictures were taken: 3G Mobile phones (~15k entries, for example iPhone 4 to 5), compact and ultra compact point and shoot cameras (~12k entries, for example Canon Powershot and Pentax Optio series). Based on this I compensated for these two groups by applying a weighted average crop factor of 7.6 and 4.8, respectively. From a similar sampling at the other end, it was apparent that this process was not necessary for long focal lengths, which were mostly taken with full frame or APS-C or APS-H cameras, which magnify the image even more.

8. Single-Lens Reflex cameras (both digital and analogue). This type of camera allows for interchangeable lenses and has a mirror system that allows the photographer to use a viewfinder to see through the camera lens in order to compose their photographs. When the shutter is pressed the mirror flips and the sensor or film stock gets directly exposed to light coming in through the lens. The acronym is often used to differentiate these cameras from point-and-shoot models, which are much smaller and have fixed (often retractile) lens, or from so-called mirrorless models, which do admit different lenses but do not have a mirror.

9. Exposure is given as the denominator of a fraction of a second, such that for example 250 is equivalent to 1/250, or 0.004 seconds.

Part II

Pixels in Motion:
The Calculation of Cinematic Time

Every photograph is a representation of space but also of time. In analogue photography, reflected light reacts with silver halides dispersed in gelatin; in digital photography it is converted into electric charges through diodes on an image sensor. In both cases there is a shutter, mechanical or electronic, that regulates the intake of light over time. The time that takes to expose a photograph is usually only a fraction of a second, just enough to capture 'an instant'. If one records these instants continuously one after the other and keeps them as a sequence, it is possible to unroll this series of instants as a continuous flow at a later time, thereby reinscribing past durations into the present. At its most basic, this is the technical principle behind the cinematic image.

Along these lines, it is possible to characterise the cinematographer (the device) as a machine that 'temporalises' space, conferring the photographic image an extra dimension where it gains recognisable beginnings and endings, as well as a perceived duration. Moreover, this perceived duration need not always coincide with our actual embodied experience of time, what we often refer to as 'real' time, and in fact, that it very often does not is one of the most significant affordances of the cinematic image. The ability to manipulate recorded durations, more specifically to contract them, dilate them, or otherwise re-arrange them, allows the production of *cinematic time*, a type of conceptual time that we can understand as distinct from our own internal sense of time but that can nevertheless be experienced within real time, over the course of a couple of hours at the movie theatre, for example.

Cinematic time holds in this way a very peculiar type of relation with real, lived time, and the alignments and misalignments between the two

84   CINEMA AND MACHINE VISION

have been a central concern to philosophers and moving image scholars for the past century. How is it, for example, that viewers can make sense and derive meaning from fragmented representations of time and space? Is this an innate ability, or something that is learned? In a well-known passage from *Film as Art*, Arnheim lays out this problem as follows:

> One might expect the spectator to be overcome by a physical discomfort akin to sea-sickness when watching a film that had been composed of different shots. [. . .] Yet everyone who goes to the movies knows that actually there is no sense of discomfort [. . .] If at one moment we see a long shot of a woman at the back of a room, and the next we see a close-up of her face, we simply feel that we have 'turned over a page' and are looking at a fresh picture. (Arnheim, 1957, pp. 27–28)

It appears paradoxical that we lend such credibility to the photographic image's ability to faithfully temporalise space, but at the same time are not immediately disoriented when time and space representations come at us fragmented and disjointed. This seemingly natural ability to piece moving images together is observable in young children, who seem to follow films without ever having been formally taught 'how to watch', not at least in the ways they have to be taught to read or write. Several explanations have been put forth to account for this apparently spontaneous ability. One influential account in cognitive film theory is that our ability to understand cinematic time and make sense of films more generally is owed to how our viewing is carefully structured through internal and external conditions:

> In watching a film, the spectator submits to a programmed temporal form. Under normal viewing circumstances, the film absolutely controls the order, frequency, and duration of the presentation of events. You cannot skip a dull spot or linger over a rich one, jump back to an earlier passage or start at the end of the film and work your way forward. Because of this a narrative film works quite directly on the limits of the spectator's perceptual cognitive abilities. (Bordwell, 1985, p. 74)

According to this view, in seeing a film one becomes a willing subject of its time-space manipulations. Viewers enter into a sort of contract with filmmakers whereby they are offered only some pieces of a space-time puzzle and are trusted to fill in the gaps themselves. To guide viewers in this interpretive process, the pieces are carefully ordered as a sequence that indicates a set of relations between characters, places, events, but also movements, colours, and sounds. As far as we are able to match and map these relations, they structure our viewing and guide us in the resolution of the puzzle, which, from this perspective, entails little more than our accurate inference of the missing pieces; the ones purposefully withheld from us. Colloquially we call this 'following the plot' of a film – to derive its internal structure through external scaffolding and internal mental schemas.

By restricting internal relations or assuming less common external schemas, films can present more challenging space-time puzzles to their audiences: some are overtly presented as puzzle films, like David Lynch's *Mulholland Drive* (2001), while others will resist being 'solved' in these terms altogether – the films of Stan Brakhage, for example. When it comes to popular narrative cinema, it is safe to say that viewers will not be confused by every close-up, jump cut, or ellipsis presented to them, at least not intentionally. Instead, they are likely to strike a bargain with the films and willingly concede that the missing fragments of space-time must have happened *off-screen*, in an imagined fictional temporality that was not recorded but that is implicitly conveyed. Over time, the techniques used to organise these fictional timelines become conventional and settle into larger recognisable forms and their corresponding film-making styles.

In this section I explore how film style and cinematic time can be studied through computational methods, and how by mobilising these methods critically it is possible to inform and reshape film theory. I focus on three specific entanglements between film theory and computation, explored critically and technically as a trio of experiments designed to 1) think about film poetics through distant viewing; 2) represent continuity editing through sonification; and 3) interrogate latent temporalities though generative machine learning techniques.

My goal is not to present a comprehensive account of any of these practices; I focus instead on the ways they address (or trouble) epistemic assumptions about cinematic time. By drawing out links between the three experiments, I weave a larger argument about the computational production of cinematic time: how the temporal form of moving images is being re-programmed computationally, the new set of technical meanings created in this process, and the ontological and epistemic displacements that this transformation entails.

CHAPTER 4

Statistical Distance and Emotional Closeness in Film Style

The point of departure in my search of a computational theory of spectatorship that accounts for cinematic time is the link between formal analysis of film style and the practice of 'distant reading/viewing'. In the case of film, I take my cues from historical poetics (Bordwell, 1989, 2008; Bordwell and Carroll, 1996) and neoformalism (Thompson, 1988); in the case of distant viewing, I take Arnold and Tilton's formulation (2019), but contextualise their definition within the frameworks of distant reading (Moretti, 2013, 2007) and macroanalysis (Jockers, 2013).

Initially, distant viewing appears to share some of its core epistemic commitments with the formalist agenda in the study of film, most obviously in their favouring of inductive reasoning. Both distant viewing and formalism are also purportedly analytical approaches, meaning they break films into smaller units and isolate specific properties as variables in an attempt to discern organisational patterns from a wider corpus of films. So far, this corpus has been relatively small in non-computational film scholarship, but the desire to take 'distance' from exemplary films and close interpretations is undoubtedly a significant part of what animates new formalisms in theory and in practice. Cinemetrics, the database of average shot lengths in films, is a good example of this affinity, but the desire for distance can be traced back to Bordwell, who explicitly sets his agenda against what he calls 'doctrine-driven' criticism, which he himself criticises invoking a bottom–up and data-driven *doxa*:

> When theory projects downwards to the datum, the latter becomes an illustrative example. The result may have rhetorical force, as vivid examples often do, but because of the underdetermination of theories by data, a single instance is not particularly strong evidence. (Bordwell and Carroll, 1996, 19)

Conversely, distant viewing, insofar as it inherits from distant reading, shares with formalism an implicit mistrust of 'top-down' inquiry, the cannons it establishes and the cultural elites that promote and police these cannons, often from positions of personal authority. Franco Moretti, who coined the term, made the argument about the canons of literature being only a 'minimal fraction of the literary field' (2007, pp. 3–4). And Matthew Jockers, with whom Moretti co-founded the Stanford Literary Lab, similarly argues for what he calls a 'macroanalysis' of literature: 'not simply as an examination of seminal works but an aggregated ecosystem or "economy" of texts' (2013, p. 32).

Sustaining their respective critiques of interpretive frameworks in the fields of literature and cinema, these approaches enlist methods from the sciences, most notably empirical inquiry and reliance on data as evidence. The main epistemic gambit here is that while subjective experience and interpretation of films vary widely at a higher level – for example in individual value judgements about specific meanings, themes, or genres – the medium's underlying set of low-level techniques are empirically falsifiable, and common to most texts/films. One can disagree on whether a film is a masterpiece or not, the formalist would argue, but an ellipsis will always be an ellipsis, a close-up is not a long-shot, and most popular narrative films include ellipsis, close-ups, and long shots in one way or another.

In this same tenor, Moretti claims that fewer elements allow 'a sharper sense of their overall interconnection. Shapes, relations, structures. Forms. Models' (2007, I). And this is in turn the logic at work in distant viewing, which according to Arnold and Tilton:

> calls for the automatic extraction of semantic elements of visual materials followed by the aggregation and visualization of these elements via techniques from exploratory data analysis. [. . .] These extracted elements do not attempt to capture all of the elements of an image; as mentioned, the interpretive act of coding images is necessarily destructive. The metadata here, also, does not directly attempt to measure higher-order meanings such as the themes, mood, or power dynamics captured by an image. However, much like the relationship between words and cultural elements in text, these elements can often be discerned by studying patterns in the extracted features. (2019, pp. 4–5)

So, what, exactly, are these extracted features? And how do they answer questions the formalist film scholar might ask? Arnold and Taylor built an open-source library to conduct this type of analysis, they call it the Distant Viewing Toolkit (DVT). Looking under the hood, and at the time of writing, the following computer vision methods were bundled in the library, some of which will probably be familiar to the reader by now:

- Shot detection
- Object detection
- Face detection

- Face identification
- Colour analysis
- Image similarity
- Optical flow
- Shot distance analysis

This is a mixed bag of tasks. In the DVT's technical documentation (DVT, 2019), these tasks are separated in *annotators* (that work directly on the frames) and *aggregators* (that take annotators' outputs as inputs): 'The annotator algorithms conduct the process of "viewing" the material whereas the aggregator algorithms perform a "distant" (e.g., separated from the raw materials) analysis of the visual inputs' (Arnold and Tilton, 2020, p. 2).

Extrapolating from this distinction, we can similarly separate the tasks in two groups, according to how close they are to the images and the kinds of outputs users can expect from these operations. Object and face detection and recognition are distant in the sense that they aim to *name* something, while motion estimation and colour value calculations are used to *describe* something else. In philosophy, the difference between words that name and words that describe is a well-established problem, but for our purposes here it is sufficient to say that in computer vision the former largely depend on the latter, such that lower-level features like colours, borders, and textures feed into higher-level representations such as objects and people. In natural language this is arguably the reverse: we often use names as referents to general forms to avoid having to describe perception in minute detail in order to communicate with others. If I describe the cactus in my office, for example, I say it is on the windowsill, comment on its shape, its colour, its size, how many prickles it has; if I name it, I just call it 'Iggy the Cactus'.

When applied to film analysis this difference comes to the fore. Critics, for example, can easily and immediately name objects and people they see on screen: this a bicycle, that is a thief; this is Venice, that is Mexico City; she is Penelope Cruz, he is Adam Driver. In ordinary language, we find nothing particularly impressive about this, and we would reasonably expect most critics to be able to perform this naming without much trouble. In computer vision, however, accomplishing even this basic level of symbolic abstraction is considered a significant achievement.

Conversely, computers are much more precise at producing low-level descriptions about categories to which natural language does not easily attach, such as degrees of motion, qualities of sound, or properties of colour. Human critics struggle to describe these using natural language and build classifications, for instance categories that accurately describe the colours of one scene as they compared to the colours of another; or how dynamic, bright, or textured moving images are compared to each other. Consider for example the difficulty in accurately describing 'yellowness', or 'slowness' in ways that are communicatively effective and empirically verifiable.

This should come as no surprise to any film or computer vision researcher, but it does contribute to explain why film scholars who use computational methods might tend to be less impressed by state-of-the-art face recognition and are more interested instead in motion estimation (Rodriguez, 2019) or colour analysis (Flueckiger and Halter, 2018; Flueckiger, 2012), as well as the access and visualisation of these properties (Kuhn, 2018; Kuhn et al, 2015). And conversely, why AI researchers will tend to be less interested in optical flow and shot boundary detection, problems that they largely regard as having been solved.

In closer inspection, the motivations and assumptions mobilised by these two research programmes and their communities are not as aligned as they first appeared, even if they share an affinity for inductive reasoning and seem to have a common object of inquiry. It is not immediately clear if film scholars and computer scientists are working on the same problems addressing them from different directions, or rather on a different set of problems altogether. I suspect Arnold and Tilton would argue for the former, given how they align their work to 'bridge the semantic gap' (2020, p. 3). I tend to be more sceptical. Although I share their enthusiasm for exploring the area between moving image studies and computation, in my view, the tools from the toolkit do not address key questions in the broader study of moving images; for instance, what exactly do we know when computers are said to detect an object or recognise a face? Is this the same type of knowledge critics have when they perform the same tasks? How about other tasks that are not perceptual?

From the tasks automated in the DVT, only shot detection and shot scale are analytical categories innate to the study of film; the rest are imported from computer vision and then given some role to play in the distant viewing of films. Arnold and Tilton (2019) claim that 'state of the art' (p. 4) algorithms are 'approaching human-like accuracy' (p. 5) and that computer vision systems 'can now perform as well as or better than manual expert annotations on narrowly focused tasks' (p. 3). But where does this set of narrow tasks come from, and why would we want to use them specifically on films? The methods Arnold refers to in the quotes above come from the medical sciences: specifically, to classify skin lesions, diabetic retinopathy, lymph node metastases, and pneumonia.

STATISTICAL DISTANCE AND EMOTIONAL CLOSENESS 91

Film studies borrow from scholarship in art, literature, linguistics, psychology, and indeed the natural sciences. But the academic success of the discipline has arguably also been staking what, precisely, from these disciplines is relevant to the study of film. In this it shares with digital humanities a critical stance towards the unexamined use of diagnostic and forensic technologies. And so, when Arnold and Tilton claim that the DVT addresses the needs of scholars by 'packaging together common sound and computer vision algorithms in order to provide out-of-the-box functionality for common tasks in the computational analysis of moving images' (2020, p. 1), it begs the questions of what are these needs and who is this community of scholars?

Focusing on the shot scale module in the DVT, we can start by asking why distinct types of shots are so central to film analysis, and how are these being modelled computationally. Shot scale matters to critics for historic and aesthetic reasons. Close-ups, for example, were very rare before 1900, when cinema arguably looked more like recorded theatre. Some of the earliest known examples of close-ups are experiments in the films of George Albert Smith, 'As Seen Through a Telescope' and 'Grandma's Reading Glass', where Smith incorporates them in the narrative to convey the point of view of his characters as they look through a telescope and a magnifying glass, respectively (Gray, 1998). Only a decade later, the close-up had gained its place in the filmmaker's stylistic repertoire; its use was normalised through the works of popular directors such as D.W. Griffith (Young, 2010). Today, a popular film with no close-ups is incredibly rare. The close-up, writes Mary Anne Doane, has been seen as

> the guarantee of the cinema's status as a universal language, one of, if not the most recognizable units of cinematic discourse, yet simultaneously extraordinarily difficult to define. [. . .] The close-up, together with an editing that penetrates space and is at least partially rationalized by that close-up, seems to mark the moment of the very emergence of film as a discourse, as an art. (2003, p. 90)

In the DVT, shot scale is defined as a proportion between the frame and the boundary box of a detected object (usually a face). For a close-up (CU), the proportion is 50 per cent, for a big close-up (BCU) it is 70 per cent. Arnold acknowledges some of the technical limitations of this approach, namely that these proportions are given at the frame level, and therefore there is no straightforward method to generalise to account for camera movement or multiple subjects. Also, for long shots (LS), where the detection threshold is set at 5 per cent, face detectors perform very poorly, particularly in low definition or grainy footage (Arnold, 2019).

Despite these limitations, because this module of the DVT is based on an existing category of film analysis, it is possible to use it to access at least some of what Doane has in mind. Let us consider, for example, a type of BCU that is quite popular in contemporary Hollywood films, and which is often referred to as 'subjective camera' close-ups; a type of shot where the face of the performer fills almost the entire screen. It is called 'subjective' because it implies the presence and point of view of an interlocutor who is in very close proximity – think of someone leaning in towards you a little over what is comfortable. To record this type of close-up actors usually need to perform looking directly at a camera positioned right in their faces, which makes this type of shot technically challenging and often also difficult for performers. It is only in editing that these close-ups are arranged to convey the idea that actors are addressing some other character, when in fact the shots were captured by looking down the barrel of a lens.

At this degree of magnification, facial features gain a texture of their own: the slightest of movements and the smallest of wrinkles and expressions are all scrutinised and given significance. These are shots where 'the camera feels like an intruder', as cinematographer Benoit Delhomme puts it, and 'the face becomes a landscape' (quoted in Lee, 2018). The effect sought through this type of quasi-topological BCUs benefits from large screens and high-definition displays. At such scales and resolutions even performers with very terse skin show numerous imperfections that would not normally be on display: minute blemishes, scars, spots, hairs, pores, are all captured. This might seem counter-intuitive, but in popular Hollywood cinema, this kind of magnification has become its own form of spectacle, since any imperfection that might be distracting or simply not wanted can, and very often is, corrected in post-production. The result is a subtle but powerful type of visual effect: faces are shown enormous in scale and yet they appear remarkably perfect. It is as if the face had intensified to show more of it than what was there to be seen in the first place.

This type of magnification would have likely been considered excessive at other moments in the history of cinema, even obscene, as suggested by Smith's telescope, used in his 1900 film to get a furtive closer look at a woman's ankle. Today, different flavours of this frontal BCU are commonly used by high-profile Hollywood directors, for example in the films of Paul Thomas Anderson, Wes Anderson, and Spike Lee (see: *On Story 414*, 2018).

Neither looking directly at the camera nor the close-up are in themselves new techniques. The former is relatively more common in documentaries, in pieces to camera where presenters address the audience directly, albeit not in BCU, for example in one of David Attenborough's BBC nature documentaries. The latter, on the other hand, is immensely popular in narrative cinema, although performing directly at the camera as if 'breaking the fourth wall' is less common. The combination of frontal direct address with the BCU in popular narrative cinema, or at least its revival, is more of a recent phenomenon, one that can arguably be traced to the early 1990s, in particular to the films of Jonathan Demme (Wickman, 2015).

With this in mind, I modified the DVT shot scale module to include an additional BCU category, where the bounding box of the face was over 98 per cent of the frame, my intuition being that there would be few of these shots and that they would likely be the type of overblown BCU for which Demme became known. I ran this tool over the three films Demme shot in the 1990s: *Silence of the Lambs* (1991), *Philadelphia* (1993), and *Beloved* (1998).

One of the best examples from this analysis is from *Silence of the Lambs*, in the now famous scene where police academy trainee Clarice Starling (Jodie Foster) meets serial killer Hannibal Lecter (Anthony Hopkins). In this scene, Lecter talks to Clarice behind a glass wall, and asks her to get closer. As she does, the framing of the shot-reverse-shot pattern gets progressively tighter, leading to the well-known 'Demme close-up of Lecter (See Figures 4.1 and 4.2).

Face detection is useful in this instance because unlike other categories of analysis in film, the close-up is one technique in the study of cinema in which identifying and looking at shots in isolation has in fact been used as a method. One of the reasons for this is what Doane calls 'the

Figure 4.1 Shot-reverse shot in *The Silence of the Lambs* (1991)

Figure 4.2 Demme close-up of Anthony Hopkins in *The Silence of the Lambs* (1991)

theoretical fascination with the diegetic autonomy of the close-up, the repeated assertion that it escapes the spatio-temporal coordinates of the narrative' (Doane, 2003, p. 107). In other words, it is precisely because the Demme BCU fills the screen in a way that severs the face from its context that, as Balaz reminds us, the 'expression on a face is complete and comprehensible in itself and therefore we need not think of it as existing in space and time' (Balaz, 1952, p. 61). Balaz and Doane are representative of a rich tradition in film scholarship that already admits the close-up as an autonomous unit of analysis, and for which detecting, isolating, and then aggregating these shots does indeed make sense.

The other aspect to note is that through this method one can only get candidate shots. I had to manually select from these the ones that more clearly showed performers looking directly at the lens, as opposed to just large faces. It takes some experience and careful observation to ascertain if a performer is looking directly into the lens or just slightly off, and there is no task in the toolkit for this. I also found that in many cases the bounding boxes drawn around the faces simply occupied all (100 per cent) of the vertical space in the frame, but very rarely was the same true for the horizontal space. This is to say, faces, insofar as bounding boxes outline them, tend to be portrait or square in shape, and therefore calculating shot proportions from the horizontal instead of the vertical dimension of the bounding box would likely yield quite different results, as would close-ups of objects other than faces, whose shape might be oblong.

And these proportions are of course also set in relation to the shape of the frame, which has evolved too over the years: from 1.33:1 for much of the silent era up to the so-called Academy ratio with the advent of sound, through to the wider formats after the mid-1950s – Cinerama, Polyvision, Cinemascope – and now presumably also to square, or vertical formats for mobile phones and digital platforms such as Instagram or TikTok videos. And some films, although rare, use more than one aspect ratio, for example Wes Anderson's *The Grand Budapest Hotel* (2014) (see: Laskin, 2015) (Figure 4.3).

Furthermore, looking at the candidate shots it is immediately apparent they are not just fully frontal faces, but in many cases are also photographed in a specific manner, namely with a very shallow depth of field, the eyes are in sharp focus but other parts of the head like the ears are blurred. This narrow focal range further contributes to separate the face from the background (and the body).

These observations highlight how proportion is only one aspect of the close-up, and how even something as seemingly trivial as encoding proportion is contingent on medium-specific factors. Deep engagement with the DVT further throws into question if computer vision systems can perform as well or better than humans. And the answer, much like the encodings, largely depends on what we believe humans do when they analyse a film, as well as on what we can reasonably expect computers to replicate from this activity. In other words, statements of performance ought to be qualified in terms of the 'art' in question when we speak of 'state of the art' in these systems.

This is not to say nothing can be learned from using the DVT; on the contrary, I would argue that as long as we treat it less as a tool for data extraction and analysis and use it instead as a set of techniques to be opened up, calibrated, and modified for experimentation, computer vision libraries such as these can play an important role in humanities research. For instance, with some fine-tuning, the experiment I present here can be expanded to collect a dataset of these BCUs, and then use them to train a 'Demme close-up' detector, like I did for depth of field in the previous chapter. Having such a detector, one could then imagine how it could be reattached to the DVT as custom embedding, and be used to undertake a larger distant viewing exercise to trace the use of this type of shot, find other stylistic features that correlate with it, and eventually compile a broader catalogue aiming towards an empirically defined signal of Demme's influence in contemporary Hollywood.

A study of this scale is beyond the scope of this chapter; I outline it here to illustrate one case in which, with minimal modifications, the tools of the DVT can be used in direct response to an existing debate in scholarship about film style. Note, however, that this is a type of formalism that is

Figure 4.3 Three different aspect ratios in *The Grand Budapest Hotel* (1.37:1, 1.85:1, 2.35:1)

explicitly concerned with the materiality of film, with surface, texture, and appearance; with the aspect, proportion and aggregation of faces by their properties as images, extricated from their narrative contexts and largely stripped from their regular symbolic functions. In summary, this experiment shows how the tools in the DVT assume a particular ontology of the cinematic image, one that reifies surface, and therefore paradoxically fits better with Doane's revision of *photogénie* than with Thompson and Bordwell's neoformalism (for more on these two branching approaches in film theory, see: Ray, 2001).

More than a critique of the DVT, my argument is that, as it stands today, the epistemic commitments of distant viewing are far from clear. When Arnold and Tilton write that 'Interpretive strategies within the distant viewing framework are only useful if they can be applied efficiently to large corpora', and that '[e]xtensive data creation as well as testing and tuning of computer vision algorithms is often required to achieve acceptable results' (2019, p. 5), one is left under the impression that they might be more interested in the distance than in the viewing, raising the question of to whom are these results acceptable and under what conditions; what kind of film scholarship and what kind of computer vision? In other words, what are the questions being asked when we claim accurate, efficient, and useful answers? And how can we be sure, like John Tukey cautions, that we are not accepting an exact answer to the wrong question in lieu of an approximate answer to the right one (1962, pp. 13–14)?

If to analyse moving images at a distance one must indeed automate some of the viewing, which is to say, model at least some aspects of visual perception as computational processes, surely the question of what exactly is being delegated to computers (and why) must come first; what aspects of vision are being outsourced to machines, and whether and how these vision tasks in fact correspond to operations and methods used in film scholarship. I am not arguing computer vision methods ought to correspond neatly with existing categories in film theory, and in fact towards the end of this section I will put forward a case for why we might not want them to. But as novel computational systems open moving images to new forms of intellectual inquiry, part of the task from a critical technical perspective is to specify exactly what machines are doing when we say they are 'viewing' on our behalf.

Both machine vision and film analysis are already broad and interdisciplinary fields, with multiple possible couplings and technical articulations in between. Developments in this emerging in-between space will depend as much on understanding how machines are designed than on what are they designed for and for whom. As we saw in previous chapters, human vision need not be the stick by which we measure machine vision, but even if it was, we experience, think, and discuss films across such a broad spectrum of perspectives, that it is hard not to imagine an equally rich technical equivalent diversity in machine vision. To allow for such a multiplicity of computational points of view to flourish, more suitable ways to observe the emergence of a larger techno-aesthetic ecology are needed. In other words, I submit that we need a *computational poetics of film* that underpins computer vision libraries like the DVT, so that seeing films at a distance can become epistemically grounded.

devices as rhythmic alternation, recapitulation, retrogression, gradual elimination, cyclical repetition, and serial variation, thus creating structures similar to those of twelve-tone music. (Burch, 1981, p. 14)

This set of basic minimal transition units are set on a 'scale' ranging from continuity to discontinuity, and their permutation, according to Burch, creates conventional editing patterns. One example would be the well-known 'shot-reverse-shot' technique, where a single character is shown speaking to someone off-screen, and there is then a cut to show the reaction or the response of their interlocutor, thereby fully preserving space-time continuity, just like the sequence from *The Silence of the Lambs* (1991) analysed in the previous chapter. Another example is 'parallel editing', like in the famous 'baptism of fire' scene in *The Godfather* (1972), where shots of Michael Corleone (Al Pacino) are intercalated with shots of multiple murders committed at his behest. In this case continuity is preserved in time but not space, which is to say, viewers are led to understand that these events are happening in separate places simultaneously.

These patterns in turn give rise to larger structures. Elaborating on Burch, Bordwell and Thompson describe two editing modalities: analytical and constructive. In the former, events are portrayed from the general to the particular, often starting with an establishing shot that sets the characters in relation to the space they occupy and progressively cutting to tighter shots to show the details of the scene. In the latter, details are given first, often as a series of close-ups, and viewers are invited to infer the spatial relations as more details are progressively revealed. The systematic analysis of these structures over time allows Bordwell and Thompson to map these styles onto larger historical traditions. Analytical editing, with its emphasis on space-time continuity, they argue, is the dominant form in classic Hollywood cinema, while constructive editing is more commonly found in directors from the French New Wave, like Robert Bresson (Bordwell et al, 2017, pp. 234–238; Bordwell, 2012).

It is worth noting this formal approach has its own internal debates and contradictions. For Burch, for example, editing is first and foremost a matter of internal coherence; 'a kind of music [. . .] what counts in film is the *mise-en-scène*, and that narrative is a kind of convenient support that has no importance whatsoever' (Burch, 2002). For Bordwell and Thompson, meanwhile, narrative comes first, and editing is seen as a process that gives content to external narrative schemata. As we shall see towards the end of this section, this tension between internal and external structuring forces of film form runs deep in different strands of film theory, and manifest too in different approaches to model film as a computational object.

viewers infer not only the presence of the shark, but its relative position and speed (*Jaws*, 2010).

Directors, filmmakers, and authors of various kinds organise temporal units in their films in different ways depending on the type of production; its scale, genre, planned distribution and exhibition outlets, et cetera. In smaller independent productions, directors themselves might write, shoot, and edit their own footage; Hollywood blockbusters on the other hand will often work from a script, have several parallel shooting units and a team of editors.

These examples show that more than a job entrusted to a specific person, or delegated to a fixed station in the assembly line, the temporal structure of a film is designed more generally by filmmakers throughout the pre-production-post-production continuum; between early planning and final fitting. From this point of view, the ability to order these temporal units, regardless of whether they have been photographed or not, can be seen as the core process required to produce meaningful cinematic temporal forms. In line with this analytic approach, we can then consider the act of relating one shot to the next to be the most basic expression of this ability, and further conclude, echoing the Soviet montage theorists like Kuleshov, Pudovkin, and Eisenstein, that cinematic time is produced precisely when filmmakers design an imagined relation between shots.

A contemporary exemplar of this formal-analytical approach to the analysis of film structure is the influential work of Noël Burch. With a background in music, Burch observes that film directors and editors often select from a relatively limited and stable palette of possibilities when assembling a sequence of shots, and that the interplay between these options over time can produce the effect of continuity, like a continuous complex melody is composed out of a small set of individual notes. He calls this organisational process *découpage*, from the French *découpé* 'to cut-up', alluding to a literary technique whereby fragments of texts are rearranged so as to produce new lines and potentially new meanings, only for Burch, instead of sequences of words, filmmakers cut-up strips of celluloid (Burch, 1981, pp. 3–4).

Through this concept, Burch classifies the ways in which a film can be edited by identifying all possible space-time articulations that describe a minimal relation that exists between any two consecutive shots, like the 'notes' of a film:

> a set of formal 'objects' – the fifteen different types of shot transitions and the parameters that define them – capable of rigorous development through such

processes are usually mediated by a script and subordinated to the director, who has the most general perspective on all aspects, including performers, sound, music, special effects, et cetera.

Although the temporal form of film can be said to be the result of a collaborative effort between almost all actors in this production line, it is fair to say that directors, and to a degree also editors, have the most influence over how shots and sequences are organised. Editors in particular appear to be the main responsible figures in making shots 'fit' with each other during post-production. However, if we take shots and scenes to be abstract temporal units rather than instantiated pieces of footage or bytes in a hard drive, it is clear that their organisation begins much earlier in the production process, often before shooting even takes place; in the form of a script, a storyboard, and other forms of pre-visualisation.

Some directors meticulously storyboard every shot of their films in the order in which they are meant to fit together, de facto pre-editing them before anything is recorded. Bong Joon-Ho, for example, is known for making storyboards so complete that '[t]hey look like mangas' (Yeun in Jung, 2019). So much so that his storyboard for *Parasite* (2019) was published as a stand-alone graphic novel (see: Vlessing, 2020). Arguably, the temporal structure of his films is largely decided in advance, with all other production activities subordinated to fit this initial, comic-like, blueprint.

On the opposite extreme there are those who abhor storyboards, like Werner Herzog, who calls them 'the instruments of cowards who have no faith in their imaginations and are slaves of a matrix' (Herzog in Cronin, 2002, p. 104). Herzog's faith is placed instead in his imagination during and after shooting. For his documentary *Grizzly Man* (2005), he worked with over 100 hours of archival footage shot over the thirteen summers by 'bear whisperer' Timothy Treadwell during his time in the Alaskan forests (Bradshaw, 2006). The temporal structure of this film, and indeed much of its emotional impact, was designed *a posteriori*, in the way Treadwell's video tapes were selected and cut by Herzog and his long-time collaborator, editor Joe Bini.

What is more, the organisation of shots and sequences can even change as a result of chance and ingenuity during the shooting process itself. A now classic example is when the mechanical shark in *Jaws* (1975) malfunctioned. The filmmakers had to radically alter the script, which had the shark appearing in frame constantly throughout the film. Steven Spielberg's solution was to imply the presence and movements of the creature through music: the now iconic two-note crescendo score of John Williams, paired with underwater point of view shots, which together help

CHAPTER 5

Computational Analysis of Continuity Editing

One of the limitations of the DVT for the study of cinema is its focus on analysing frames primarily as still images. Save for shot boundary detection, there are no other methods in the toolkit explicitly concerned with how images are organised in time. But as we know from several decades of film theory, the order, frequency, and rhythm of moving images are fundamental to how they are enjoyed and understood.

Temporal structure in film is usually broken down analytically into sequences, scenes, and shots. These are units with which filmmakers and film editors design an intelligible whole from a pool of possible parts, most often recorded in various locations at separate times and in a different order. *Casablanca* (1942) is set in the eponymous north African city but was filmed at the Warner Bros studio lot in California (Francisco, 1980, p. 139). In *Mary, Queen of Scots* (2018), the characters played by Margot Robbie and Saoirse Ronan are shown to sustain a rivalry for over seven years, but they shot their only scene together during a single day of overlap in their respective schedules (Blyth, 2019). In *Dunkirk* (2017), events occurring on air, sea, and land, during an hour, a day, and a week, are presented simultaneously by cross-cutting between the timelines (Debruge, 2017). Space-time elision and manipulation are fundamental aspects of filmmaking and spectatorship, from production to pleasure to analysis.

Film production tends to be a capital-intensive enterprise, organised as an assembly line in which highly specialised and interconnected professionals converge. In this line, cinematographers are responsible for shooting all the individual pieces, designing their appearance and ensuring consistency through lightning, cameras and lenses; they control the photographic aspect of the shots. At the editing stage, film editors arrange these individual shots into scenes and sequences; they fit all the smaller moving pieces together to form a larger moving picture, by adjusting their individual duration and reordering them as necessary. Both of these

COMPUTATIONAL ANALYSIS OF CONTINUITY EDITING   103

Table 5.1 Burch's 5 × 3 matrix, as per Frierson

Time / Space	Continuous	Ellipsis (definite)	Ellipsis (indefinite)	Time reversal (definite)	Time reversal (indefinite)
Continuous	CC	CE	CEi	CR	CRi
Contiguous	CtC	CtE	CtEi	CtR	CtRi
Discontinuous	DC	DE	DEi	DR	DRi

But let us focus for now in what Bordwell and Burch have in common: the idea of film analysis as a form of pattern recognition, where larger patterns can be inferred from smaller unit relations, all the way down to a finite set of minimal units, namely shots. This line of thinking appears immediately amenable to algorithmic implementations; for example, Frierson (2018) has noted that Burch's system amounts to a 5 × 3 relational matrix (Table 5.1), which allows to describe the space-time articulations between shots through a pre-programmed rule-based system of classification:

From a data analysis perspective, the relation between any two consecutive shots can be defined using this matrix, and we would obtain as a result a signal of continuity-discontinuity over time. And given enough samples, patterns in this signal could be used to identify conventions and larger structures common to directors, genres, or time periods.

This inductive approach is compatible with distant viewing and reminiscent to the logic of Cinemetrics, but in close inspection there is a very significant difference: the metrics of Cinemetrics and the tools of the DVT act upon an immediately observable and measurable property of shots (for example their duration, or their colour), while Burch's matrix describes a set of latent relations between shots, across time, and in terms of their interpretation by a viewer. In other words, Burch is interested in the invisible relations that make the visible shots meaningful. A sceptical reader might object and say measurements are simply the result of a more stable set of conventional relations, but even if this is the case, the relations between shots proposed by Burch are neither directly observable nor immediately measurable, and thus need to be considered as relations of a second order: contingent on external schemata, such as an understanding of cinematic time and how it is structured in concert with an internal and subjective concept of time.

It follows that what Burch has in mind cannot be calculated from the shots alone; while shot duration can be treated as a visible trace of the film production process and thus construed as a signal that can be directly extracted from the material object of the film, the concept of cinematic continuity implicates a viewer external to the film, an interpreter who labours to piece it together using their previous knowledge of film form, their implicit understanding of film as a medium, and their internal sense of time as a way to regulate its elision and manipulation. What Burch has in mind and what he endeavours to make explicit in his classification is not just how films are made, but how they are seen. And the traces of film watching are neither visible nor contained in the films themselves, but emerge from the contact between films and their audiences; their meanings are co-constituted through the activities and modes of attentive and structured watching.

Therefore, in order to model a 'computational Burch', we need both the edit points that separate one shot from the next and an annotation of what viewers infer to be in-between the shots. This second signal is much more elusive because it needs to be encoded from a subjective unconscious process that appears to leave no traces. The question for us is how to make this process explicit so that we can model it computationally. From the terms laid above, we can say that a Burchian computational method suggests an integrated practice, namely the extraction of shot boundaries (which is possible through the DVT) and the crowdsourcing of manual annotations about shot transitions (which is not).

Let us try this idea through an example of this workflow applied to *The Godfather*. Following Burch, our first task is to split the sequence into its constituent shots. This can be done manually, as was the case in Cinemetrics, but we can also employ known methods to automatically compute shot boundaries. Most of these methods, including the DVT aggregator, are based on frame-to-frame histogram calculation: hard cuts are detected when the difference in pixel values changes abruptly between frames (Hong Lu and Yap-Peng Tan, 2005; Joyce and Bede Liu, 2006). Depending on the specific method employed, some transitions such as dissolves or wipes are harder to detect, and similarly, sudden changes in luminance of the video feed, such as depictions of explosions or flashes, can yield false positives.[1] These caveats notwithstanding, automated shot boundary detection methods are generally reliable *vis-à-vis* manual annotation, which by comparison is slower and much less consistent in the types of errors it produces (see: Hanjalic, 2002 for more on shot boundary detection methods). As with most computational methods, the key is to make an informed decision about the kind of errors one is willing to live with.

Although it is possible to perform shot boundary detection using the DVT, I found that the open-source Python library PySceneDetect (Castellano, 2020) offers more control, as it allows the fine-tuning of various parameters to the source material. Using this library, I processed

COMPUTATIONAL ANALYSIS OF CONTINUITY EDITING 105

Table 5.2 Shot segmentation results

Shot	Start frame	Start timestamp	End frame	End timestamp	Duration (frames)	Duration (seconds)
1	0	00:00:00.000	718	00:00:29.947	718	29.95
2	718	00:00:29.947	1674	00:01:09.820	956	39.87
3	1674	00:01:09.820	1913	00:01:19.788	239	9.97
4	1913	00:01:19.788	2152	00:01:29.756	239	9.97
5	2152	00:01:29.756	2391	00:01:39.725	239	9.97
...	...	...	...	...	...	...
1425	245939	02:50:57.706	246017	02:51:00.959	78	3.25
1426	246017	02:51:00.959	246089	02:51:03.962	72	3.00
1427	246089	02:51:03.962	246165	02:51:07.132	76	3.17
1428	246165	02:51:07.132	246414	02:51:17.517	249	10.39
1429	246414	02:51:17.517	247470	02:52:01.561	1056	44.04

Table 5.3 Cinemetrics-like breakdown analysis

total number of shots	1429
longest shot	104.69
shortest shot	0.58
range	180.5
average shot length (ASL)	7.22
median shot length (MSL)	4.09
length ratio (LR)	0.57
standard deviation	9.64

The Godfather to break it down into individual shots. Table 5.2 shows a snapshot of the resulting data-frame. Table 5.3 shows basic metrics in a format comparable to Cinemetrics.

Using this list of shot boundaries, we can split the video stream and compose a shot-by-shot table, rendering the first, middle, and last frame of every shot as a thumbnail JPEG image. With this table at hand, let us now turn our attention to the aforementioned baptism sequence (shots 1296–1364), where we can visualise the parallel editing pattern more clearly: the film alternates between shots of Michael Corleone in church at the baptism of his nephew, and shots showing the preparation and execution of the planned murders of competing mafia bosses. The rhythmic back and forth is punctuated through sound design, by keeping the organ music from the church over the whole sequence and having the baptised baby crying during the preparations. As the scene reaches its climax, the crying stops, Michael is asked by the priest three times if he renounces Satan, and with every affirmative answer, the film cuts to a different murder scene.

106 CINEMA AND MACHINE VISION

Table 5.4 'Baptism of Fire' shot by shot fragment from *The Godfather*

Shot	Length (secs.)	First frame of the shot	Middle frame	End frame of the shot
1340	1.585			
1341	3.337			
1342	2.085			
1343	4.087			
1344	1.585			

The editing pattern underwrites Michael's growing power by showing his influence expanding to separate places simultaneously, and the sequence is also widely recognised for its climactic juxtaposition of religious ritual with violent crime, as Michael becomes godfather to his nephew in church and simultaneously steps into his new role as *the* godfather of a criminal operation (Jones, 2009). In Table 5.4 we see an example of the editing pattern, as well as Bordwell's analytical editing in action: shot 1340 shows a close-up of Michael, shot 1341 shows someone coming into a parlour in Las Vegas where a competing crime syndicate boss, Moe Greene, is being massaged; shot 1342 gets closer to Greene as he put on his glasses to see who is coming into the room; and shot 1343 gets even closer to his face as he gets shot. The sequence goes from the general to the specific and then cuts back to Michael at the church, and then the pattern repeats.

Using this table and Burch's matrix, I manually annotated the sequence with shot transitions. Table 5.5 shows these annotations for the final seven

COMPUTATIONAL ANALYSIS OF CONTINUITY EDITING   107

Table 5.5 'Baptism of Fire' sequence from *The Godfather*, annotated with Burch's continuity matrix

Shot	Length (secs.)	End frame of the shot	Space	Time	Burch class
1359	5.797		Continuous	Continuous	CC
1360	1.752		Discontinuous	Continuous	DC
1361	2.628		Discontinuous	Continuous	DC
1362	2.336		Discontinuous	Continuous	DC
1363	2.002		Discontinuous	Continuous	DC
1364	4.504		Discontinuous	Ellipsis	DEi
1365	4.796				

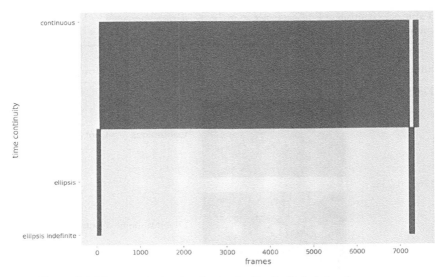

Figure 5.1 Time continuity visualisation in *The Godfather*'s baptism sequence

shots, as the murders and the cross-cutting pattern comes to an end (shots 1359–1365).

I encoded these annotations by assigning them values on a scale from −2 to 2, where positive values represent continuity and negative values discontinuity. Using these values and the shot durations I plotted a signal for time and space articulations, as seen in Figures 5.1 and 5.2.

Note that while the patterns above reflect the parallel editing technique, they are not representations of the shots themselves, but rather of the relations between them as inferred by a viewer, in this case me. The key assumption Burch makes is that these categories are, if not objective, at least subject to empirical verification. And the advantage from this perspective is that these categories, unlike higher-level ones, are presumed to be shared among viewers, making errors and inconsistencies a function of how well the annotators understand the classification criteria and how closely can they follow it, as opposed to their subjective interpretations of what the film means more generally.

These patterns give an indication of interplay between intrinsic and extrinsic forces in the editing of the film; between production and consumption; between what is there to be seen in the shots and what inferences we 'inject' in between them. In this way, this is a model of continuity that includes the shots as well as the cognitive and affective 'glue' that binds them, or in other words, the invisible that makes the visible meaningful. Taking Burch's claims to their logical conclusion, we can go further and

COMPUTATIONAL ANALYSIS OF CONTINUITY EDITING 109

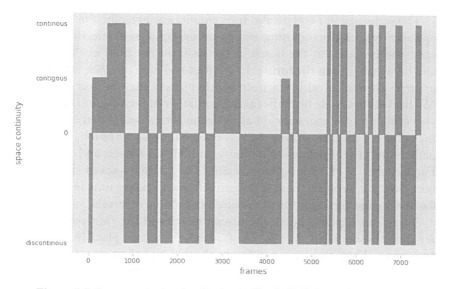

Figure 5.2 Space continuity visualisation in *The Godfather*'s baptism sequence

turn to sound as a channel to represent these temporal relations; we might want to hear rather than see continuity. The signals I encoded are coarse but can be used to produce a basic sonification of continuity. One significant advantage of sonification over visualisation of multivariate time series is that sound allows for multidimensional polyphony, meaning the ability to assign multiple variables to individual 'voices' or tracks, and 'stack them' one on top of the other so that they play simultaneously. Combining shot boundary detection with manual encodings and pixel value data, such as optical flow, could make for a distinctly richer signal to enable the sonification of continuity. Moreover, as far as sonification can also be analysed as a sequence of images in the form of a sequence of spectrograms, it too can be configured as training data for AI systems that 'listen' to continuity in films.

I did not get this far in my experiments, but following the encoding pattern in *The Godfather*, I manually annotated and created a sonification of the last sequence of *Dunkirk* to compare them through sound.[2] This sequence is constructed by cross cutting between several characters across different timelines: Tommy and Alex, who are returning soldiers on a train passing through Woking; Dawson and Peter, father and son from Weymouth, who helped evacuate the soldiers; and Farrier, a pilot who defended the evacuation from the air over the beach at Dunkirk, running out of fuel in the process.

The sequence in *Dunkirk* also uses parallel editing, albeit in almost the opposite way: by juxtaposing events occurring at separate times in the same three spaces; at the beach in the past, on the train in the present, and in Weymouth in the future. In contrast to *The Godfather*, which plays in strict chronological order over approximately the one year that takes Michael to supersede his father as the godfather of the title, in *Dunkirk* the viewer follows the characters in asynchronous time scales that converge at the climax of the film, during the rescue operation in the beach. After their paths cross, the timelines of Tommy and Alex, Dawson and Peter, and Farrier, start to slide out of sync again. The last sixty-seven shots of the film cross cut between these sliding timeframes, eliding time in a series of flashbacks and forwards, or what Burch calls 'time reversals'.[3]

As we can see (and hear), the discontinuities in the *Dunkirk* sequence are more pronounced than in *The Godfather* and take place in both time and space. They also have a different rhythm and their own type of *crescendo*. Their effects are radically different, even when the cross–cutting editing technique they use is formally similar.

Almost all of Christopher Nolan's films are structured around the careful manipulation of cinematic time through temporal abridgements of various kinds. Bordwell calls this Nolan's 'formal project', which he argues consists of 'exploring what the technique of cross–cutting does to story time' (Bordwell and Thompson, 2019). But even if in *Dunkirk* these time displacements are overt, the underlying mechanism, according to Burch, is not particular to climactic sequences, complex plots, or formally inclined filmmakers. His conjecture is, rather, that in nearly all popular narrative films cinematic time is constructed by elision; by carefully selecting what not to show, or rather how not to show it, in such a way that viewers can still infer that which has been omitted.

Bordwell later elaborated on this notion from a narrative perspective, arguing that filmmakers manipulate these inferences by controlling how the 'whole' story is presented to viewers as an organised series of fragments, or a plot – if one can follow the various pieces of the plot one can in principle understand the story. From this it follows that the same story can be plotted in a number of ways, through differentiated patterns for withholding information from the viewer, or degrees of narrative restriction, as Bordwell calls them. In a typical murder-mystery story, for example, the identity of the killer can be kept from viewers until the end (restricted narration), or viewers can know from the start who the killer is and are instead left to wonder if and how they will get caught (unrestricted narration) (Bordwell, 2006). And the two types of plot will elicit a different aesthetic response even when the underlying story is the same. The key factor in the production of meaning from this perspective is how to organise over time the seen and the told against the unseen and the untold, and in this, editing does play a crucial role.

Notably both Coppola and Nolan work in close collaboration with their editors, the former going as far to say editing is 'the essence of cinema' (Coppola, 1994). For *The Godfather* he employed a total of six editors to cut over 'a maze' of ninety hours of footage (Lebo, 1997). For *Dunkirk*, Nolan worked with his long-time editor Lee Smith, who went on to win an American Academy award for the film, and who Nolan often credits for making his complex treatments of cinematic time understandable to popular audiences: 'What editors do is to me very mysterious and therefore very exciting. At its best, editing is invisible – or extremely mysterious – and its effect is very difficult to explain' (Nolan in Giardina, 2011).

This assumption that good editing is 'invisible' is widely held among critics and audiences, the implication being that when shots flow one after the other without the viewer noticing, cinematic time is created and/or preserved. The great mystery as to how this happens can be partially dispelled by thinking of editing as a material process of assemblage, as if it were the carpentry of an Alvar Aalto chair or a building designed by Zaha Hadid, whose surfaces are polished to the point where joints and seams disappear onto smooth and continuous surfaces that blend into each other, and are seen as being naturally integrated into an individual building or piece of furniture.

To the visual caress of the film viewer, the transitions between shots appear smoothed out, as the joints are cleverly concealed and often not perceived at all when the film unfolds in time. But the appearance of smoothness, as Roland Barthes reminds us, 'is always an attribute of perfection because its opposite reveals a technical and typically human operation of assembly' (1993 [1957], p. 88). By undertaking even the least demanding of editing projects, or simply by watching a student film where the techniques of continuity editing have not yet been fully mastered, one is quickly reminded of the amount of work that goes into achieving this continuous effect in practice, and just how manufactured and contrived the cinematic flow of imagery in narrative cinema actually is.

By eschewing visibility, both computing and sonification bypass the gaze that is focused on the continuous surface of film and reveals its inner workings, isolating its seams, joints, and hinges, so that their patterns can be apprehended as a high-dimensional sound map. With supplementary information about how the sound representation was created, attentive listening, and some practice, one can hear and compare sequences and films in a manner analogous to how one would interpret a graph or a diagram.

And this practice in turn would contribute to explain how (cinematic) time is designed 'between the shots' as much as through them.

In principle, sonification is compatible with distance-based methods: to achieve it we created an interpretive code, extracted and aggregated features, and found patterns through data analysis techniques. Simultaneously, however, the computational Burchian is engaged in a self-reflexive and creative endeavour; first, by recognising that to understand meaning-making, an account of viewers is needed too. From this perspective, the computational modelling inspired by Burch is additive as much as destructive: some features are ready to be 'mined' but others had to be 'sculpted'. A conceptual framework of film's temporal structure, its units, and conventions is mobilised to inform this modelling, which then facilitates engineering of higher-level features such as continuity. Data in this process, as Lisa Gitelman (2013) reminds us, is not just extracted but created and recreated at every step, which is to say, there is as much of a miner as there is of a jeweller in the labour of a computational film scholar.

A second observation in this process of modelling film continuity computationally is that distance-based readings and viewings often lack an internal awareness of how their underlying algorithms gained their automation powers in the first place, which is to say as a function of what was seen and encoded previously – the human vision on top of which computer vision is built. It is the viewing and not the distance that requires more critical attention from this point of view, as there are few encodings and little data to account for film spectatorship, and no corresponding task in computer vision.

To create these annotations manually is an arduous and time-consuming task, as it was for Salt when he measured film reels in feet and inches back in the 1970s. This is the epistemic bargain at the heart of machine vision: in order to step back and look at film at a distance, one needs to first step close and look at it in the eye; in order to automatically extract one has to manually model. But herein also lies the great promise of machine vision: to make data not only of the images that were shot, but also of how they are seen, and by whom. These other dimensions of meaning-making can also be encoded as data, which suggests that such a computational spectatorship is entirely feasible. As of writing, this type of aesthetically sensitive machine vision has not yet been designed, but as AI diversifies its epistemic configurations, I believe that it will.

Notes

1. In the example of The Godfather (1972), the longest shot (no. 792) is actually a montage of several shots with dissolve transitions.
2. Sonification experiments can be accessed here: https://on.soundcloud.com /Ym7ca
3. At one point in his *Theory of Film Practice*, Burch questions whether flash-backs are not simply a form of inverted ellipsis: 'Are not jumps forward and backward in time really identical on the formal organic level of a film? Are there not ultimately, then, only four kinds of temporal relationships, the fourth consisting of a great jump in time, either forward or backward?' (8). In the case of *Dunkirk*, however, the difference is relevant, as it is indeed in most of Nolan's films, so I kept the original 5×3 matrix and assigned specific values to time reversals for the sonification.

CHAPTER 6

Duration, Motion, and Pixels

So far, I have discussed the production of cinematic time in the context of formal-analytical frameworks to film. As mentioned earlier, there are two significant assumptions that go with these approaches: first, that films are broken down to their constituent units for analysis, meaning frames, shots, sequences; and second, that the viewer submits to a pre-programmed temporal form, for example narrative continuity. In this chapter I question whether and how these assumptions hold under the epistemic displacements brought about by new forms of inductive computing such as deep learning.

Elsewhere I have argued (2012) that computational methods can accommodate radically different theoretical frameworks in moving image studies. Elaborating on this argument, I submit that there are at least two complementary ways to understand the problem of using computers to 'see' films for us: what we may call the classical analytical approach, in which the goal is to train computers to perform like critics, and which amounts to designing systems that encode and reproduce existing categories of film analysis. And what we may call generative revisionist approaches, whose goal is to design systems that open new categories and reshape critical practice.

There is no inherent advantage to either approach, nor are they mutually exclusive. They do, however, present distinct advantages and limitations at different junctures. While formalist approaches to film were among the first to embrace the computer as an analytical tool with which to answer existing questions, today, global networked computation is less of a tool and more of a condition under which new questions can be asked and answered. Moretti had some of this in mind when he wrote that distant reading:

> *is a condition of knowledge*: it allows you to focus on units that are much smaller or much larger than the text: devices, themes, tropes – or genres and systems. And if, between the very small and the very large, the text itself disappears, well, it is one of

DURATION, MOTION, AND PIXELS

those cases when one can justifiably say, Less is more. If we want to understand the system in its entirety, we must accept losing something. (Moretti, 2000, pp. 57–58)

There is an economic aspect to this logic which sits well with big data analytics. Arnold and Tilton are concerned with the very large, and so is Jockers, who in fact overtly models his *macroanalysis* on economics, referencing John Keynes and Milton Friedman (Jockers, 2013). But the other, often neglected aspect of this distance is the very small, which can also make the original text disappear and reappear in ways that can produce knowledge, albeit in a different sense.

These tensions of scope find their correspondence in the ways film theorists have understood the production of cinematic time, particularly in the assumptions of shots being the basic-most unit of film analysis and narrative continuity the dominant schema with which to organise these units. Cinemetrics and the Distant Viewing Toolkit (DVT) leverage data analysis and deep learning to sustain the primacy of the shot and the dominance of continuity editing, but these same technologies can also be used to question the formalist *doxa*, and to give computational currency to competing ideas about cinematic time. The most notable among these are the approaches indebted to the philosophy of Henri Bergson.

Even more than the formalists, the debates inspired by Bergson's ideas about time are broad, heterogeneous, and beyond the scope of the present work (see: Guerlac, 2017 for a general introduction). Here I shall only focus on his concept of duration (*durée*), the significance it has for cinema, and in particular the consequences for the computational encoding of cinematic time.

One of Bergson's central claims is that empirical inquiry of continuous phenomena necessarily ignores duration, since the flow of time and motion needs to be interrupted to enable measurement:

> The indivisibility of motion implies, then, the impossibility of real instants; and indeed, a very brief analysis of the idea of duration will show us both why we attribute instants to duration and why it cannot have any. (2004 [1896], p. 223)

The type of continuity Bergson is keen to restore in critical debate is in direct opposition to Zeno and his paradoxes about the fragmentation of instants and the impossibility of change.[1] This might appear at first to be a philosophical rather than a computational question: either time is continuous and we break it down into measurable parts, or it is in fact composed of a sequence of instants in constant succession one after the other tricking us into thinking it is continuous; either way, the reader might ask, why does this distinction matter for the critical technologist researching cinematic time?

Bergson's notion of duration animates scholarly debate in Film Studies because, among other things, it gives the temporal form of moving images both a historical and a technological dimension. Mary Anne Doane for example, channels Bergson in her investigation of cinematic time, as she observes how technologies like the cinematographer are profoundly linked to the standardisation and rationalisation of global time at the turn of the twentieth century. Cinematic time, argues Doane, was born with industrialisation, with the railway and the telegraph, which required a consistent way to organise time across territories, and with the factory, its assembly lines, and punch-card routines to measure 'man-hours'. As time became a measure of production in industrial societies, its meaning was radically altered: no longer an infinite continuum that simply 'passed', but a differentiable and quantifiable resource that could be 'saved' or 'spent' (Doane, 2002, p. 4).

To manage time in this way, according to Doane, meant not only rethinking it as discrete but also to make it representable and to an extent visible. To visualise the passing of time one has to stop it, to freeze its ebb at given intervals so as to record it in discrete units, and this is a distinctly Bergsonian argument: that to measure time one has to change its meaning. Nowhere is this more apparent than in the technologies of cinema, where every second is segmented into a number of frames so that time can be experienced as uninterrupted during projection: 'The representation of time in cinema (its "recording") is also and simultaneously the production of temporalities for the spectator's time. The cinema is perceived as both record and performance' (Doane, 2002, p. 24).

This double function of cinema as a recorder and a producer of time, between faithfully capturing time and creatively manipulating it, has been at the heart of scholarly debates for the past hundred years, and it comes back in full force under the aegis of digital technologies, which radically alter our perception of time.[2] The door is left open to ask: if frames, shots and scenes are constructed historically as conventions related to the development of technologies of cinema at the turn of the twentieth century, what new temporal forms are possible under the logic and affordances of global networked computation?

Tying these threads together, let us get back to Moretti and the very small. Before they were digital objects, moving images could only be reduced to frames, photograms that flowed one after the other through the projector. But this is no longer the case; today digital moving images flow in a different sense altogether, through digital networks as continuous streams of data and through computational engines that process them in much smaller units: as number arrays. From a data science perspective this can be seen as a question of granularity, of the sampling rate at which we are able to perceive units to be discrete; the higher the sampling rate and the smaller the unit, the more we can say a signal resembles a continuous flow and appears to us as a continuum as opposed to the concatenation of its parts.

In this sense, one of the least observed powers of digital moving images only comes into focus not at a distance but in very close proximity, and this is a familiar territory for scholars who take after Bergson. The flow of moving images amounts to a stream of data: a sequence of numbers that describe every pixel of every image of every frame of every shot, like droplets of water that now percolate through the much larger mechanical sluices of capture and projection to form a continuous river with no apparent gaps. So, it is not only a matter of scale or perspective, distant or close readings; that computational technologies have atomised images into minute particles has more profound ontological consequences and effects in our categories of knowledge. In a literal sense, a flow of pixels now threatens to erode pre-existing temporal structures used in the analysis of film. This is not to say frames and shots are no longer relevant, but rather that what we think of as a shot is being conceptually redefined from a recording to a calculation; from the cut and the edit point to the modulation of pixel values over time.

The act of 'cutting' films, both actually or analytically, and the logical pieces that result from this act are still in place, but the outlines of the pieces and the relation between them are being reshaped either explicitly or implicitly at the level of pixels, which can be drawn one after the other algorithmically and without holding any isomorphic relation to anything other than themselves. The smallest unit in digital films is not a photogram but a tiny bucket of numbers; for example an orange pixel [255, 153, 51], a blue pixel [68, 46, 179], or a yellow pixel [255, 255, 7].[3] The cut and the shot as categories of analysis are equivalent from this perspective to using a pair of scissors on a stream of water: it is technically possible, but less effective at producing meaningful segments for analysis.

More than cuts and edits, what binds moving images together today is the set of millions of calculations that describe the relations between these tiny buckets of numbers over time. Film can thus be described as a time series of pixel values, and the gaps between shots that Noël Burch sought to define, or the intervals between frames that greatly concerned Bergson, are now to be found between pixels.

So, what is there between pixels? As we discussed in earlier chapters, not every pixel drawn at every time-step is described using the same logic: some pixels need to be drawn in full, some inherit from previous states;

some are the result of a photographic process, but others are only the result of calculations. What lies between pixels is a rich network of logical relations which are too small to observe with the naked eye, and too complex to describe through the existing technical language of film. To access this network, it is necessary to engage moving images at the molecular level; to track their flow through the instruments of computing, but also to design new temporal units, and their corresponding critical vocabulary.

There are examples that already hint at the dissolution of the logical distinction between frames and shots, even in popular cinema. One such example is in the trend of elaborate long takes in the recent films of Alfonso Cuarón, where several separate shots are digitally composited together to look like single uninterrupted sequences (Udden, 2009). This technique is stretched to the duration of a whole feature film in Sam Mendes' *1917* (2019), which is edited in a way that suggests the action is captured in a single continuous shot (Siegel, 2019).[4] These editing techniques are not in themselves new; the idea has been around since at least 1948, when Alfred Hitchcock used a similar concept for his film *Rope*. But while Hitchcock had to disguise shot transitions using close-ups every ten minutes (the length of a film reel), Cuarón and Mendes used computers to digitally 'paint' over the seams between shots, manually injecting correspondences between individual pixels, or effectively *un-cutting* film algorithmically.[5]

The pressure put upon classical temporal structures is even more overt in animation, perhaps because in animation space on screen needs to be drawn, not captured, and the idea of a shot as a recording was therefore already weak, even before the rise of digital technologies. A prime example of this weakening of shots can be seen in the films of Satoshi Kon, in the abundant examples of the type of complex transitions he uses, fluidly zooming in and out of different spaces and pulling and pushing his characters along with/through the transitions (Figure 6.1).

There is no Burchian category for what Kon does to space-time transitions, in part because the Japanese director is not constrained by recorded time in the way live action filmmakers are. But this is also increasingly the case with live action films because their pixels too are often rendered rather than recorded, not captured but drawn in post-production. Digital images are in this sense closer to tapestry than to photography, not so much the result of pro-filmic events, but a steady stream of pixels that fall into place like the patterns in a Jacquard loom.[6]

This becomes apparent in analogue computing and in examples of algorithms without software. One such example is the project known as *r/place* (PLACE, 2017). In this project a shared canvas of 1000 × 1000 pixels was set up for registered Reddit users to fill in during the course of

Figure 6.1 Complex editing in *Paprika* (2006)

three days. Any given user could only edit (change the colour of) one pixel at the time, at intervals varying from five to twenty minutes. During the seventy-two hours of the experiment, users collaborated and competed to create an evolving tapestry of graphics, from national flags, game artwork, political propaganda, to fictional characters, memes, and abstract 'voids' of colour (see: *PLACE timelapse*, 2017).

The pixels in this project can be said to have been drawn 'by hand'. Distinct communities of users coalesced on various parts of the canvas at separate times to produce coherent imagery one pixel at a time. In themselves, individual pixels appear meaningless, but over time and in in aggregate they gain their meaning from the contact they make with their neighbours, thereby creating 'a latent structure of emergent relations' (Rappaz et al, 2018). Furthermore, the emergence and erasure of images over time suggests that this latent structure can be construed as a set of micro-narratives:

> Tension between *r/ukplace* and *r/mexico* grew when a cactus was built which began extending up into the dress of r/ukplace's depiction of Queen Elizabeth II, but negotiations brought about a peaceful resolution and a non-aggression pact between the two powers. In the final hours of Place, a Void Core was created in the left hand side of this territory and quickly expanded to cover the flag and destroy the pixelart, but was beaten back by a combined effort of *r/mexico* and several surrounding factions. (Rytz, 2019)

By placing them and picking their colour, users are in effect annotating every pixel manually, performing micro-calculations of space which in aggregate amount to the rendering of larger images. In this project users become human computers whose processing power is distributed in a cluster of many 'human-cores', and the resulting moving images are both digital and manufactured; at once manually hand-painted and algorithmically rendered.

The case of *r/place* is illuminating because by altering the division of labour between humans and machines it stretches the temporal dimension of the process through which images are made to flow, pixel by pixel, to a scale where the discrete set of units and their relations becomes apparent. On this distended time scale, we can focus on the very small; for example on the local pixel variances that influence neighbouring pixels and reverberate through the images as they change, which is to say, as they move.

This idea of the cumulative effect of minute local variances sounds eerily similar to the sort of ineffable internal rhythm of moving images which some filmmakers and editors invoke, usually to argue that it can only be 'felt' or otherwise intuitively grasped:[7] 'Rather than film editors impose their rhythm on the images, the images and sounds impose their rhythm on the editors, restrict them as to where and how the film can be cut . . .' (Van Leeuwen, 1985, p. 217). And perhaps the filmmaker that most eloquently embodies this idea is Andrei Tarkovsky, for whom editing is the uncovering of a 'self-organising structure' dictated by internal rhythm:

> Editing a picture correctly, competently, means allowing the separate scenes and shots to come together spontaneously, for in a sense they edit themselves; they join up according to their own intrinsic pattern [. . .] Rhythm, then, is not the metrical sequence of pieces; what makes it is the time-thrust within frames. And I am convinced that it is rhythm and not editing, as people tend to think, that is the main formative element of cinema. (1989, pp. 116–117)

Talking about the editing for his film *Mirror* (1975), Tarkovsky recalls how after a lengthy process and many frustrating attempts, one day 'the material came to life; the parts started to function reciprocally, as if linked by a bloodstream [. . .] the film was born before our eyes' (1989, p. 116). His language here is eminently Bergsonian: the flow of blood is like the flow of time, a continuous stream of internal forces that cannot easily be made discrete.

A computational Bergsonian would argue that by treating images as streams of data it is possible to process them in their 'liquid form', to reshape them and squeeze them as number arrays through a different type of machinery such as artificial neural networks. When the frames of a film undergo the process of convolution, we can say these flat surfaces soften, 'loosening into pixels' whose local relations are calculated as a filter scans the surface of the image, like a flying shuttle in a loom. In other words,

DURATION, MOTION, AND PIXELS

images give up their fixed spatial coherence to gain some of the powers of pure sequentiality.

The sceptic, on the other hand, would respond like Zeno responded to Heraclitus, and argue that this continuous flow is merely an illusion; that however small, units are nevertheless discrete and that their internal relations can be abstracted 'out of time', stripped from their duration as mathematical expressions. Furthermore, a materialist sceptic might also object to the notion of an unrecognisable array of numbers being an image at all and would probably argue for a sharper distinction between images and representations.

Meanwhile, for a creative technologist the paradox takes a more practical dimension: computer programs are structured as a set of individual logical steps, yet their powers ultimately depend on performance and execution at 'run time'. If a program does not 'run', or halts at an unexpected point, it is usually an indication that something is not working correctly. Conversely, if a program runs continuously, the set of steps disappear, and the individual parts remain unnoticed. For those involved in this logic, images alternate between states without much philosophical fuss, their flow becomes a flow of numbers modulated by logical gates and computational overheads.

In deep learning images are represented as multidimensional arrays of specific shapes before they pass through a neural network. A single image shaped [512, 340] pixels would need to be reshaped to a tensor of a shape such as [16, 3, 340, 512], where 4 is the batch size (how many images will be passed to the network at once) and 3 is the number of channels (typically one for each RGB channel in a colour image). As this tensor 'flows' through the network it is constantly reshaped: channels are likely to increase while height and width usually decrease. At some of the deeper layers the tensor could be shaped something like [16, 786, 17, 32], and whatever is left of the image at this point is more like an unrecognisable mush of numbers. And finally, in order to be interpreted again, this four-dimensional representation needs to be 'flattened' as it is squeezed out of the network, for example in a vector of as many categories as the model was trained to detect.[8]

Flows in deep learning are computationally expensive and increasingly complex; tensors are now being pushed through sophisticated 'backflow' modules such as inception or residual modules (Szegedy et al, 2014; He et al, 2015), and more recently also attention mechanisms (Vaswani et al, 2017). At the same time, common frameworks to manage this type of tensor arithmetic are making easier the integration between different models, architectures, and concepts. A notable example of this technical flourishing in deep learning are unsupervised or self-supervised methods like generative adversarial networks (GANs), where two mirrored models compete in a loop against each other so as to approximate any given non-linearity in a dataset (Goodfellow et al, 2014).

When applied to images of faces, GANs can be used to create synthetic images, some of which are photorealistic, colloquially called 'deepfakes': images that are not the product of any specific pro-photographic event. Deepfakes look like photographs, and thus enjoy some of the epistemic advantages of photography despite not being recordings of anything. Floridi (2018) has suggested that a more accurate name for these images would be *ectypes*: 'a copy, but not any copy, but rather a copy that has a special relation with its source (the origin of its creation), the archetype' (p. 319).

However, what is remarkable about deepfakes is not just that they are records without recording, but how this transformation comes to be. GANs achieve this effect through a type of time compression that subordinates historical time to computer time, a process that collapses history into processing cycles, thereby letting images that were recorded in the past bear upon the pixels that are yet to be plotted. By leveraging this latent network of connections between images across time, images gain 'a power to turn back on themselves. They are the object of a perpetual reorganization, in which a new image can arise from any point whatever of the preceding image' (Deleuze, 1986, p. 265).

So where does this leave cinematic time? Through this potential for perpetual reorganisation at the level of pixels, and by virtue of generative techniques such as *GANerated* imagery, the classical temporal structures of cinema become profoundly eroded. This is not to say film analysis need not be concerned with frames, shots, sequences, and continuity editing, but rather that a much more subtle but consequential transformation is occurring at the micro-level, one that in visual culture we can identify in how the cinematic gradually gives way to the datamatic.[9]

Datamatic time is not measured but generated, it is the time produced by calculation without quantification, simply because it is brought into existence in an already quantified world, where representations are always atomised and always contingent. In the same way that cinematic time was structured through the rationalisation of time at the turn of the twentieth century, and we learned to construct and enjoy films under the temporal logic of the assembly line, today we are again restructuring time under the logic of atomised, distributed production, the order of the hyper-connected global social factory. The rupture from the cinematic to the datamatic mirrors this restructuring and points to an epistemic shift, from the analysis of *kinostructures* (patterns of motion) to the integration of *chronogeneses* (creation of time). And in light of this shift, the history

Figure 6.2 Flying pelican captured in motion by Étienne-Jules Marey c.1882

of cinema becomes all the more relevant, particularly its early techno-aesthetic development.

A case in point is chronophotography. This is the name given to a set of techniques developed during the later part of the nineteenth century, intended originally for the scientific study of locomotion. The practice involved the use and development of devices to visualise motion, instruments such as the Thaumatrope, Zoopraxinoscope, Phenakistiscope, and Zoetrope, initially used by scientists such as Étienne-Jules Marey (Figure 6.2), a physicist and physiologist who produced some of the first images of animal locomotion rendered as a series of superimposed frames.

Marey and his chronophotographs are often cited in moving image studies as being significant precursors of cinema, his techniques already embodied in some of the key concepts that would make the cinematographer possible. According to Frizot (2001), Marey understood, at least in theory, the possibility to reverse his process to synthesise motion from a set of multiple photographic events. At the same time, and according to Braun (1994), he was profoundly suspicious of this idea and never took the time to pursue it, as he was much more invested in analysis by division than in synthesis by conjunction, and profoundly mistrusted cinema, which he saw as illusionistic and contrary to the scientific precision he was after in his experiments (1994, p. 255). Doane calls this 'Marey's dilemma', and recognises in it one of the foundational problems in the emergence of cinematic time:

> What Marey's dilemma makes apparent is how the normalization of vision conceals an intense epistemological work of fragmentation. The reconstitution of a naturalised movement is a laborious process subject to certain standards for the reconstruc-

tion of time. [. . .] fragmentation of motion and time was historically the condition of the possibility of cinematic time, and the instantaneous photograph is still its crucial substrate. (2002, pp. 210–213)

Today we find a new form of intensified epistemological fragmentation, bidding to normalise vision under the algorithmic regime of the datamatic. The technical substrate of datamatic time, however, are not machines to capture light, but pixels and tensors, which were also initially mobilised for scientific inquiry but are now finding their way into culture more generally. Practitioners of these recent technologies of vision can be said to be retracing Marey's steps *volte-face*, creating their own kinds of computational *chronographs*, a type of moving image that *releases* time instead of fragmenting it.

One of the best examples of this logic is synthetic animation, for instance '3D photography', which takes a single RGB image as an input and outputs a video with generated camera movement: 'a multi-layer representation for novel view synthesis that contains hallucinated color and depth structures in regions occluded in the original view' (Shih et al, 2020). This method uses adversarial learning for generative in-painting based on previous work by Nazeri et al (2019) to effectively create what can be called deepfake zooms and dollies.

In filmic and video recording, as the camera moves around a subject, various parts of the background are visible at any given point. As a camera pulls in for a close-up, for example, the subject will fill the available screen space, thereby occluding whatever is behind them, and there is of course no pixel information about the parts of the scene that are occluded. However, through adversarial in-painting it is possible to generate approximate values for at least some of the pixels missing had the subject been in a slightly different position on-screen. In combination with a generated depth map that separates foreground from background, it is then possible to simulate restricted camera motion, like pans, dollies, and zoom-like effects.

What Shih et al call hallucination is the plotting of pixels using a computational representation learned adversarially, and motion is created through the 'unrolling' of such latent representational space, where pixel values can be predicted and generated. The effect may look like a dolly shot, but it is not attached to any specific pro-filmic event; there was no dolly equipment involved, no camera, no recording, and no real-time corresponding duration. Time in these computational chronographs is generated by calculation rather than recorded.

Using this method, I created a chronograph from a still frame of *Jaws* (1975). The still comes from a famous dolly-zoom shot in the film, just at the moment when chief of police Martin Brody (Roy Scheider) realises

Figure 6.3 Top: synthetically generated dolly zoom in *Jaws* (1975). Bottom: mechanically/optically generated dolly zoom

there is a shark attack underway (Figure 6.3). Some technical context is necessary here. The dolly-zoom is a technique that consists of zooming in on the lens while tracking back with the camera (or vice versa), thereby keeping the subjects in the foreground the same size relative to the frame while simultaneously widening or flattening the background. This shot produces what is commonly known as the 'vertigo effect' (after Hitchcock's use of it in his 1958 film *Vertigo*), and it is often used in popular cinema for its disorienting qualities: the viewer is tricked because although motion is obvious, it is not immediately clear where this motion comes from, if neither the camera nor the subject appear to be moving. What moves is the background, and just how much of it fits in the frame.

The effect produced by the computational chronograph reminded me of the dolly-zoom effect in cinema. Although the background is not optically reshaped but just expanded or contracted in 2D, and the subject of course remains still, the two clips show an uncanny family resemblance (Figure 6.3).[10]

This experiment shows how cinema aesthetics finds new computational bodies, and how technicity can jump from one regime to another. This quintessentially cinematic effect, that originally required a dolly, a lens of variable focal length, and considerable practice to coordinate their inverse operation, can be approximated algorithmically from a single still image. The results are for the moment lower in quality and resolution, as the generation of only a few frames requires considerable compute power, but it is early days for this kind of neural in-painting technology and it is only a matter of time before high-quality moving images generated using these and similar synthesis techniques become mainstream.

The acceleration in the development of image synthesis is also being fuelled from the hardware front. In the past decade, chipset manufacturer NVIDIA has used its prominent position in the computer graphics market, initially oriented to gaming, to supply AI research and development with incremental processing power. The company has been building cards that can handle the type of high-performance matrix arithmetic that is needed to render games, but optimising it for deep learning operations (NVIDIA, 2020). A few days before NVIDIA announced its new line of chipsets in 2020, game developer Epic Games announced their new *Unreal 5* game engine, which allows designers to import photorealistic graphic assets as virtualised geometry illuminated by in-engine dynamic lightning (EPIC GAMES, 2020). In tandem these developments suggest the intensification of the feedback loop between synthesised imagery and computer vision in the coming years, as training data can be synthesised from photorealistic 3D models, and this in turn used to produce more synthesised images.

This feedback loop reduces the reliance on datasets scraped from the internet and suggests a turn to compute as a viable alternative to secure data supply chains as governments tighten regulation around the extraction and use of user-generated data. Techniques such as contrastive learning, self-supervised learning, and other approaches to data generation and augmentation signal a new stage in the development of machine vision in which it becomes tightly coupled with image synthesis and generation. This convergence suggests we might be much closer than we imagine to an *ectocinema* of hallucinated imagery, in which the ability to interact with vast latent visual spaces is available directly to users (for a fee of course). This ectocinema is a medium whose temporal forms we are only beginning to outline, and which will likely be shaped under the techno-aesthetics of datamatic time.

In the meantime, my experiment shows how one of the core tenets of formalist film scholarship is reversed through deep learning: motion is not fragmented into a sequence of individual frames, but rather any single frame already contains the potential to release motion, so long as this frame is cast in a latent space. Datamatic time is not segmented and analysed, but predicted and synthesised. From an industrial perspective, synthetic imagery of this kind is already having a profound effect in how visual production is organised, initially in the production of still images in the fields of art and design, but already serving as the building blocks of rendered virtual worlds and interactive systems. Variations of the neural in-painting method I described above are already integrated in creative workflows and have gone in the space of only a few years from technical demos to boutique tools, to full integration with larger systems such as the neural filters of Adobe Photoshop.[11]

And a new ecosystem of specialist creative AI platforms is also emerging in this space, for instance Runway ML, an early adopter in the deployment of synthetic image generation methods as a set of AI editing tools aimed at the creative industries. Their 'magic tools', as they call them, include at the time of writing: image generation, style transfer, image in-painting, video erasure, motion photographs, slow motion, and text-to-video. Video erasure, for example, allows users to 'paint' a mask over an undesired element of a video to make it disappear. Behind the scenes, the mask defined by the user is passed as an input region to a model that in-paints the background on top of the undesired element based on adjacent pixel information; this operation is repeated and tracked across multiple frames to generate the output video. The same model can be used in reverse to extend the background of any image, as in my dolly-zoom example. And similarly, by interpolating synthesised frames in-between, it is possible to render hallucinated motion from a photograph, or inter-frames to an existing sequence to make any video run in slow motion. In all of these cases, motion is being synthesised, not by recording past durations, but as a function of calculation of pixel relations in high dimensional space. In other words, through the enveloping of visual production into inductive computing, every image is already a moving image.

If I am correct about this, one can imagine in the near future how cinematic discourse, its forms, grammar, and temporal units, will loosen their grip on the structuring of time, and indeed on narrative. GANs, diffusion models, and similar techniques for image synthesis might still exist then, but the images produced through them will probably not be called 'deep-fakes' nor even 'deep' anymore, but simply images, since most will enjoy the same potential to be 'set in motion'. What would have changed then is not what these images are, but what we think the originals were. As much as the images themselves, it is this broader shift in the social and cultural uses of imagery that this mode of production affords that will change the status of pre-generated imagery. Profilmic moving imagery will come to be seen in the future as an exception, a niche type of media drowned under layers upon layers of computationally generated moving imagery. I believe early forms of neural in-painting like the one I show here will be seen then as we now see Marey's experiments, and like him, perhaps we ought to be suspicious of it as the instrument of a science of culture, but also hopeful about its possibilities as a creative medium.

From an arts and humanities perspective, the question extends well beyond the analysis of films using deep learning methods. A computational spectatorship of film ought to include the new temporal structures that are emerging through the mass adoption of these technologies, all the while prompting us to reimagine the future and, more tantalising still, the past of cinema, under an algorithmic governance of the visual.

Notes

1. In fact, Bergson engaged Zeno and his paradoxes, specifically the arrow paradox, with which Zeno wanted to disprove the existence of motion. See Bergson (1998 [1907]). 'Zeno was the perfect nemesis for Bergson' writes Doane, because he (Zeno) was invested in the denial of movement, change, and plurality. His paradoxes were designed to demonstrate the absurdity of a common sense belief in the reality of such concepts' (2002, 173).
2. For more on how digital technologies alter our perception of time, see Wajcman (2015).
3. Given in RGB values.
4. There is a break point about two thirds into the film, when the lead character loses consciousness for what can be presumed to be a few hours. Although there are no hard cuts, and the film just fades to and from black, this ellipsis arguably divides the film into two separate long takes.
5. This stylistic trend is not limited to Hollywood blockbusters; consider for instance feature films that are actually accomplished in a single shot, perhaps the most notable of which is *Russian Ark* (2002) by Alexander Sokurov. (See: Ravetto-Biagioli, 2005.)
6. For a longer discussion on the relation between computing technologies and looms, see Essinger (2004).
7. See (Pearlman, 2015, p. 9) for more on editing and intuition.
8. This example is taken from the Pytorch model used in Chapter 3.
9. I borrow this term from Ryoji Ikeda. However, in this context I use it to describe a modality of vision, related but beyond the aesthetics of his video pieces and installations.
10. To appreciate the comparison these clips really need to be seen in motion: https://vimeo.com/420998448
11. See: https://helpx.adobe.com/photoshop/using/neural-filters.html

Part III

AI and Criticism:
Aesthetics, Formats, and Interactions

One of the classical tenets of artificial intelligence is to model computer systems to simulate human behaviour. However, in pursuit of many of the same objectives, there is a parallel and complementary process that consists of modelling human behaviour to accommodate several types of AI systems. In this third part of the book the emphasis shifts to this other complementary impulse, as we move from using computers to analyse films and towards rethinking film criticism and scholarship practice computationally. In this line of thinking, I propose we re-examine the role of the critic, from analytical tool bearer to a critical technologist of moving images, a role similar to what Simondon calls 'a mechanologist' (2017[1958], p. 19).

To explore this change in roles, I stage an encounter between critics and computers based on a different set of assumptions about the function each part plays in the co-constitution of machine vision. And from this encounter I outline a type of critical practice informed by an emerging kind of techno-aesthetic imagination, one which I provisionally call *macroscopic*.

This encounter is staged in three parts. First, I address the problems of interfacing with cultural objects and traces that are cast in high-dimensional space, asking how to explore and question visual worlds that have already been seen for us, but not directly by us. In the next chapter I consider the current and future roles critics might play in the production of and interaction with these worlds, as well as the kinds of questions that can be asked from moving imagery by this critical-technical avant-garde. And finally, I introduce the idea of AI as a medium of inscription: a protean space for expression as well as analysis through which critics can document and narrate their interactions with inferred visual worlds.

CHAPTER 7

Algorithmic Films as Data Analysis

One of the side effects of a distant reading of films or the cultural analytics of moving images is that their explicit commitment to large corpora usually means in practice an implicit alignment to a political economy of data where scale becomes both technically necessary and epistemically sufficient to account for meaning-making. We observed this economic logic at work in distant viewing, where distance becomes a condition for knowledge no less than an appeal to the authority of induction. The epistemic strategies of data and computer science, exported to other disciplines through their various techniques, devices and practices, pose in this way a challenge to theoretical frameworks and modes of critical practice that rely heavily on deductive reasoning, close readings of media texts, and hermeneutics.

The meta-disciplinary insurrection brought about by the rise of inductive computing is set against a historical backdrop of quantification, datafication, and their derived calculating devices and techniques – digital computers and machine learning included. Numbers themselves, as Porter reminds us, need to be understood as 'technologies of trust' (1996), which are very often used to exercise or resist power in different contexts. Quantification can be used, for instance, to constrain individual and personal authority by redistributing it to several quantification and calculation processes, and conversely, the more individuals are entrenched in positions of authority, the more they 'can afford to be looser with numbers or even to block the intrusion of quantitative technologies that constrain their judgment and limit their power' (Espeland, 1997, p. 1109). Similarly, an appeal to quantification and calculation in the form of statistics, for example in 'points-based' processes or 'data-driven' decision-making, is often the recourse of those who wish to justify their choices by challenging the subjective judgements of individual critics. The notions of consensus and transparency that data and statistics can conjure and mobilise can be leveraged by the populist against the expert or the bureaucrat against the despot: while individuals might be biased, unreliable, and decide on whims and prejudices, opinions in aggregate and the calculation of majorities present themselves as viable counterweights to individual authority.

Viewed as a form of computational statistics, machine learning technologies have been instrumental in the assault on the authority of individual experts. Take a common training exercise in machine learning and data science courses, in which students are given a dataset of physico-chemical properties of wine samples labelled by their ratings and are tasked to train a model to predict the quality of out-of-sample wines (KAGGLE, 2019). With adequate implementation and some adjustments, these models train well and can be accurate. Students are empowered as they realise that their models can predict wine quality without ever having to open a bottle. Why, then, trust an individual sommelier, if the model can perform just as well? From this perspective, time and resources would be better spent on improving the computational model: implementing the most effective learning architecture, optimising training cycles, and, above all, getting more and higher-quality data. In this way, knowledge about how to model computational critics appears preferable to the knowledge needed to become a critic, inevitably bound to individual subjective experience, whereas a large computational model can be trained to abstract judgements from a multitude of critics distributed in time, space, and across cultural backgrounds and levels of experience.

It is important to note that there are also internal tensions and epistemic struggles within AI research communities, notably between so-called symbolic and connectionist approaches, and between supervised, unsupervised, and self-supervised training environments. In the above exercise, for example, researchers who originally proposed the task of wine quality prediction and assembled the dataset argued that a type of algorithms called support vector machines (SVMs) outperform other methods, including neural networks (Cortez et al, 2009). Meanwhile, neural network proponents, who were for decades a marginal group in AI research, argue their methods – now rebranded as *deep learning* – are much more effective at dealing with massive quantities of data from the 'real world', as opposed to the toy worlds of symbolic AI (Cardon et al, 2018, p. 27).

Deep learning initially challenged what Haugeland (1989) called 'Good Old-Fashioned Artificial Intelligence' – a paradigm of symbolic approaches, rule-based algorithms and expert systems, that were popular in the 1980s. As we saw in earlier chapters, the success of deep learning goes hand in hand with the large-scale datafication of cultural production in the first two decades of the twenty-first century. The complementary factor in this process is a turn to induction. By passing sizeable portions of cultural artefacts through inductive machines, the corporate harvesters of cultural data mobilised the political powers of consensus, effectively challenging a regime of knowledge-making through large computational models of correlation and inference. As the effects of corporate AI become more widely felt and its extractive practices better understood, trust in these companies, their business and computational models, and their influence in the governance of self and other, as Aradau and Blanke put it, is being increasingly questioned (2022).

Hubert Dreyfus, who was one of the most notable critics of the first wave of connectionist AI in the early 1970s, wrote that while machines learned from a model of the world, for humans the model was the world itself (1992, p. 266). His injunction relies largely on an ontological distinction between the world and its various models; however, as the scale and complexity of the models exceed our individual ability to fathom their size and identify their edges, the fantasy of a map of culture that is as large as culture itself gains epistemic and practical currency. It is no longer just a matter of measuring the world to analyse it using statistics, but almost the reverse, a larger world that is already quantified and requires vast powers of computing to make sense of it.

Let us examine in detail this fantasy of a model that is as large as the world in terms of images and visual culture. In film studies, it appears to fit well with Bordwell and Carroll's own vision of a world beyond (film) theory (1996). One gets the impression that they would welcome such a hyper-archive with open arms, for it would mean that films too are finally allowed to 'speak for themselves' against the individual authority of a handful of theorists who have monopolised critical discourse from the top down. By the same logic however, their programme of mid-level research and their own critical authority would also be undermined from the bottom up, by computer systems able to replicate the type of formal analysis they champion. This is the double edge of inductive computing; it feeds from the cultural production that it later attempts to make obsolete; it dispenses with individual experts only after it has ingested and abstracted their expertise. In closer inspection, the idea of a large model of film that is as large as all existing films is as enticing as it is threatening to non-computational film scholarship.

In his short story *The Library of Babel*, Borges describes an infinite library that included every possible book, to which the first reaction of those who had access to it was of 'unbounded joy', for they felt in possession of a treasure (1998 [1941], p. 115). A similar point can be made of a cinephile who finds themselves in control of a set of all possible films:

every form of narrative structure, camera angle, performance style that has ever been committed to celluloid or recorded in digital formats being a part of it, waiting to be discovered or re-discovered in its relations to all others. Assuming this hyper archive was all-encompassing, it would include thousands of films of under-represented cinemas and lesser-known filmmakers, 'hidden gems' as the presenter in MbM puts it, that would have never seen the light of day under the tyranny of professional critics and their normative cannons. Such a *Cinematheque of Babel* would encompass all cinematic representations across all ages and be a paragon of diversity and inclusion.

But Borges describes a darker side to this library. In his tale, he also warns about its users going mad trying to make sense of such a place, as they realise that any systematic approach to find or articulate anything of value would be impossible. Viewers of the *Cinematheque of Babel* might well be stoked by the same anxieties, the vertigo produced by the collapse of difference and mourning the loss of the hidden. Borges' parable can be read today almost as a work of science fiction, including the exhilarating enthusiasm of vast access followed by the abject panic of what this all-encompassing collection means for those with finite lives and memories. How can a critic navigate or make sense of millions of years of video circulating online? What kind of judgement might they be able to formulate when confronted with the vastness of a hyper-archive?

Before moving images became ubiquitous online, a major part of the critic's job was to find and track films; to watch more than the average viewer by attending screenings, travelling to festivals, and various other exchanges with their communities. Television, VCR, and DVD first altered the circulation and distribution of films, making them increasingly available beyond the experience at the theatre (Elsaesser, 2005). Later, digital technologies and the internet radically transformed every other aspect of cinema, including criticism, which expanded from trade publications and newspapers to an ever-growing ecosystem of blogs, podcasts, videos, and dedicated websites (Frey and Sayad, 2015). Today, in the wake of inductive AI, could film critics not be replaced by a computer model, much like the sommelier? Assuming they resisted to be automated out of a job, and organised in large groups to scour the hyper-archive like Borges' 'inquisitors', randomly sampling the endless vaults for years, how would they configure their findings without resorting to creating new canons? And if they again made canons, would that not negate the advantages of having access to a model of the cinematic world that is as large as that world itself?

As disciplines in the arts and humanities adopt AI to study culture at scale, they inherit a share of these imagined horizons and the hopes and

ALGORITHMIC FILMS AS DATA ANALYSIS 135

anxieties that come with them. At the same time, these fantasies predate deep learning, and indeed the internet, which as we have seen are built on top of previous technical regimes. Some thirty years before YouTube and Netflix, and roughly at the same time as Dreyfus was mounting his critique on connectionist AI, filmmaker Hollis Frampton wrote about a hypothetical machine comprised of 'the sum of all projectors and all cameras in the world' endlessly running and growing 'by many millions of feet of raw stock every day'. He conjectured that such a project would lead to an 'infinite film' that would collapse the world into its model:

> The infinite film contains an infinity of passages wherein no frame resembles any other in the slightest degree, and a further infinity of passages wherein successive frames are nearly identical as intelligence can make them. [. . .] If we are indeed doomed to the comically convergent task of dismantling the universe, and fabricating from its stuff an artifact called *The Universe*, it is reasonable to suppose that such artifact will resemble the vaults of an endless film archive built to house, in eternal cold storage, the infinite film. (Frampton, 2009, pp. 114–115 [1971])

Unburdened by the strictures of actualised systems, Frampton's idea of an infinite film reveals a more subtle point about connectionism and about induction, as he hints at a transformation in kind as well as scale; an ontological displacement that is only now being felt in our interactions with large computational models. In his infinite film, moving images are disaggregated into their individual frames, and arranged not by author, context, or theme; there is no genre and no narrative classification to this collection of frames, only an algorithm that sorts every frame along an axis of similarity-difference. Frampton has a distinct inductive inclination coupled with a differential sensibility, meaning that he resists top-down categories, inherited 'film grammar' conventions that structure film making and viewing, and aims instead for emergent bottom-up properties that can be observed through the recurrent calculation of difference. To enact this logic, Frampton organises images along various axes of difference, eschewing explicit references to the contents of the images in favour of tuning into a para-linguistic signal that arises between them.

Perhaps his work is most revealing now because for him cinema was already back then a machine made of images, and making films meant to interact with this machine as a critical technologist, before this practice became available through code, data, and digital computers. Many of his films show this commitment to algorithmic thinking executed through analogue computing, often as a set of constraints designed to explore programmatically a collection of moving image clips.

For example, for his film *Zorns Lemma* (1970), Frampton collected thousands of film clips of random words in signs, posters, and storefronts

136   CINEMA AND MACHINE VISION

recorded in Manhattan: 'ACME', 'AQUARIUM', 'AGENT', 'ALARM' [. . .] 'BARBECUE', 'BARBER', 'BARGAIN' [. . .] 'SQUARE', 'STOP', 'STORAGE', et cetera. He then devised a recurrent structure for the mid-section of the film, so that forty-five minutes are broken into 2,700 one-second shots, each of a different image corresponding to a letter of the alphabet. The process repeats 100 times over, and as clips with less frequent starting letters like 'Q', 'X' and 'Z' start to run out, these segments are filled with images, some of which allude to the letter but have no written text in them, for instance a person changing a tyre is shown instead of the letter 'T'. The result is generative and hypnotic: through constant repetition an attentive viewer can learn the pattern and anticipate the substitutions, so that by the end of the film one is still 'reading the film' even though there is no text left to read, only images. The first letter to run out is 'Q', which is replaced by a smoking chimney that repeats over ninety times thereafter; the most common letter and therefore the last one to run out is 'C', which is replaced by a pink ibis flapping its wings, which we only get to see once (Frampton in Gidal, 1985, pp. 94–97).

By prompting the viewer to deconstruct the algorithm that shapes the film, Frampton is training the viewer to interact with the film, prompting the isolating of variables and finding of patterns that allows us to treat moving images as datasets before this became a necessary condition for their computational production and analysis. Because of this, his work affords a rare view at an emerging type of inductive technical practice still untethered from digital devices:

> I do most of my work in such a way that I supply a certain amount, I make a container, and for the rest of it, the film – the work itself – generates its own set of demands and its own set of rules [. . .] But it wasn't simply a question of, say, getting more ambitious, wanting to order larger and larger amounts of material. There are ways of doing that. Rather, it was a question of finding some way the material would order itself that would have something to do with it and that would also seem appropriate to my own feeling about it. (Farmton in Gidal, 1985, p. 99)

My contention is that this way of thinking about imagery, as a vast visual substrate that can be made to self-organise and its patterns be prompted to emerge through recurrent operations, is enacted today through generative AI systems. And the main challenge, as Frampton anticipated, is not of distance or scale but of interaction; of finding creative ways to redistribute agencies between the various parts of the human–machine continuum and to design the container that allows a degree of control in the self-organisation of the material.

One of such ways is by rethinking inputs and outputs and the logical units of processing and analysis. Specifically, that in order to enable self-organisation, moving images need to be pulverised, which is to say, broken down into minute particles and stripped from previous structures: 'data is not made available to the perception of calculators in a "raw" and "immediate" form, but rather is subject to atomization and dissociation in order to transform it into the most elementary possible standardized digital signs' (Cardon et al, 2018, p. 29). And this is precisely the epistemic bargain struck by the group of 'neural conspirators': we can model increasingly large parts of the world through computers so long that the world is formally encoded and logically dissociated from its context, vectorised and represented into multidimensional number arrays that are amenable to deep learning, but which by the same token become intractable to direct human interpretation.

More than models that are as large as the world, current AI systems depend on this more subtle but crucial epistemic gambit: to apprehend the world they need this world to change. In other words, to understand culture through AI requires us to reshape cultural artefacts and their relations into computable units. This re-encoding of culture goes much deeper than digitisation or datafication; it requires that all material culture and traces of our interactions with it are reduced to isomorphic tokens, so that every token can be set in relation to any other, and their positions and differences calculated in a coherent representational space. This is the vectorisation of culture.

Seen in this way, inductive computing and its neural methods are technically and historically contingent; not aiming to approximate a human-like way of apprehending the world, but instruments of world-making in their own right. And the worlds created through these AI systems are thus revealed to be profoundly ideological, presented as totalities when they are in fact reductions, vectors that only make sense in a self-contained and self-identical representational space. Such reduction is a structural feature of computational models, and not in itself a problem, but arguably precisely what makes them useful in the first place as *reductions that reveal*. The problem is, rather, that these reductions are always incomplete, and that the source of their incompleteness is not often apparent, and sometimes even deliberately concealed. And this is also a structural issue, as the pre-processes of tokenisation and encoding tend to privilege data signals that offer the paths of least resistance: words over sentences, clicks over opinions, pixels over shots, film ratings over critic reviews, etc.

Armed with this understanding, we can begin to dismantle the fantasy of an infinite film. More than a map that is as large as the territory, the hyper-archive can be better understood as the result of what Alan Blackwell calls 'a sublimated anxiety about a universal interface' (2010,

p. 396). To process films and television through inductive computing we need to reshape them into computable units, while at the same time trying to keep these units under some form of control so that they respond to us, much like Frampton described. Critical views of current AI systems have mostly focused on their actual or potential nefarious effects, a more nuanced theoretical critique complements this by addressing the problems of what Blackwell calls 'interacting with an inferred world' (2015). This is, in my view, the underlying anxiety outlined by Borges: the empowerment of scale vis-à-vis the disempowerment of interaction; interfacing with a world of films that have been seen for us but whose representation we cannot directly access or explicitly control.

Somewhat paradoxically, the *Cinematheque of Babel* in the digital age would not contain any films as such, it would be comprised instead of computable artefacts, number array representations whose distance relations can be calculated reducing the representations to their similarities. The reader might get some distinctly Deleuzian echoes from this idea, which implies that to get a distinguishable signal of difference through calculation requires repetition, or in other words, that reducing moving images to the same kind of calculable tokens makes differences noticeable. The upside of this logic is that, if we are successful in such intervention, every image will enter into a latent relation with every other image in the archive – we would have effectively created Vertov's box, or Frampton's container. Being and operating in a container that appears to have no exterior is the fundamental technical and ideological gambit of AI, and is what enables its relational-analytical powers and creates the rational illusions of completeness and infinity.

A concrete instantiation of this idea is a film archive processed in a way similar to how Frampton imagined, in which every film is broken into its constituent frames, and every frame is arranged according to a calculated difference. In terms of their visual appearance, frames that are similar would cluster together, whereas dissimilar frames would be far apart. Initially, similar frames would be consecutive frames, as they would be almost identical. But in time and over a larger corpus, similarities would begin to emerge between frames from different films: clusters of hands, close-ups of actors, several types of lenses, colour treatments, grain textures, et cetera. And differences too would become apparent, even in consecutive frames. In higher dimensions, the archive that self-organises begins to warp and fold into itself, like Paris in *Inception* (2010), or the farm world in *Hyperbolica* (2022).

The problem of course is that we do not experience the world in high-dimensional space any more than we reason directly through vectors when watch films. For these relations to be observed, and patterns of difference to be recognised, the archive needs to be flattened again and its dimensionality reduced to 2D or 3D space that we human observers can perceive and interpret. To solve this problem of dimensionality reduction, computer science and engineering have developed a series of projection techniques, often inspired or directly taken from topology. Techniques such as Principal Component Analysis (PCA) (Wold et al, 1987), T-distributed Stochastic Neighbour Embedding (t-SNE) (Maaten and Hinton, 2008), or Uniform Manifold Approximation and Projection for Dimension Reduction (UMAP) (McInnes et al, 2020; Narayan et al, 2021) are used for this purpose, to afford interpretable views of high dimensional spaces.[1] Using techniques such as t-SNE or UMAP allows us to visualise and explore the film archive as a topology of learned features that is graphed by measuring the distance between one and every other frame, and this graph in turn shows latent structures in the form of clusters and continuities. This is, at a glance, the route or cultural analytics of distant viewing as it employs machine vision and AI: the re-inscription of complex time representations into interpretable 2D and 3D space.

We must take care to understand, however, that the relations plotted in this space are qualitatively different to the ones described in a regular chart. Data points in these visualisations are not plotted according to an external scale, but are instead projected onto a 2D or 3D plane through the t-SNE or UMAP algorithms, which calculate the position of data points at different steps according to their respective hyper-parameters, in the case of t-SNE, for example, *perplexity*[2] while in UMAP users can control *nearest neighbours*,[3] and *minimum distance*.[4] The cluster size and distance between clusters will depend not only on the underlying data distribution, but on how the user configures the projection. The spatial dependencies shown by these dimensionality reduction techniques are therefore only meaningful in relation to themselves and can show vastly different versions of the same underlying data depending on how the technique is applied. Under certain configurations, these dimensionality reduction algorithms will not show any structure, even if there is one, or will produce clearly defined structures out of random noise.

The broader point I want to make through this dive into the technical aspects of interacting with latent spaces is that this type of manipulation is a significant departure from other forms of quantitative analysis and their epistemic frameworks. The data practices and techniques of inductive computing are much more performative and interactive than other types of computational statistics, in that there is a more explicit feedback loop between the expectations of the user and the renderings produced by the algorithms. It is common for instance to go over many iterations to test different combinations of data/hyper-parameters/targets, to evaluate if the latent space allows for the kind of self-organisation that is useful to solve a specific problem and meaningful to how such a problem was defined in the first place. In other words, latent space navigation needs its subjects to perform an iterative minimisation of error of their own in coordination with their machines. Techniques like t-SNE and UMAP are necessary precisely because they enable such coordination; they afford agency over otherwise inaccessible manifolds. Conceptually, these data embedding activities can and probably ought to be seen as creative practices, closer in kind to sculpture than to statistics.

In mathematics, embeddings are a core concept in manifold geometry, and refer to objects that contain other objects, and to the shared properties between the container and contained (Nicolaescu, 2007). But the word 'embedding' has an older history; it was first applied in the eighteenth century to describe the condition of fossils in rock. Recovering this geological etymology, a useful way to think about embeddings is to consider them shapes or structures 'trapped' between data strata, and simultaneously to think of embedding as the action of 'casting' these shapes into solid rock. In two commonly quoted aphorisms attributed to Michaelangelo, the Florentine artist is said to both have 'seen the angel in the marble and just set it free', but also that a block of raw marble 'can hold the form of every thought an artist has'. In one version the angel lives in the artist's mind, in the other it lives in the rock. Embeddings in machine learning embody this double meaning, and its models are designed as a dialogue between analytical and creative practices. On the one hand the analytical impulse asks us to uncover a structure that was there waiting to be set free, while on the other, a creative impulse demands that we sculpt something out of layers of noise. The emphasis one chooses will likely depend on the context, of one's background and inclinations, yet the broader argument here is that inductive computing cuts both ways: it folds both the object and the subject in a concerted interactive process.

Once we think of these as interpretive-sculptural processes, subjectivity and the need for explanation return in full force. The question is not only or mainly about ever more sophisticated methods and tools for revealing patterns in data, but about the ways of interaction with AI models, and the new forms of cognition and emotion they afford. What is needed from this perspective is to identify and understand these emerging forms of algorithmic reasoning and emoting enabled by machine vision, and the visual imaginaries they bring into existence. My intuition is that this cannot be accomplished through cultural analytics and its distant reading operations alone, which operate inside the container and can therefore not explain its constitution. If we aim to turn co-relations into explanations, we need a framework that accounts for the set of creative practices that go into the constitution of AI systems, a system to narrate how the subjects are folded into the objects.

I submit that certain types of algorithmic films already do some of this successfully. I mentioned already the films of Dziga Vertov and Hollis Frampton, and other significant referents are the experimental documentaries of Harun Farocki, in particular his three-part installation, *Eye/Machine* (2000–2002), in which he coined the term *operational images*, images that 'do not represent an object, but rather are part of an operation' (2004, p. 17). Farocki's work ignited debates in media scholarship about the production and circulation of images increasingly outside the realms of human viewing and control, visual regimes that 'require neither human creators nor human spectators' (Blumenthal-Barby, 2015, p. 329) as they are produced through the eyes of an automaton that 'replaces the human robotically' (Foster, 2004, p. 160). This idea of an economy of images that has left humans outside the loop is an extreme version of Vertov's original observation of how the movie camera afforded points of view that were unavailable to humans, thereby extending vision beyond human faculties. This in turn sat well with post-humanist media theorists and media ecological approaches, giving currency to their critiques of media essentialism and anthropocentrism.

I share some of the commitments of post-humanists to expand the field towards complex and dynamic systems that include an ecosystem of non-human actors, but I am more sceptical of the leap that posits machine vision as a form of non-human vision, and by that same token I am less persuaded that the images produced and regulated by AI systems are necessarily or mainly operational, at least in the sense that Farocki defined it. Besides, there are several other works that already cover operational images at length (Parikka, 2023; Hoel, 2018; Pantenburg, 2016). Instead, here is where I believe a technical understanding about how the automation of vision is achieved becomes fundamental. As I show in earlier chapters, dismantling inductive machine vision reveals many human actors and nested layers of labour. We are certainly just one of many actors operating in larger environments but shifting the focus away from the human subjects that co-constitute AI risks downplaying, and even effacing, key power relations between designers, owners, users, and all others who are affected by these systems.

It is not that operational images make humans unaccountable – there is undoubtedly a political project in Farocki's use of images of war in his

Eye/Machine – it is, rather, that when we redistribute aspects of vision to other elements in the system, it is easy to forget that we ourselves are also part of this system, and by downplaying the human in the loop, the power relations between seers and the seen become harder to pin down. In this I am closer to the media ecologists and the notion of culture as a complex system than I am to the post-humanists, if and when they lean towards anthropophobia. Machine vision of the kind described in this book is arguably one of the most overtly anthropocentric assemblages, drawing from and catering to human knowledge and desires, often to the expense of the planet and its other inhabitants. Disassembling the technologies that enable machine vision into its technical and historical constituents reveals human intervention at every step and reveals automation to be an intimately human process. The main challenges with AI today lie within, not beyond, the human.

It follows that my interest in algorithmic films is not that they channel non-human actors, but that they contain the instructions for their watching through the familiar logical gateways of difference and repetition, and how this allows them to thematise and give content to human algorithmic thinking. And this capacity is not circumscribed to avant-garde or experimental documentaries either but is a visuality (a visual rationality) that is also present in other forms of popular media; for example the supercut, which I have argued is a computational form of the video essay (2023). The supercut consists of an editing technique in which short video clips with common motifs or salient stylistic characteristics are extracted from their original context and are sequenced together in a montage. The commonalities are highlighted through repetition and interpreted by viewers as a form of aboutness, meaning the thematic content of the supercut.

Popular supercuts abound online in numerous non-professional compilation videos in different video platforms.[5] Tohline (2021) traces the history and aesthetics of the supercut, highlighting the ways in which it intensifies attention, and theorising it as a visual expression of what he calls 'database episteme':

> [. . .] the supercut entails not simply a mode of editing, but a mode of thinking expressed by a mode of editing. [. . .] Just as capitalism treated workers as machines as a prelude to workers being replaced by machines, so also supercutters simulate database thinking in apparent anticipation of a moment, perhaps in the near future, when neural networks will be able to search the entirety of digitized film history and create supercuts themselves, automatically. (p. 3)

Although as I have argued, machines do not create by themselves, Tohline is right in that modes of thinking can be expressed as modes of editing.

Algorithmic films, as a more ecumenical genus, prompt us to acknowledge our position as viewers engaged in the pleasurable decoding of images along a temporal axis. And this is a singular affordance of films; they can conjure the conditions of necessity by which we feel and expect that some images ought to follow others. By putting images in time, we endow them with relations of continuity, which is a stronger form of relation than contiguity or proximity. Perhaps continuous images in time appear to be more densely related than proximities in space because time cannot be frozen or experienced in reverse; it can be manipulated to appear reversible, or altered such as in fast, slow, or reverse motion, but this is always a manipulation of past duration, whereas our conscious perception of time as we watch these images unfold can never be stopped. Space can come at us simultaneously, time cannot.

This is why algorithmic films might be the right complement to data projections like t-SNE or UMAP. The types of relations they can create between images can arise too from high-dimensional spaces but are eventually arranged along a temporal axis that provides a structuring order: a temporal container in which contingent proximities can solidify into thematic and even narrative forms. And these forms are needed for the configuration of explanations, which require stronger forms of causality than the aggregate of co-relations.

Narrative, whether explicit or not, is a better container for causal explanations, it allows for counterfactual understanding and the configuration of subjects who can give meaning to the data projections and are able to put forward answers to why data looks the way it does, giving the models created by AI a moral dimension. Algorithmic films satisfy in this way the creative and sculptural impulse at the heart of machine vision and can be understood at the same time as an effective analytic practice and a dimensionality reduction technique in their own right.

Notes

1. One significant difference between PCA and the other two is that PCA is a linear projection and therefore cannot capture non-linear relations in data.
2. Van der Maaten and Hinton describe perplexity as 'a smooth measure of the effective number of neighbours' and indicate that 'typical values are between 5 and 50' (Hinton, p. 2582). It can be thought of as a measure of the number of neighbours for any given data point. One of the purposes of t-SNE is to avoid what is known as 'the crowding problem', which occurs when points in high dimensional space are forced to 'fit' into lower-dimensional spaces. There simply is not enough room in fewer dimensions so the points end up

overwhelming the space. To prevent this, t-SNE calculates the local euclidean distance between points and then 'spreads it out' as points are projected.

3. The number of approximate nearest neighbours used to construct the initial high-dimensional graph.

4. The minimum distance between points in low-dimensional space. Again, to mitigate the crowding problem.

5. See for example: 'The Wire – Donut Supercut' (https://youtu.be/kkMFaWg 5rXY). A compilation of all the scenes of a small-time car thief character from the television series *The Wire*, or 'American Restaurant Chains in Movies and TV – Supercut' (https://youtu.be/_Aw8ruEm7Fo). Many more examples are available in Tohline's comprehensive study of the format.

CHAPTER 8

Aesthetic Judgements and Meaningful Dissensus

Research shows that the ways in which we describe AI in popular discourse are highly distorted and often have more to do with applications and effects in specific contexts than with the general functioning of the technology. A recent report on public perceptions of AI highlights this disconnect from the reality of the technology: 'fictional and many non-fictional narratives [about AI] focus on issues that form either a very small subset of contemporary AI research, or that are decades if not centuries away from becoming a technological reality' (Cave et al, 2018, p. 14).

In the case of AI, the ways specialists use to describe the functioning of the systems are, as Agre suggests, deliberately and strategically ambiguous. As a discursive practice, he argues, AI is less concerned with abstract concepts of intelligence and is configured instead as the activity of 'building systems whose operation can be narrated using intentional vocabulary' (Agre, 1997b). This intentional vocabulary matters, as it can be very telling of the expectations and anxieties about AI, and over time these declared intentions, whether real or not, become interwoven with broader popular narratives about the role of these technologies in society.

One of the issues that came up constantly during the development of MbM was precisely the question of whose intentions was our system attempting to model. Answers to this question oscillated at various points between replicating the functions of a critic or an editor; one who analyses moving images and produces some form of evaluation, or one who manipulates them to produce sequences and programmes for others to watch. We knew that it would require some imagination on the part of the viewer to see the computational processes as equivalent in function to those of a critic or an editor, but the hope was that at least some aspects of these functions could be described using vocabulary common to these activities. The goal was to strike a balance between describing the system in a way that was both informative of the actual computational processes

146   CINEMA AND MACHINE VISION

and also expressive enough so that these processes could be more widely understood by a general audience.

Part of this description was done through the graphics we overlaid on the generated clip sequences, which were meant to suggest a dashboard-like graphical user interface (GUI) that showed computer operations as they were being performed. But another significant part was written as a script, and delivered by the presenter, Hanna Fry. Her role, as we conceived it and in line with the documentary tradition of the BBC, was to ask on behalf of the audience: 'How does the machine *choose* what we're about to see?' and answer the question with 'the machine . . .':

- "*looked at* more than a quarter of a million BBC programmes . . ."
- "*examined* the programmes . . ."
- "*ranked* each of those quarter of a million programmes . . ."
- "*selected* 150 . . ."
- "*split* each one of those up into little bite-sized chunks . . ."
- "try and *create* its very own BBC Four mini programme by chaining those chunks together."

Although this way of describing computational processes using intentional vocabulary is quite common, MbM allows these terms to be put to the test by an audience. Watching the programme, viewers are invited to question and decide if and to what extent the language used by the presenter corresponds to their expectations about the formal modes of address posed by the sequences, and if the intentional descriptions given are sufficiently similar to their own intuitive understanding of what it means to 'look at', 'examine', 'rank', or 'create'.

These are activities a general audience would reasonably expect critics to perform: to see the material, analyse it, and assign value to it. Similarly, to create a coherent programme by selecting and piecing together pieces of footage is how they might colloquially describe the job of a film or television editor. Language opens in this way a shared discursive space within which communication about computational processes can occur, and in doing so it inaugurates a discursive and epistemic horizon of belief that ranges from radical scepticism, as in computers cannot actually 'look at' images, to technological determinism, as in the computer creates its own TV program. The technical aspects of system-building and formal languages become in this way deeply entwined with popular media and natural language.

In this discursive space, Agre observes how AI technologists often use language's ambiguity strategically and to their advantage, terms like 'examine' or 'create' are used to communicate externally by appealing to their general meaning, while internally these words are used in their narrower meanings, closer to a formalisation that is more amenable to encoding and computation. Some common criticisms of AI from a humanities perspective focus on the inexact or deliberately elastic use of terminology, injunctions such as computer systems not in fact being able to 'watch' programmes or pass aesthetic judgements of their own, or the fact they can only be said to do so insofar as one admits the often narrow formalisation of vision and taste implicit in their design.

However, these criticisms miss a larger point about language, which as Agre reminds us, is also instrumental to the internal communications necessary for the development of AI systems as a matter of craft:

> What matters practically is not the vague issue of what the words 'really mean' but the seemingly precise issue of how they can be defined in formal terms that permit suitably narratable systems to be designed [. . .] The vagueness of AI vocabulary is instrumental in achieving this effect. [. . .] It does permit AI's methods to seem broadly applicable, even when particular applications require a designer to make, often without knowing it, some wildly unreasonable assumptions. (Agre, 1997b)

His observations on the strategic use of intentional language are directed at AI researchers, but the implications extend in reverse to the humanities, where technical modes of inquiry can also reveal unreasonable assumptions. In the case of MbM, once we devised a way to traverse the television archive, the concatenation and rendering of clips as new sequences became trivial from a technical perspective, and this unexpected proximity between 'the walk' and 'the assembly' processes put pressure on our initial belief of a sharp distinction between critics and editors. If the terms used to describe the computational processes correspond to what we intuitively consider two separate activities, but in our formalised system are almost logically equivalent, does this not suggest that our initial assumptions need revision?

Film and television critics tend to be a step removed from the market-driven, capital-intensive imperatives of film production; their activities are usually carried out at the consumption end of the life cycle of audio-visual products. This is often seen as beneficial to the fulfilment of their function as adjudicators of value, at once part of the industrial apparatus of cinema but at an arm's length of the production of any particular film. Filmmakers by contrast are very much invested in particular films, their livelihood depends on the commercial success of their production, and they are therefore considered not to be in the best position to pass balanced or impartial judgements about their films or those of others. We socially uphold this separation between critics and makers, between those tasked with creating moving images, and those who professionally assess them, and we reserve distinct intentional vocabulary to refer to their activities.

Computer systems designed to replicate critics and creators reflect these differences. A computer that is said to 'make' films is likely to be designed as a generative system, several examples of which can be found in art practice and experimental media, from projects like *JanBot*, described as 'the first filmmaking bot' that splices together trending topics in the news with clips from the EYE Museum's *Bits & Pieces* collection of orphaned film fragments (Delpeut and Klerk, 2018);[1] gallery installations like *The Pirate Cinema* (2014), which 'produces an arbitrary cut-up of the files currently being exchanged' through peer-to-peer file sharing platforms; and other fringe projects such as *sCrAmBlEd?HaCkZ!* (2006), deliberately designed and overtly promoted to make copyright infringement easier: 'one has to cut, copy, paste and arrange. All that takes precious creative energy and a lot of time. Enough of that.'

In film and media studies, projects such as these have been categorised at various times under the prefixes of 'cybernetic' or 'expanded' cinema (Youngblood, 1989), 'soft' or 'database' cinema (Manovich and Kratky, 2005; Manovich, 1999), or more recently 'generative' cinema or 'algorithmic' editing (Grba, 2017; Enns, 2012). In AI research circles, these projects are often examined under the subfields of 'computational creativity', whose goal is 'to model, simulate or replicate creativity' (Jordanous, 2014) and more generally to study systems that 'unbiased observers' would deem creative (Colton and Wiggins, 2012; Colton et al, 2011), or more recently 'Creative AI', which theorises 'the problem of artistic and creative practice as enabled by AI technologies' (Bunz et al, 2023).[2] The general operation of these systems is usually narrated as *creation as/by generation*.

Conversely, systems in which a computer is said to be taking on the role of a film critic are often designed to output tokens of recommendation, for example a personalised suggestion based on a predicted rating, or a predicted probability that a given user might want to watch a given film of TV show. Recommender systems like these are now commonplace in many streaming services and other online platforms, even non-commercial ones such as *MovieLens*, which 'helps you find movies you will like', or crowd-sourced projects like *The Movie Database*, which mirror the aggregation and recommendation logic of major streaming platforms, industry databases, and e-commerce sites. The operation of these systems can therefore be narrated as *recommendation as/by prediction*.

These operations of evaluation and recommendation traditionally occur after production, once these cultural artefacts and products are made available to their audiences, and there are considerable financial incentives to develop and fine-tune recommender systems based on predicted preference. In the film and television industries, even a marginal increase in viewership can mean a significant gain in revenue, and as discussed in previous chapters, this dynamic has been exacerbated by streaming platforms competing for market share. This is the narrow meaning of criticism, which takes signals such as 'likes', up or down thumbs, user scores, stars, or percentages, in order to track and predict user behaviour. From a marketing standpoint, these signals are sufficient to drive consumption. However, from a broader perspective, criticism can be cast as a problem of computational aesthetics, understood here as 'the research of computational methods that can make applicable aesthetic decisions in a similar fashion as humans can' (Hoening, 2005).

Aesthetic judgement as a computing problem is usually traced back to Birkoff's *Aesthetic Measure* (1932), subsequently elaborated as 'information aesthetics' (Bense, 1982 [1965]), 'algorithmic aesthetics' (Stiny and Gips, 1971), or 'computing/computational aesthetics' (Machado and Cardoso, 1998; Machado et al, 2008; Greenfield, 2005). However, the notion of abstracting the 'conventional wisdom of criticism' (Litman, 1983) by empirical means in order to adjudicate on the merits of specific cultural artefacts is part of a much older tradition, one that includes experimental aesthetics dating back to the nineteenth century and extends further back to the philosophy of art and meta-criticism. For our purposes, we want to trace this idea back to David Hume's essay *Of the Standard of Taste* (1910 [1757]), which is one of meta-criticism's foundational texts.

In this short work, Hume defines the paradox of taste as one of the central problems in modern aesthetics. He recognises that we treat taste in two seemingly contradictory ways: on the one hand we concede that aesthetic preference is subjective, and therefore judgements of taste – as far as they are not accessed through properties of objects but rather sentiments that arise from our appreciation of these objects – cannot be compared in value. I prefer Velázquez, you like Picasso instead, *de gustibus non est disputandum*, meaning, roughly, that there is no accounting for individual taste. On the other hand, Hume observes, common sense simultaneously tells us that some works must be more valuable than others, or at least we seem to equally endorse this proposition in our behaviour, by elevating some works above the norm, creating anthologies and canons of 'classics'. Confronted with this paradox between individual subjective judgement in matters of taste and collective consensus about some works being more pleasing than others, Hume suggests the need for a standard: 'a rule, by which the various sentiments of men may be reconciled; at least, a decision afforded, confirming one sentiment, and condemning another'. In his view, only such a procedure would allow conflicting parties to come to some form of resolution in matters of taste.

The way he conceives of such a standard is highly original and arguably inaugurates the field of empirical aesthetics. Simply put, he claims that although we cannot condemn sentiments, for they are real and refer to nothing beyond themselves, we can try to assess the critic's ability to channel these sentiments in a consistent manner, and then *aggregate* these judgments to abstract a *model* with which to evaluate any given work of art. And he spends the rest of the essay discussing the criteria a 'true critic' must meet in order to be counted in the standard:

> Strong sense, united to delicate sentiment, improved by practice, perfected by comparison, and cleared of all prejudice, can alone entitle critics to this valuable character; and the joint verdict of such, wherever they are to be found, is the true standard of taste and beauty. (Hume, 1910 [1757])

This solution appears at first to risk circularity: where and how would one find these ideal critics? But for Hume the way out of the paradox is via an empirical account of criticism. While the individual judgements of critics are subjective, the means by which they arrive to these judgements can be observed, measured, aggregated, and compared. Hume's strategy is to 'bridge the gap between fact and value by making the standard of taste a matter of empirical discovery' (Carroll, 1984, p. 183). To do this, his standard eschews transcendentalist definitions of beauty used to identify major works of art, and suggests instead the engineering of a probabilistic inductive system with which to compare works and pass judgement; a set of instructions (an algorithm) and of constraints (targets) that, when applied to critics *en masse*, abstract their subjective judgements for the very practical task of settling aesthetic disputes.

Modern recommender systems inherit from these assumptions, not least in their probabilistic approach and normative functions. In some striking ways, Hume's logic prefigures that of a machine learning technologist. He parsed the problem of taste into the narrowly defined task of settling disputes, and to achieve this objective his standard did not have to produce a definitive ruling, only a sufficient degree of consensus. So long as this degree was reached, the standard could be said to work, which is to say, to be doing what it was designed to do, as Agre would have it. The only real problem Hume foresaw was if consensus could not be established, which in current terms would translate to the model not converging or over-fitting, meaning it either would not perform above randomness or it would not generalise well to out-of-sample inputs.

In an analogous way, a recommender system need not have an internal representation of what is good or pleasing for all or even for most. For it to work it only needs to be accurate to the point where its users are inclined to view a recommended item a degree above than they would a random item, and from that threshold onwards the more its predictions move away from randomness the better; its performance and indeed its usefulness become a matter of optimisation of error. In this way the *Standard of Taste* echoes the aphorism now commonly repeated in machine learning circles: 'all models are wrong, but some are useful.'

In a different sense, however, recommender systems are almost the inverse of Hume's standard. He wanted to abstract a general rule from the aggregated subjectivities of critics, a process that could be applied to every aesthetic dispute. But recommender systems are designed to produce predictions tailored to individuals; their overall goal is not to resolve disputes but to bypass them altogether in order to maximise individual consumption. Once again, similar intentional language is used ambiguously to convey almost opposite meanings. If some of these computational models are indeed useful, what they are useful for? And for whom? These questions point to the discursive dimension of AI systems that Agre was after.

Treating recommender systems as proxies for criticism is inaccurate because their design precludes canons of taste from being constructed, challenged, or overthrown collectively, as personalised recommendations place individual preferences over social consensus about the quality of cultural works. In other words, for these systems it does not matter if a work is critically considered to be good or not, what matters is whether the user of the system likes it. Personalisation of this kind is not far from a user-centred design approach, which in principle caters to users' real needs and desires, but that has been also linked to confirmation bias and intellectual isolation (Pariser, 2011; Bail et al, 2018). The risk of reducing people to users and society to markets is to disconnect individuals from their collectives, to sever individual preference from the regulating forces of public discourse and limiting the possibility of establishing broader social agreements. In short, this reduction erodes the *demos* of sociality. One of the implications for film criticism is that by negating its social dimension, systems such as these can lead to critical atrophy.

Noël Carroll's reading of Hume helps us tease out this social dimension of criticism and how it is negated by recommender systems. He claims that the Scottish philosopher conflates liking and assessing: one can assess, Carroll argues:

the symbolic density of a given poem with no special sensation of pleasure or enjoyment and with no disposition to be moved to like the poem [. . .] just as one can note that a given checkmate is a masterpiece of ingenuity while neither being moved by it nor taken with chess in general. (Carroll, 1984, p. 188)

Critics need not like what they assess nor assess only what they like, Carroll argues. In fact, their personal preferences would be of little relevance to us were it not for the fact that they are critics, which is to say, audiences find value in their recommendations precisely because in some level we can access, understand, share, and question their assessments. This is also the reason Carroll downplays the distinction between academics, journalists, and reviewers. For him, and to a considerable extent in this book also for me, the only requirement a critic must meet to be defined as such is to be committed to backing up their evaluations with reasons: 'criticism is essentially evaluation grounded in reasons' (Carroll, 2009, p. 8).

Because reasons are as important as evaluations, there is a very reasonable expectation for a critic not to withhold their reasons, but rather lay them out for public view. As with other types of popular media, criticism about film is decidedly social in this way: it elicits agreements requiring critics and audiences to meet in a discursive space and to engage in imagined conversations about the experience of watching films. The dialogue one imagines having with a critic is from this perspective as valuable, if not more so, than their judgements. We expect a critic not only to tell us whether a film is pleasing or worth watching, but *why* they think that is the case, and *how* they came to that conclusion. In other words, we demand a verdict no less than an *explanation* about the verdict. Moreover, we enter into these imagined exchanges expecting explanations of a particular kind: we engage critics with a disposition to be persuaded by informed and well-organized propositions that we assume were formulated to test our beliefs, about our individual perceptions, but also about the critic's knowledge, nuance, and rhetorical ability. In some level we want to be persuaded, or at least we allow ourselves the possibility of being influenced by a critic who pushes the right buttons for us.

For the same reason, the dialogue with critics also affords us the opportunity to question their reasons and their reasoning styles, to test a critic's authority against our own inclinations, temperament, and taste. The modern critic, argues Terry Eagleton, should become 'the co-discursing equal of his readership, his perceptions tempered by a quick sense of their common opinion' (Eagleton, 2005 [1996]). 'Co-discursing equals' does not imply critics and audiences are equivalent or interchangeable, critics can and often do speak from a position of authority, usually enabled by various forms of platform that allow them some distance from their audi-

AESTHETIC JUDGEMENTS AND MEANINGFUL DISSENSUS   153

ences. The point is, rather, that whatever authority critics might possess is not imposed all at once, but is instead exercised over time, constructed, and constantly refreshed through repeated conversations, both with and among critics as well as with general audiences who might endorse or reject their positions. When we read the reviews of Manohla Dargis, Nelson Carro, or Mark Kermode, whatever trust we, as audience, place in their assessments is cemented through a sense of aesthetic consistency built over the repeated conversations we imagine having with them about films; even when we do not in fact watch together, meet, or speak directly with them, they nevertheless appear to speak directly to us.

The configuration and access to this shared social space for aesthetic assessment, as both a common network of inter-subjective meanings and a framework of accepted modes of evaluation, is a fundamental aspect of criticism. Through their repeated assessments, critics create the common ground for the building of consensus but also the conditions for meaningful dissensus about the merits and shortcomings of specific works. Criticism has in this way a dual function – it is normative as well as subversive; it enables broad social consensus and cannon making, as well as galvanising disagreement and the subversion of cannons. Modern criticism in Europe, according to Eagleton, was 'born of a struggle against the absolutist state' in the seventeenth and eighteenth centuries:

> A polite, informed public opinion pits itself against the arbitrary diktats of autocracy [. . .] Every judgement is designed to be directed toward a public; communication with the reader is an integral part of the system. Through its relationship with the reading public, critical reflection loses its private character. Criticism opens itself to debate, it attempts to convince, it invites contradiction. (Eagleton, 2005, pp. 9–10 [1996])

The conversational and oppositional aspects of a critic's function highlighted by Eagleton are worth recovering for our purposes here because together they serve to explain how a critic's evaluations become valuable precisely *because* they are publicly made and can be publicly contested. To declare something to be beautiful in a critical manner is binding in a way that greatly exceeds individual preference, simply because beauty demands commitment from all parties involved, including those who want to disagree. The beautiful includes by necessity the threat of its denial, it builds itself against the constant risk of contradiction, which in turn makes its endurance all the more poignant. In short, criticism demands what Alan Badiou calls *fidelity*: 'the transition from random encounter to a construction that is resilient, as if it had been necessary' (2012, p. 44).

Recommendation without assessment is sterile for aesthetics because it negates this potential, and in so doing, precludes access to the recursive social reorganisation of taste. Therefore, a computational aesthetics that is concerned with beauty and the beautiful is ill-served by focusing only on the aggregation of fleeting signals of pleasure. In other words, criticism in its wider sense is valuable because it aspires to stand the test of time, whereas 'likes', 'thumbs up', and 'stars' only have to stand the test of click-through rate. And so, by admitting tokens of prescription that cannot be meaningfully connected to processes of evaluation, we are likely to confuse the beautiful for the pleasurable, and to ignore how the former greatly exceeds the latter.

As they are currently designed, recommender systems are missing a key aesthetic dimension in their enactment of criticism. From a computational humanities perspective, the question is how to restore this dimension in our interactions with computers; how to incorporate the subroutines of critical assessment into digital and computational practices in the age of AI?

An initial move could be to look at the text behind the ratings: to seek and extract the data that contains a critic's reasons. There are a few datasets that are sourced from film reviews written by professional critics, notably the ones introduced by Pang and Lee (2005). These have been used for various forms of natural language processing; for example sentiment analysis. Let us briefly consider this approach through the following excerpt from Peter Bradshaw's review of Shane Carruth's *Upstream Color* (2013):

> [The film] is invigoratingly freaky and strange, with a Death-Valley-dry sense of humour somewhere underneath – though a little derivative sometimes. More than once, Carruth gives us a close-up on a hand ruminatively stroking a surface: very Malick. And the shots of creepy creatures swarming under the skin are very Cronenberg. (Bradshaw, 2013)

Depending on the method used, sentiment analysis performed on this review yields negative or inconclusive results:[3] 'a little derivative', 'freaky', 'strange', 'dry sense of humour', are either predicted as negative or too low in magnitude to be meaningful.[4] Yet if one is accustomed to film criticism and to Bradshaw's reviews in particular, it is clear that his stance on the film is very positive, the expressions 'Malick-like' and 'Cronenberg-like' are the key terms needed to understand Bradshaw's stance on the film.

By summoning the works of these directors, Bradshaw gives readers much more than a positive or negative adjudication; he opens a whole horizon of themes, styles, and associations that can be mobilised in one's own appraisal of the film in question. The critic is passing a judgement on the film, but he is also laying out a map with which to understand his assessment, and in this sense he acts as a guide as much as a judge; showing the reader around as if they were walking together through the edifice of cinema, pointing to where a film might be placed in relation to others, and to how certain aspects of it can be best appreciated from specific vantage points. Bradshaw does not deny his fondness for the film, which he rates with four out of five stars, but the key is that he is giving this rating *a content*, grounding it in reasons that are made explicit. And these reasons are not picked up by the rating itself nor by sentiment analysis performed over the text of his review.

As I have argued, this implicit content of criticism is crucial because it is what enables audiences to test their own beliefs against the critic's, and thus redefine their taste: it is not just that if one enjoys the films of Terrence Malick and David Cronenberg one might also find Carruth's work appealing, as a recommendation engine might have it. The critic's proposition is, rather, that one way to find the appeal of *Upstream Color* is by watching it through the aesthetic vocabularies of these other directors and other films. And this is a proposition that viewers can verify for themselves and even challenge if they are aware of the works mentioned, or by watching them retrospectively.

Carroll (2009) elaborates on how critics go about explaining themselves. He defines four basic 'component operations' to criticism: description, classification, contextualisation, elucidation, interpretation and analysis (p. 84). Together, he argues, these activities ground critical evaluation (p. 153). These processes are not organised so much as a method but rather as a functional repertoire from which critics avail themselves. As a result, operations may overlap; not all of them are needed at all times, but according to Carroll at least one of these ought to be present in a piece for it to count as criticism: 'without saying something about the work of art by way of discussing it in terms of one or more of these operations, the critic's remarks would be virtually uninformative – little more than a gesture of thumbs up or down' (p. 85).

In Bradshaw's review we can locate description in the lines 'a close-up on a hand ruminatively stroking a surface', and 'shots of creepy creatures swarming under the skin'. However, all the other operations are found in condensed form in the expressions 'Cronenberg-like' and 'Malick-like', Bradshaw mobilises our prior knowledge of films and filmmaking and its various signifiers to classify, contextualise, and to an extent interpret other films. Readers and viewers are in this way prompted to unfold these operations by themselves. One might conclude for example that

Upstream Colour is thematically closer to the body horror films of David Cronenberg, but stylistically owes more to Terrence Malick's contemplative editing and visual style. And these conclusions are modulated too by previous criticism of those other films (see for example Kermode, 2012; Dargis, 2003).

My contention here is that, in a reversal of terms, critics can be said to conduct 'wet embeddings', meaning they serve as human interfaces for audiences to interact with high-dimensional visual worlds. By skilfully manipulating what we could call aesthetic manifolds,[5] critics can embed films into other films, images into other images; they can bring entire iconographies to bear upon a single shot, decompress a scene into its multiple historical constituents, and compress it again into a model that is instantiated in other films and by other filmmakers. This is one of the most salient powers of critics, and one which can be understood as mapping one aesthetic topology onto another, carefully and effectively selecting the local aesthetic variations through which different films can coalesce in contingent clusters, families, or neighbourhoods.[6]

We could argue that in his review, Bradshaw is putting forth two possible ways to cast *Upstream Color* in vector space, and is suggesting the corresponding neighbourhoods where this film can be placed in relation to others. If we were to model this operation computationally, we could try an embedding of plot summaries, which might place the film closer to *Shivers* (1976) or *Videodrome* (1983), whereas an embedding of image features might put it closer to *The Tree of Life* (2011) or *To the Wonder* (2012). Further still, the connection with the Malick films might prompt a different critic elsewhere to experiment with other embeddings, for instance one of lens technology such as the one I propose in Chapter 3. Arguably, this could reveal an even more subtle stylistic connection to some of the films photographed by Emanuel Lubezki, who worked with Malick in his later films. This is hypothetical but entirely feasible with existing technology and shows how more than a rating or a verdict, from a humanities perspective it is the interactive feedback loop that the systems affords where some of the core operations of criticism take place.

To return to our original question about the intentional language used to narrate the operation of AI systems, we can now posit that a system that is said to model the behaviour of a critic can be redefined as one that performs a contingent network of embeddings, meaning a sequence of connections between multiple latent spaces organised as an explanation with which to ground an aesthetic judgement. This is admittedly a much more ambitious conceptual blueprint for a computational critic, but new insights and potential new directions present themselves by taking on the explicative aspects of criticism.

First, this framing opens the earlier stages of vectorisation and the conditions of access, manipulation, and interaction with latent space as sites of critical inquiry. Secondly, and at a more general level, focusing on human-computer interaction can help expand the scope of critique, from 'bad data – bad effects' to a complex systems-oriented 'network of networks' approach that provides a nuanced view into nested meaning structures and contingent connections between various levels, actors, and timelines. A focus on interaction enables a critique of the processes that occur between the data and its effects, and this can in turn contribute to loosen the loggerheads between subject- and object-centred epistemics in cultural analytics and distant reading/viewing.

On this last point, I propose to redesign the critic-machine nexus by placing critics in the stage of machine learning engineering that best matches their reasoning styles. This idea is aligned to Agre's interactionist methodology, and in particular to what he calls *machinery parsimony*. According to Agre, rather than an attempt to replicate high-level human mental capacities such as analysis or creativity, the first port of call for interactionist AI is a detailed account of the dynamics of real agents as they interact with their actual environments. Real agents 'lean on the world', he argues, meaning they rely on 'advice' from their surroundings through constant interaction, and because the dynamics of these interactions can be studied empirically, 'Deeper understandings of dynamics can lead to simpler theories of machinery' (1997a, p. 63).

Agre's interactionist approach to AI assumes that an agent's intelligence is never fully – or even mainly – contained in their minds, brains, processing units, or codebases, but rather that what we observe as intelligent behaviour is an emergent property arising from the agent's perception and interpretation of 'the signs and sight lines and sources of advice that the world makes available' (p. 63). Therefore, and if Agre is correct, the insights gained through the observations of interaction can be used as heuristics to simplify, or, more precisely, guide the simplification of computational systems that model the behaviour of complex organisms.

Following this approach, my argument is that Caroll's core components of criticism are realised, at least in part, through a critic's ability to lean on past experience, knowledge organised through social interaction, but most strikingly, on the circulation of the films themselves. As far as films can mobilise large and coherent sets of signifiers, they can be treated as artefacts used to facilitate complex forms of communication and technical cognition; they are not only the object of criticism but are used by critics as externalised visual imaginaries with which to express and communicate with audiences, enabling them to mobilise intersubjective webs of meaning. I believe, in other words, that to a significant extent critics already treat films as machines made of images; as visually encoded models of the world with which to interpret and navigate a vast visual cultural milieu that includes other types of images and other models; critics are already able to treat films as both physically actualised technical devices and interconnected environments for meaning-making.

Perhaps this is more apparent now, under the dynamics of AI and its social factory of vision, because there is greater reciprocal correspondence between machines used to render and analyse imagery, and images used to produce new machinery. As argued in previous chapters, a computer vision model is a socio-technical assemblage made of annotated images, and the same can be said of film if we consider their cultural environments are rich in annotations. The main difference strives not in the devices in which their machinery is actualised, but in the kinds of machinery and the organisation of the assemblage: as a representational system, film is governed by deductive reasoning, and as a technical practice it is organised as the design of duration through temporal operations of control such as recording and editing. Computer vision, on the other hand, at least in its current form, is fundamentally inductive, and is controlled through prospective operations such as feature extraction, vectorisation, and visualisation techniques. In the case of films, the computer is used to unroll time and create latent duration; in machine learning it is used to flatten time and create latent spaces. And as shown in Chapter 6, these processes are now also increasingly connected through feedback and recurrent mechanisms such as attention and adversarial architectures in the design of contemporary AI systems. Such systems increasingly use images to generate machines to generate images in a dynamic of mutual reinforcement.

This level of reciprocity is only possible because images are never isolated; they enter social circulation and gain their content historically by attaching and detaching to and from their referents, which can of course be other images. This is the process being replicated, albeit in a restricted manner, by the computational production of contingent latent spaces that can be traversed, explored, and shared; plugged and unplugged from different networks and other such spaces. From a techno–aesthetic perspective, we can argue that inductive computing is encountering representational problems with which art history and media studies have long contended, and conversely, that study of moving images is rediscovering one part of its technical history as scientific machinery. Database cinema and algorithmic films are, in my view, symptomatic of this reciprocity between aesthetics and computation.

Under this realignment, I propose to reimagine film criticism as a series of reflective conversations mediated by machine. Computational utterances in which critics can actively (and technically) exercise their narrative powers through their interactions with AI systems. By narrative powers I mean a critic's ability to organise the set of core operations described by Carroll into high-level vignettes arranged in a sequence that plays over a temporal axis. In other words, to use a critic's capacity to control latent time to help them deal with the interpretation of latent space, and vice-versa, to offload to computers the processing bandwidth required for perception and low-level feature matching. Through this redistribution of labour, critics could externalise their embedding activities to a realised computational system, and simultaneously AI systems would not need to aim for causality, for they could lean on the sequential structures provided by the critic. Research under this logic would be constituted as a concerted programme of feedback between the spatial renderings of a computer and the sequential directions of a critic.

In practical terms, these redrawn dynamics presuppose the creation of systems where critics can create, explore, and compare latent spaces through an interface that is familiar to their modes of inquiry, and which allows them to: a) control the process of design and creation of latent spaces; b) explore and compare multi-modal and inter-connected latent spaces; and c) store, reuse, and reproduce their interpretive operations in a shared environment.

These design principles are not meant to be exhaustive, nor preclude eventual evaluation or prediction; on the contrary, the idea is to ground tokens of prediction and evaluation in a technical practice whose operations are concomitant with the core operations of criticism. The first two of these capabilities are already available in terms of technology, even if not fully realised for the purpose of film criticism. The third requires more attention, as it involves the creation and/or re-signification of a set of conventions that allow these interactions with already seen worlds to be followed, not only by other critics, but by wider audiences and in a way analogous to how we can follow a film review or an essay.

The *raison d'être* for this third communicational aspect of AI criticism is to create the conditions necessary for meaningful dissensus, a discursive space in which critics can be challenged and disproved, so that they are tethered to the public realm in which they need to 'strive for what is binding' (Han, 2017a, p. 80), which is simply a different name for Badiou's fidelity. Such an agora is needed for a standard like the one Hume imagined, and it cannot be constituted as a lump sum of individual preferences or consumption behaviours; it requires conversation, negotiation, and resolution between actors, a type of sociality and active participation in the co-constitution of a *demos*. The way many AI systems are currently designed tends to collapse this space and bypass this larger purpose of criticism rather than enabling it. But this again need not be so; the design of these systems is not fixed, and it is never full or complete, even when it is made to appear like it is. As AI systems are rolled out at scale and become a key part our cultural infrastructures, possibilities for intervention will still arise at the site of design and interaction.

Notes

1. At the time of writing, JanBot had 'edited' 17933 videos in its 1128 days of existence. Before going to press, it was announced that the project would come to a close, with some of the generated videos being minted and auctioned as NFTs (non-fungible tokens).
2. See: https://creative-ai.org/info
3. I tested it using 'text2data' via its API, and the Python library 'TextBlob'.
4. Magnitude refers to the overall volume of sentiment expressed in the text, regardless of whether it is positive or negative.
5 In mathematics, a manifold is a space that is topologically isomorphic to Euclidean space. This allows the mapping of complex topologies onto Euclidean projections, much like we observed in the examples of t-SNE.
6. I am using 'neighbourhood' in its regular meaning, but also alluding to the concept in topology, defined as a set that contains a point so that there is a consistent 'padding' all around that point.

CHAPTER 9

AI as Media

One of the challenges of radical reciprocity between computation and aesthetics is the configuration of shared vocabularies and the design of common instruments and methods. In this ninth chapter I will outline one possible configuration that synthesises previous discussions and is driven by interactionist AI and computational aesthetics at their encounter with film and its theoretical frameworks. This will in turn lead to a broader reflection on the future of technical and analytical work in the humanities and lay the case for aesthetic thought to be integrated in the design of AI systems.

Elsewhere (2019) I made the argument that this moment of rapid technological intensification in AI, during which its various reasoning and technical regimes are deployed and spill into wider culture, deeply echoes the early years of the twentieth century, when electricity and new technologies of vision were repurposed by artists and entrepreneurs to configure the technical milieu of what was later going to become cinema. These early years are of especial interest to film historians because neither the technical nor the aesthetic conventions of the medium were yet fixed; there was still a lot of experimentation with equipment, styles, and formats of exhibition and distribution. Films were seen at the time as technical demonstrations rather than narrative vehicles, 'the cinema itself was an attraction' argues Tom Gunning (1990, p. 383); a spectacle in which audiences went to screenings to see the cinematographer in operation rather than the films.

In the last decade creative applications of AI have undergone a similar process, quietly percolating into culture at first, as inductive computing took hold and its techniques and equipment became more accessible to groups of early adopters outside of specialised laboratories, and eventually gaining critical mass and enough momentum to draw patronage from established art brokers (Bogost, 2019; Christie's, 2018; Sotheby's, 2019) and prompt major museum exhibitions such as *Hello, Robot* (2019) at the

V&A in Dundee, *AI: More than Human* (2019) at the Barbican in London, *Entangled Realities* (2020) at HeK in Basel, and *Uncanny Valley* (2020) at the de Young in San Francisco. My intuition is that, like in the early 1900s, a wider public was drawn to these works and these exhibitions to see the machines in action more than to enjoy the art or other creative outputs in their own right.

These exhibitions and the early AI art market are symptomatic of a moment in the social deployment of general-purpose technologies, a stage when their functioning is not yet common knowledge and can be thus presented as a spectacle in itself. As we move deeper into the twenty-first century and creative AI is no longer a novelty but increasingly an essential dimension of our social and cultural environments, there comes a second stage of large-scale mass rollout, when AI goes from the art gallery to late night TV (Horton, 2023). With this broader deployment into everyday life, AI becomes less of a curiosity and more of an infrastructure we rely on, rapidly woven into every other system at a pace that seems both inevitable and uncontrollable. AI today is morphing from a socio-technical assemblage to a fully formed cultural condition, and the symptoms of this transformation are the inflated hopes and anxieties placed upon it.

Between these two moments, somewhat of a Cambrian explosion of formats, conventions, and standards is occurring. In parallel with the development of AI technologies themselves, the interfaces, cultural norms, and rationalities to transform inductive computing into its own kind of mass media are being created. And herein lies in my view a fantastic opportunity for film and media studies. Practitioners in these fields are well positioned to understand the emergence of new media, and not only cast their historical lens to it, but in this case also actively intervene and contribute to shape these rationalities, along with their new formats of production-consumption, and indeed of criticism.

Following this approach, we might also take a step back to reflect how before the study of film was accepted as an academic discipline, legitimated, and rewarded under the institutional frameworks of the university, critical thought about film had been closer to the operation of machinery, often in open dialogue with engineering and the sciences. There was a time when film theorists were not academics but technologists, and perhaps no one embodies more this spirit than soviet filmmaker and theorist Dziga Vertov, who was active in the 1920s promoting his theory of the *Kinoglaz* (cine eye/mechanical eye). Influenced by futurism, journalism, and the political climate after the October Revolution, Vertov saw himself as a techno-artisan; an engineer tasked with the building of a new type of cinema that would be factual and informative, expressive and simultane-

AI AS MEDIA 163

ously ideological (Tode and Wurm, 2006 [1947], p. 85; Vertov, 1984 [1922], p. 59).

Malcolm Turvey (2014) notes how Vertov's works (written and filmed) elude categorisation under the philosophical problems of classical film theory (Carroll, 1988). Because he was both a realist and an illusionist; he wanted his films to shape the consciousness of the masses by capturing real life as it was, unmediated by theatrical devices such as acting, staging, or over-laboured melodrama, and at the same time he set about doing this through a sophisticated avant-garde practice, deploying innovative techniques that heavily distorted visual representations, making them more complex and charged with meaning so as to advance the political project of communism (Petric, 1978).

Although the ideological content of Vertov's practice has been largely dismantled, his influence as a technologist has not waned; on the contrary, it has found echo in fields beyond film, in the research programmes of areas like cultural analytics (Manovich, 2013) and digital humanities (Heftberger, 2018). His enduring appeal stems from having inhabited worlds that were later split: film theory and practice, documentary and narrative, avant-garde and popular spectacle, social realism and especial effects. And today his highly original unified technical craft finds fertile correspondences under the aegis of digital technologies, especially with the cross-domain technicity of AI technologies and the emergence of new subjectivities. In an often-cited passage Vertov powerfully evokes and prefigures the emergence of synthetic media and its new subjects:

> I am kino-eye. I am a builder. I have placed you, whom I've created today, in an extraordinary room, which did not exist until just now when I also created it. In this room there are twelve walls shot by me in various parts of the world. In bringing together shots of walls and details, I've managed to arrange them in an order that is pleasing and to construct with intervals, correctly, a film-phrase, which is the room. (Vertov, 1984 [1922], p. 17)

Confronted with the radical transformations brought about by computational technologies, it is perhaps unsurprising that scholars are turning to early film history, to a time before theory was severed from machinery, perhaps in a more or less conscious attempt to recover a long-lost technical practice, and to recast it now in digital environments. The role of the critic needs to be redesigned in concert with the design of new types of machinery. As Colangelo suggests:

> [Film scholars] must do something that the audience does not and cannot do themselves, while making their analysis accessible to said audience in some way. The

164 CINEMA AND MACHINE VISION

> scholar, once dedicated to tracking down archival reels and editing tables instead
> might create algorithms and interfaces that produce new observations of film to
> justify their position. (Colangelo, 2017, p. 144)

Through this book I aim to contribute to this type of radical reciprocity and interdisciplinary practice. Yet I also recognise we cannot all be the Vertovs of our time. I do not suggest that film critics and scholars learn programming and start training their own machine vision models, although I suspect at least some of them are already doing this and might become much better theorists because of it. Similarly, I do not expect computer vision scientists and engineers to read Laura Mulvey, Donna Haraway, or the collected works of Rudolf Arnheim any time soon, although, again, I suspect some do and benefit greatly from this in their practice.

In tandem to this cross-fertilisation between disciplines, my proposal consists of designing the scaffolding that assumes data as infrastructure and AI as media. I believe that a radical reciprocity between aesthetics and computing can be externalised in aesthetically sensitive systems that are informed by, and at the same time structure, aesthetic thought. Such systems would allow their users to interact with AI in a way that leverages their existing reasoning styles and current practices, which is to say, use computer models as a medium of inscription, a 'powerful, transportable mode of communication that can be easily reconstructed and defended' (Espeland, 1997, p. 1108).

In the case of film, this would amount to scholars becoming the interface in a larger ecology of interconnected multi-modal systems. This is not a futuristic cybernetic scenario, but something we can already approximate through existing implementations that increasingly afford interaction and control over computers through culture. The most visible example of this trend is large language models (LLMs), computational models trained on vast amounts of data gathered from the internet which are then set up as generative systems. LLMs can take natural language inputs, or prompts, and output images, code, or other styles of natural language. Broadly speaking, this is the same idea that underpins automated language translation and autocompleting functions, which are now commonplace in many digital applications.

One can easily imagine a LLM designed or adapted to discuss films and interact with audiovisual material. Let us consider an example using ChatGPT,[1] a system that was first released in June 2020 and has since become one of the most popular large language models available. ChatGPT was trained on vast amounts of internet text and is owned by a private company, confusingly called *Open AI*, which was recently staked

AI AS MEDIA

165

by Microsoft. The system is available for public use through a web interface as well as a growing ecosystem of plugins. Interacting with ChatGPT takes the form a 'prompt' which is inputted by the user as a query, a direct request, or an instruction, in natural language. The system takes this input and generates a response based on a large probabilistic model that predicts the language tokens that are likely to follow the prompt. For our purposes here, we can think of systems such as these as autocomplete on steroids:

> Prompt:
> Write a review of the film Jurassic Park (1993) in the style of film critic Mark Kermode
>
> Generated response:
> At its core, Jurassic Park is a cautionary tale about the dangers of playing God, as the characters grapple with the ethical implications of cloning extinct species for the sake of entertainment and profit. This underlying theme adds weight to the action sequences and gives the film a thought-provoking edge that sets it apart from other blockbuster films of the era.
> Jurassic Park is a classic adventure film that still holds up today as a thrilling and thought-provoking ride. Spielberg's direction is masterful, the special effects are groundbreaking, and the cast is excellent. If you haven't seen it in a while, it's definitely worth a revisit, and for those who have never experienced it, it's a must-see classic that has rightfully earned its place in cinematic history.

Besides producing a perfectly competent review, one aspect that stands out is that the generated response assumes the film is not a current release, and this is one of the limitations of the system: it has a relatively narrow historical window because of the data used to train it. Kermode began reviewing films in 1993; if he reviewed Jurassic Park then his review might have not ended up online for ChatGPT to include. However, he did review the re-release in 2011, and the model appears to reflect this.

At the same time, what the model abstracts from the billions of internet text samples which it has seen is not always clear and can often be factually inaccurate or downright fabricated.

> Prompt:
> Write a review of the movie "Hard Candy (2005)" reflecting the views of film critic Pauline Kael and in her writing style
>
> Generated response:
> Upon viewing "Hard Candy," I am left with a complex set of emotions. While the film's subject matter and execution are undeniably challenging, I cannot help but feel that the film is ultimately unsatisfying.
> The film follows a teenage girl named Hayley who meets a man named Jeff online and agrees to meet him in person. Hayley suspects Jeff of being a paedophile and takes it upon herself to expose him and bring him to justice. The film's central

themes of vigilante justice and the dangers of online communication are compelling, and the performances by Ellen Page and Patrick Wilson are exceptional.

However, the film's handling of sexual violence is deeply troubling. The film's graphic depictions of violence and torture can be difficult to watch, and its portrayal of female sexuality as a weapon is problematic.

Furthermore, the film's resolution leaves something to be desired. The ambiguous ending may leave some viewers questioning the ultimate message of the film and whether justice was truly served.

The synopsis of the plot is accurate, including the names of the characters and performers. Similarly, the generated review seems to reflect Kael's distaste for violence and presents a plausible argument to support such view. Kael, however, died in 2001, so she did not get to see this movie, and the language, for those who were her avid readers, sounds uncharacteristically flat. As compelling as the generated review might be, it is in effect a fabricated piece of text that technically amounts to a bunch of words probabilistically put together by what Bender et al (2021) call a 'stochastic parrot':

> Text generated by an LM is not grounded in communicative intent, any model of the world, or any model of the reader's state of mind. [. . .] This can seem counterintuitive given the increasingly fluent qualities of automatically generated text, but we have to account for the fact that our perception of natural language text, regardless of how it was generated, is mediated by our own linguistic competence and our predisposition to interpret communicative acts as conveying coherent meaning and intent, whether or not they do. (p. 616).

Interestingly, Bender and her co-authors reference literature on human-computer interaction to support the passage above, drawing specifically from social and affective computing studies that show how people develop emotional responses and form beliefs when they interact with computer systems, even when they (the human users) are fully aware that these systems do not have emotions or beliefs of their own. According to Weizenbaum (1976), a key distinction between the synthetic reviews and the ones made by human critics is that, despite their similarity, the computer model *selects* the words it will use, but the human critic *chooses* them. While selection can be formalised and calculated without much trouble, choice implies a moral agent capable of holding beliefs about the world and to a significant extent about itself.

And yet, this fundamental difference is of little consequence for how most users interact with many AI systems and respond to them. User behaviour suggests that they have almost no trouble endowing said system with knowledge, intelligence, and agency. Collins and Kusch (1998) describe this dynamic as Repair Attribution and all That (R.A.T.), which, they argue, is psychological miscalculation that occurs when users fail to understand how much work they put into their interactions with computers: 'one may think that a system with which people can interact easily is a social creature. But it is not a social creature unless the pattern of skill use is roughly symmetrical between all parties' (123).

Bender et al are correct in pointing to how this dynamic of ascribing human-like properties to systems is exploited by the companies who design these systems, as well as noting the risks of rolling them out at scale when, for example, LLMs can reproduce and amplify hegemonic worldviews present in their training data, or be tricked into exposing information that would otherwise be restricted or kept from the public domain for different reasons, including public safety. By the same token, however, these works and similar works in affective computing show that users might find value and even pleasure in interacting with these systems, despite, or even because they are aware these systems are not human agents. In the case of the synthetic film reviews like the ones shown above, even if they are uttered by stochastic parrots, they nevertheless say something about the film, about the critic, and about the model. Furthermore, generated text like this also says something about the prompter, who even in full awareness of these reviews being hallucinated can respond to them. The meaning-making process is altered, but the meanings themselves do not disappear as we find ourselves reading machine-generated text; they transform instead into something else.

Treating AI as a medium echoes Weizenbaum's ambivalence, and the Vertovian double bind by which media reflects and magnifies the real through the design of plausible fictions. Treating AI as medium for creative expression is probably a more honest account of its technicity, in how it relies on a human being in the interaction loop and how in turn this diverges qualitatively from more descriptive branches of computational statistics. Following this logic, my sense is that we ought to treat these generated texts as outputs of an LLM no less than as inputs of our embodied 'wet machinery' – we seed the system, but the system then seeds us back. In aggregate and in time these feedback loops of interaction become conventional and are eventually thematised into aesthetic forms.

What is new in affective and social computing under this new wave of generative AI systems is that interactions with computer systems are increasingly programmed and controlled through culture in a broader sense. These are, arguably, the early days of cultural computing in earnest, when we ourselves become the interface that connects various computing systems together through communication and control protocols that are not distinct from how we communicate with other humans. The most significant consequence of this shift towards cultural computing is not that computers learn to think or create by themselves, but rather that interfacing with systems through culture opens new horizons of interactions for non-specialist users.

What is more, these cultural protocols of interaction and exchange include not only natural language but also other meaning-making abilities, such as the interpretation of images and the configuration of visualities that co-constitute linguistic rationalities. Because LLMs operate in high-dimensional space, it is also possible to turn natural language inputs into images and vice-versa, which is to say, not only to automate the perception and description of the visible, but to imagine new visibilities; to synthesise latent images through systems that can take text descriptions as inputs and produce matching images as outputs. Examples of these systems include *IMAGE GPT* (Chen et al. 2020), *DALL·E* and its successor *DALL·E 2* (Ramesh et al, 2021, 2022), *Image* (Saharia et al, 2022), *Flamingo* (Alayrac et al, 2022), and *Stable Diffusion* (Rombach et al, 2021), developed by an open-source AI community and whose code and model weights were publicly released in 2022: 'Stable Diffusion is a text-to-image model empowering billions of people to create stunning art within seconds. It is a speed and quality breakthrough, meaning it can run on consumer GPUs' ('Stable Diffusion launch announcement', 2022).

The release of *Stable Diffusion* paved the way for image generation as a viable model for the mass production of images, and is having a significant impact on digital art, photography, videography, architecture, and other creative domains, prompting debates about authorship, creative agency, copyright, and the value of images as data. At the time of writing, the second version of *Stable Diffusion* is used in thousands of applications by millions of users around the world, from curious individuals tinkering with the web interface, to companies running the models in their production pipelines. At the same time, *Stability AI*, the startup company credited for creating these models, has been the target of lawsuits by artists and established image archives for copyright infringement (Vallance, 2023).

Underpinning their commercial success and fraught legal status, the computational models produced by these companies afford non-specialist users a mode for *visual production through verbal interaction*, and these interactions can themselves be used as data that can be fed back into the system. Through different platforms, from the command line to a Photoshop plug-in, to an interactive website, text-to-image models allow

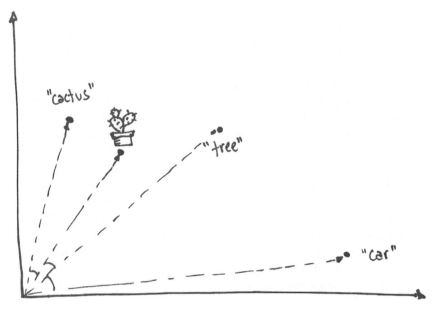

Figure 9.1 Text and images in shared vector space

us to *describe images into existence*, and in doing so we collectively serve as the wetware that enables and expands the generative capabilities of said models.

Let us unpack this logic through a high-level overview of how this kind of image synthesis works. At the heart of text-to-image models is the idea of an image synthesiser attached to a large pre-trained model. In the case of *Stable Diffusion*, the model was trained on a subset of the LAION 5B dataset of text and image pairs (https://laion.ai/blog/laion-5b/). This is then coupled with an adversarial mechanism to generate images, which involves gradually adding noise to an image to create a series of partially corrupted images. These partially corrupted images are then used to train the generator to reconstruct the original image from a noisy input. The key for this coupling to work is the addition of positional embeddings to images, an ingenious encoding technique that allows images to effectively be 'read' sequentially, as if they were text, and thus be cast in a shared vector space with text.

This allows the image generator to be progressively guided in this space, from a starting state, which can be simply noise (for example a random distribution of pixels), to progressively converge towards the target area in vector space, which is to say, render an image that approximates the description given by the user as a text input. This correspondence between linguistic and visual representations is at the heart of these text-to-image models and their new interactive affordances, which include of course the creation of synthetic datasets with which to train or fine-tune more models. An image is worth 16x16 words, as the original Vision Transformer paper states (Dosovitskiy et al, 2021).

In philosophy, there is a term to describe this type of relation between representational modes, and specifically between words and images: *Ekphrasis* – from the Greek *ek* meaning 'out' and *phrásis* meaning 'speak'. In ancient Greece, ekphrasis was taught as a rhetorical technique which consisted of producing a verbal description of an object that aimed to be as vivid as the object itself and could thus conjure an image of said object using language, or to 'paint a picture with words' in common parlance. The implications of ekphrasis as a rhetorical device meant that the technique allowed for the conjuring of absent or impossible objects, the classic example being Homer's elaborate description of Achilles' shield in the *Iliad* (Heffernan, 2004, p. 10).

For our purposes here, we can use Heffernan's modern and streamlined definition of ekphrasis as a verbal representation of a visual representation (1991), which more generally describes an epistemic cleavage between words and images; the idea, as Mitchell observes that 'Words can "cite," but never "sight" their objects' (1995, p. 152), and the persistent attempt at bridging this gap. In the wake of generative AI systems, words and images find novel forms of fluid permutation and latency in a shared representational space, albeit in high-dimensional space that is not directly interpretable to humans. We can call this *computational ekphrasis*: 'Calculation from/out of speech'.

Current AI technologies allow us to use words that can 'sight' imagery into existence, as well as images that can reply in kind. Since these models are somewhat reversible, given an image as input, like a frame of a film, a model in reverse can predict a likely prompt that would have generated such an image. Note that this is different from the object detection and recognition tasks discussed in earlier chapters, the outputted text here is not a pre-defined category external to the model, but a prediction of use based on the isomorphism of text and image tokens intrinsic to the model. A shared representational space is what affords such reversibility. Figure 9.2 is a frame from the film Blade Runner 2049 (2017), which I passed as input to a tool called CLIP Interrogator[2]. The Interrogator outputs a predicted prompt:

'a person standing in a room with a dog, blade runner 2049 colors, smoke and thick dust in the air, window in foreground, people and creatures walking, as far as the

Figure 9.2 Frame from *Blade Runner 2049* (2017)

Figure 9.3 Image synthesised using the predicted prompt in *Stable Diffusion* v1.5

eye can see, oilpunk, standing in front of a mirror, landscape mode, real hellscape in background'.

This can in turn output a similar image using Stable Diffusion v1.5 (Figure 9.3). Note how the model appears to have 'seen' *Blade Runner 2049*, which is to say, images from the film are probably in the dataset used to train it. With this in mind, if we take this kind of generative AI system as an expression of a centuries-old desire to dissolve the functional difference between verbal and visual representation, we can begin to configure an organised set of interactions between critics, films, and computer models, as an emerging technical practice in film scholarship. A crude example would be 'a symposium of robots', in which a human critic 'chairs' an exchange between models by selectively and recursively passing outputs of one model as inputs to another. The inputs and outputs can take the form of any kind of media, from text to movie clips, from code snippets to a piece of music. These exchanges could be framed as a recursive cycle of questions and answers, as the interface of ChatGPT is designed, or more provocatively, as an evolving conversation between agents that consume and produce media aiming for a metabolic state: text that creates images that creates text that creates images.

It is not so much that ekphrasis will in this way be 'solved'; words and images would remain interpretable tokens to the critic or critics chairing the 'meeting', at least provisionally. The advantage of this practice would be, rather, that such difference would be rendered functionally inconsequential through the modal translation delegated to AI. The critic would in this way be able to freeze language to operate in it all at once, as if it were an image, and to read images sequentially, as if they were speech; they will effectively be learning to sight through language and enunciate with pictures.

An informed human critic knows these systems do not hold views or beliefs of their own, but also knows that this does not preclude meaningful interactions with and among models, and by this, I mean interactions that can produce and reproduce meanings interpretable to others. They also know that these model-mediated conversations only acquire content if they are socialised and communicated to other people, who need to be able to follow such interactions and who can uphold or contest the interpretive steps taken by the convenor of this symposium, including scrutinising what becomes an input and output, and why. In such a setting, the reasons and reasonings contained in between the models, at their organic (human) joints, becomes as important to document and communicate as the generated media.

Moving image scholarship in the future might be recreated similar to how a scientific study is reproduced, this is, not only played back, but played over. And the most influential critics then will be those who can persuasively connect diverse models and navigate with confidence in ways that wider audiences and other critics can follow and understand. From this point of view, the task for media scholarship today is to co-design the conventions and formats of generative AI systems; the interfaces but also the operational conventions and ritualised practices to interact with computational media in ways that leave visible and material traces of a critic's rationalities when interacting with and between computational models of culture.

Computing devices and skills are of course involved in this process, but my contention here is that the hard problem for computational moving image studies is to develop the technical imagination to design these formats and ritualised practices of AI as a medium. In a nod to Vertov, I provisionally call this a *macroscopic* imagination: a shared techno-aesthetic way of thinking about images as computational artefacts connected in latent space

AI AS MEDIA

173

through inductive computing. Running with this optical metaphor, we can then say that if a telescope augments vision, allowing its user to see planets and stars across the galaxy, and the microscope magnifies invisible worlds of bacteria in a Petri dish, a *macroscope*, allows one to see through the aggregated eyes of many others. More specifically to 1) gather vast amounts of visual labour from human seers distributed in time and space; 2) store their aggregated seeing in a transportable computational artefact; and 3) release this synthetic vision at a later point.

Unlike a microscope or a telescope, the components of a macroscope are scattered around the globe, distributed unevenly in ad-hoc networks of organic and silicon-based actors. A macroscopic imagination would afford an understanding of both the distributedness and unevenness qualities of AI systems, as well as enable us to imagine the conditions necessary to freeze visuality in a stable computational model that can then be used as a generative engine. Moreover, such a framing, insofar as it includes people, demands we consider how we can do all this in a humane way; how we can, like Vertov anticipated, send 'an army of observers' out into the world to report and explain it in our behalf (Vertov in Heftberger, 2018, p. 79), without stripping them from personhood and emptying their views of the world from political content. A macroscopic imagination opens the question: if we could borrow for just a few moments the visual faculties of a multitude of others, what would we have them see for us? Who would we pick, and why? And on what moral grounds would we be allowed to draw from their bodies, their eyes, and their minds?

Macroscopic imagination and computational ekphrasis co-constitute each other, the latter being the technical body of the former. Ideally, a critical technical practice configured through this framework would serve creativity, criticism, and science. Visual culture critics could get one step closer to realising one of their long-standing projects: to be able to dynamically explore otherness in relation to representation. And within this larger project, film scholars could also approximate a persistent project of their own, which is to write with/in pictures. Scientists and engineers, meanwhile, could approximate a systematic science of culture, which has been an elusive programme without the explanatory powers of subject-oriented epistemologies.

To consider AI as a medium of inscription, at once descriptive and expressive of latent visualities, entails treating its generated outputs as media; transportable, representational, and interconnected artefacts of culture. There are limits to this approach, and not every token produced by every computational system will benefit from this treatment. However, the rise of creative AI suggests the broader scope afforded by computational aesthetics: the ability to blend modalities of thought through cultural mediation, to fluidly operate across object and subject-oriented epistemic regimes. Aesthetic thought, writes Simondon:

> operates and judges at the same time [. . .] the aesthetic object is both object and subject: it awaits the subject in order to put into motion and solicit in it perception on the one hand and participation in the other. [. . .] Aesthetic intention is what, to this extent, establishes horizontal relations between different modes of thought. (Simondon, 2017 [1958], pp. 201, 203, 2010)

Without the intersubjective webs meaning that structure our shared ways of seeing and feeling, and that effectively bind us across time and space through material culture, generative AI is untethered and hollow. It is the human containment of AI, its cultural envelopment, that charges it with meanings, and thus with value. We are increasingly becoming the human interface in between our para-human computational models, the wetware in a larger system whose outlines we are just beginning to understand.

Notes

1. GPT stands for Generative Pre-trained Transformer.
2. Available as a Google CoLab (https://colab.research.google.com/github/pharmapsychotic/clip-interrogator/blob/main/clip_interrogator.ipynb), a Hugging Face Space (https://huggingface.co/spaces/pharma/CLIP-Interrogator), as a stand-alone Python package (https://pypi.org/project/clip-interrogator/), and as a Stable Diffusion Web interface extension.

Conclusion:
Machines Made of Images

In this exploration of *Cinema and Machine Vision* I have identified some of the key assumptions that underwrite the design of AI systems used in the computational study of film. By identifying the aspects of vision that are delegated to computers, I located specific articulations of theory and practice that often play out as a dialectic between object and subject-oriented epistemologies: formalist and interpretive frameworks; distant and close readings; the technical conditions under which moving images are created, and what we bring to bear upon them through our collective watching and embodied interpretations. I have explored these articulations in practice through specific ways of programming and training computers to watch films; finding what these systems are doing exactly and the different actors involved in the process. In this back and forth between film theory and computational practice, subject and object positions constantly actualise each other, and this dance is at the centre of the capabilities and limitations of AI systems that are said to be watching films on our behalf.

Understood as a form of critical practice, machine-seeing films and television is in its infancy. These kinds of moving images are some of our most complex cultural products; they have rich histories, involve a myriad of combined specialisms, and mobilise layers upon layers of signifiers in highly sophisticated ways. In their current configuration, even state-of-the-art machine vision systems afford only a superficial gaze *at* films, which their wielders trade for breadth and sheer volume, often appealing to the rhetoric of scale of big data analytics inherited from the tech industry. But at least for now, we are far from replicating with computers the kinds of attention, memory and cognition needed for the high-level interpretation of films, and even in terms of visual perception alone, I have shown how computer vision is easily trumped by standard cinematic techniques which humans understand almost intuitively. If the goal is to replicate human viewing and interpretation, AI systems still have some way to go.

Yet, my research also suggests that this is a productive shortcoming. First, because AI is developing at a pace that is quickly outstripping its critics when it comes to capabilities. By the time this book is published, there will be new systems able to perform in ways that seemed out of reach at the time of writing. When I first trained a text generator a few years ago, before attention mechanisms and transformers came along, it could barely reproduce the structure of a text, making up words along the way and without any sense of context. The most I got from people when I showed them this was a lukewarm nod. Current LLMs are now able to pass professional exams and are discussed in the news as cultural phenomena. Given the resources put into AI and its strategic importance for governments across all social arenas, it is not the best time to bet against it, or to say for certain what it will not do in the future.

Beyond its development speed lies a second and more substantive reason to welcome some of the failings of computer vision systems when it comes to watching films. Taking a broader humanities view, I have invited the reader to reconsider the assumption of human vision as a benchmark for machine vision, taking an important lesson from film and media studies to understand how human vision is already technically mediated, and showed how this mediation in turn structures our diverse ways of seeing at given historical junctures. It follows that in training computers to watch films we are simultaneously training ourselves to watch like computers. Machine vision co-constitutes human vision, and under the current paradigm of AI this is enacted more as a cultural coupling than as computers that simulate human abilities and behaviours. From this point of view the classic definition of AI as computers that simulate humans admits a revision too, as we become aware that we ourselves are increasingly imbricated as the wetware component of the larger assemblages that we now call AI. Truly, we have unwittingly been made into parts of a larger and different kind of machinery whose contours we are only starting to define and whose reach so far exceeds our current models of thought.

Disassembling machine vision through the lens of film uncovers a division of labour between wet and dry elements in this larger assemblage of AI. Humans lend the system our interpretive abilities and emotive faculties; we supply judgements enabled by the sophisticated types of attention, long term memory, and embodied forms cognition developed over thousands of years of evolution and updated during lifetimes of conscious and subconscious subjective experiences. Meanwhile, we delegate to machines the encoding, organisation, abstraction, and storage of these individual experiences into objects (models) that can outlast individuals

CONCLUSION: MACHINES MADE OF IMAGES

and serve as a material infrastructure to our intersubjective networks of meaning.

A critical strategy that follows from understanding AI as a cultural infrastructure, and us as a key part of its systems, is that it is up to disciplines in the arts and humanities to challenge and redefine the 'art' part when technologists speak of 'state of the art'. The encounter between film scholarship and AI becomes more fruitful when framed from an interactionist perspective, not only as computers designed to watch films, but as critics trained to watch films through computers. Here is where I see the value of critical technical practice as a guiding principle, because it commits critics to both creating systems that work, and to explain to others what they work for, and what working means in different contexts. As I have argued, critique not only about but *through* AI is possible, but it does require technical commitment; to embrace at least some of the constraints imposed by actualised computer systems. The payoff comes in the form of a shared conjectural horizon of what one can and cannot do with AI; what works and what does not. And these limits stimulate the practitioner's creative imagination and are very often the catalysts of technical and epistemic innovation. There are moments in the history of every art, writes Walter Benjamin, 'in which a certain art form aspires to effects which could be fully obtained only with a changed technical standard, that is to say, in a new art form' (1969 [1935], p. 23). To commit to a technical standard, and attempt to import materials and concepts that seem not to fit in it, is in my view a crucial step in the redefinition and disciplinary pluralisation of the arts and sciences of AI.

At the same time, to commit to computing, even in its inductive paradigm, is not equivalent to embracing AI technologies wholesale, nor to endorse the way these technologies are currently designed and implemented. Since the making of MbM, AI has become an increasingly contentious field and, in some senses, much more unpalatable as an instrument of critique. At the technical level, it is more accessible, but it has simultaneously become increasingly obfuscated in the social and cultural arenas; with more tools, applications, and resources than ever before, but with big tech aggressively securing their supply chains and fencing off data from public view, and governments missing for the most part the larger and longer implications of a technology that draws from and in turn becomes culture. The effect of AI as it made it out of the labs and into society at large has been profoundly disorienting.

I suggested that after 2012 followed a period of accelerated epistemic transformation, when visual and computational modalities of knowledge production were put into radical contact under a novel computational paradigm. I have also argued that this moment resembles in some striking ways the birth of cinema at the turn of the twentieth century, namely in that there was a cultural and technical milieu for the emergence of a new medium, at a time when its formats and conventions had not yet been fixed. A similar window of reorientation and possibility can be seen during the first decade of creative AI, when its practices, technical configurations, and formal characteristics, are still very much in flux and in a similar state of effervescence. But there are also significant differences. Unlike Edison's Kinetoscope or the Lumière's Cinematograph, which were inventions initially tethered to their creators and their labs, contemporary AI depends on vast infrastructures of global networked computation and therefore already relies on society in a much broader sense. The cinematographer was a mechanical eye cast *on* society while inductive machine vision is a computational eye drawn *from* society; the former can reflect or obscure existing power relations, the latter embodies them. And so, although both can be framed as technologies of vision, the development of new formats and conventions in creative AI is inevitably much more heavily controlled by various social actors, including large tech conglomerates, but surely followed by government regulation and the reorganisation of their legal systems. The next decade of creative AI will be determined by the relations between different productive and creative actors, and the state, including a radical reconfiguration of 'the public' as a political category, set against the backdrop of liberal democracies struggling to redefine their positions on public health, public education, public opinion, or public ownership of what makes this machinery work.

With its generative capabilities, this new wave of creative AI puts significant pressure on the political economy of visuality; on copyright, the public sphere, and the commons, at times threatening to capture them and at times to render them obsolete. These and other frictions coupled with a huge influx of capital has resulted in very uneven development, accelerated in some fronts, and arrested in others. Parts of the technical milieu, for instance, have grown dramatically since MbM: specialised courses, dedicated laboratories, a growing number of conferences, have all sprawled in less than a decade, accompanied by what can be described as a Cambrian explosion of creative AI initiatives: from artistic use to intellectual practice to full deployments in the creative industries. With many of the frustrating intricacies of AI work as a matter of craft being rapidly smoothed out, packaged, and sold as products and services, creative applications of these technologies are now in full bloom and available to non-specialists. However, as a cultural infrastructure and a medium of inscription, the aesthetics of AI are comparatively underdeveloped. I have

CONCLUSION: MACHINES MADE OF IMAGES

shown how, contrary to popular discourse, the kind of encodings and data needed to make machine vision aesthetically sensitive is not abundant or easily found. For example, I have made the case for a vast space in the computational poetics of film that remains significantly unexplored, not due to the limitations of inductive computing itself, but rather because it has been poorly understood across disciplines, resulting in a lack of conceptual diversity in its design and implementation. We currently lack the shared conjectural space in which to question the visual regimes created through AI, as well as the technical imagination with which to intervene it. And to break ground in this space, the latest, largest, fastest AI models are not always needed. In the preceding chapters I have questioned how this emphasis on distance and scale can in fact be intellectually limiting, and how older and simpler computational techniques can often afford significant gains that reorient what we design these systems for, and that this can in turn inform alternative systems downstream. For this kind of epistemic experimentation, we need much more than access to the latest machines; we need new models of practice that take machine-building as an intellectual enterprise no less than a practical one.

The radical reciprocity between inductive computing and aesthetics I propose in this book is challenging because these are knowledge animals that move in different manners and apprehend the world at different speeds, with AI going from a peripheral branch of computer science to being the poster child of accelerationism and overblown hopes and anxieties, inside and outside of academia. Aesthetics, meanwhile, is concerned with inter-subjective types of attention, norms, conventions, and above all forms and emotions. These take time to develop and longer still to crystalise and be observed, and therefore progress in aesthetics is necessarily slower and demands a different type of commitment to technique. Aesthetics demands us to consider technical practices that render computing not only usable or productive, but habitable; the kinds of ritualised relation to technical objects that can enable *community without communication* (Han, 2020).

I hope to have made a compelling case for an aesthetics of machine vision, without which the many subjects of AI are flattened in public discourse: no longer readers, viewers, or attendants, but just users, who participate from an assemblage that feeds from their capacity for meaning-making, compressing it into computational artefacts that are then sold back to them for a profit. Without aesthetics, creative AI renders personalised visual worlds that are hollow and un-narrated; it conjures sequences without continuity and subject-less presences. These visual regimes can be very appealing on the surface, and are even portrayed and promoted as emancipatory, freeing from the authority of elitist critics and hegemonic systems of representation. But as I have argued through the lens of cinema, beneath this ideological wrapper of individual control and self-determination, of all images seen for us and tailored images then made for us, lie the extractive and rentier dynamics of corporate AI. My argument here is that creative AI without aesthetics threatens to erode the powerful social nexus between critics and audiences, thwarting the configuration of effective and meaningful dissensus and thereby negating the political dimension of aesthetic judgements. Without an aesthetics of machine vision, subjects are reduced to users, judgements to preferences, and value to popularity.

Aesthetics is slower but empowering because it provides a line of flight, an agenda for a critical form of machine vision in which we learn to see through the eyes of others across time and space without erasing the others, the time, or the space in the process. And here is where I believe film and media studies can contribute the most, with their highly developed frameworks to study visual representations of otherness as well as the power relations that these representations entrench or subvert. This alone should be a strong reason for these disciplines to participate in the project of re-imagining machine vision. Furthermore, if we take visual culture to consist of the inter-subjective network of meanings enabled by shared material cultures – this is, the design and circulation of objects that allow us to externalise our subjective visual experiences with others – AI can be thought of as expression of this inter-subjectivity, and its computational models as its objects. These computational models have distinct affordances as media; they enable the externalisation of cumulative visual experience, allowing us to 'put on tape' a coherent latent picture of the ways we see as a group, or in the case of film and TV, as an audience.

This is a remarkable affordance, not because it implies non-human intelligence or self-generating powers, but because it can dramatically extend our reach into the past and the future. One way of thinking about machine vision from a media scholarship perspective is that it allows us to instantiate ways of seeing, and it provides a material support to experiment with how things might be seen or infer how they were seen in different contexts, therein lies its power. I have argued that the storage, portability, and reproducibility of machine vision models suggest a strong genealogical connection to photography and cinema, as well as a critical point of contact with disciplines in the arts and humanities that are concerned with the politics of vision, with the unseen, the under-seen, and the power relations between the seeable and the knowable. To wield a

CONCLUSION: MACHINES MADE OF IMAGES 181

computational gaze implies taking a stance on what needs to be seen, when this seeing involves borrowing the eyes and minds of others.

This is the challenge of AI as modality of vision. A disembodied gaze cannot be trusted because it is not committed to any specific version of events. Data-points float freely and reorganise elastically, creating contingent patterns of proximity upon which inferences are made and decisions taken. These patterns might be there, but the relations they suggest s are always contingent; they can easily be made to suggest other proximities, other patterns, and other structures, and be presented all at once again and again, creating rational illusions in the process. Proximities like these are not binding in the way events organised in a timeline are. Narrative events, as I have argued, are not only contiguous but continuous; each event is affected by the previous ones and weighs heavily on the ones that follow, their ordering and rhythms matter a great deal, making each event bound to the others in powerful ways. This quality is useful to both epistemics and aesthetics; the types of relations created by continuity qualify beliefs, *committing* contingent facts and events into strong relations that are understood and cannot be easily undone. These relations of necessity elicit in us the especial kind of attention and memory that we reserve only for that which we believe can *last*, and which is therefore worth externalising into material culture.

This is where I think machine vision can be influenced by media. Films in particular elicit a peculiar hybrid modality of vision; this is one of the main reasons for their enduring erotic appeal. Films can fork time by splicing and (re)presenting discontinuous sequences of events at the level of shots. But each frame in every shot is tightly bound in a continuous sequence that is internally and mechanistically structured; frames cannot elude their strong bonds with each other without ceasing to be frames. We trust films as recordings of past duration because of the strong relations between frames, but we equally admit their capacity to dilate and compress time at the level of shots and sequences. The interplay between these two properties makes films both structured and elastic, mechanistically bound but expressively designed.

Pixels on the other hand float freely; one cannot say that any pixel is in a strong relation with any other. They can be moved, rearranged, generated, and regenerated to fit any design; their representational powers are derived from the fact that they can be made to be contiguous in any direction and that such contiguity is always contingent. Pixels have no internal temporal form we can understand or relate to; their flow is unbound. But just like frames were once photographs, the argument I present here is that we simply have not yet created the temporal forms that can endow the free flow of pixels with the strong relations necessary for aesthetic significance. A temporal line, writes Han (2017b), 'has a direction, a syntax [. . .] The lack of pre-given temporal structures does not lead to an increase in freedom, but to a lack of orientation' (pp. 13, 32). And these temporal forms might not be intrinsic to pixels as digital objects, or to their computational environments; they might not arise in the way temporal forms in cinema once did. But to watch films through computers prompts us to think about what these new temporal forms might be, enabling the technical practices and modes of interaction that orient us in the latent visual spaces created by AI.

The initial thrust may be to simulate cinema; for example in the text-to-video or image-to-video systems that output a type of parametric animation, where the parameters can be inputted as text or another image. But eventually, the temporal forms that stick might be those that locate and exploit emerging conditions of viewership. Perhaps we will re-discover the pleasures of making images narrate without sequences, by learning how to interpret painterly tableaux of a novel kind, made interactive by directed prompting, in-painting, and zooming. In seeking to model computationally what moves us about moving images, we are compelled to think and feel through a new kind of machinery.

I now find myself thinking of *Made by Machine* in a similar way to how I think about the manual of experimental television from the 1930s, as a product of its time, a thrilling stage of experimentation and possibility, shortly before technology becomes mass media. If MbM was going to be made again today, it would undoubtedly be quite different, in some sense less experimental and surely much more ambitious, with an expanding set of techniques and resources and a different audience too. My hope is that whoever gets to make it and watch it finds in this book an honest account of what it was like to learn to see by machine.

References

Bibliography

Abell, C. (2010) 'The Epistemic Value of Photographs', in C. Abell & K. Bantinaki (eds) *Philosophical Perspectives on Depiction*. Oxford: Oxford University Press, pp. 81–103. doi:10.1093/acprof:oso/9780199585960.003.0004.

Agre, P. (1997a) 'Toward a Critical Technical Practice: Lessons Learned in Trying to Reform AI', in Geoffrey Bowker et al (eds) *Social Science, Technical Systems, and Cooperative Work: Beyond the Great Divide*. New York: Psychology Press, pp. 131–158.

Agre, P. (1997b) *Computation and Human Experience*. New York: Cambridge University Press. doi:10.1017/CBO9780511571169.

Alayrac, J.-B. et al (2022) Flamingo: a visual language model for few-shot learning. doi:10.48550/arXiv.2204.14198.

Amadeo, R. (2017) *YouTube's 'VR180' format cuts down on VR video's prohibitive requirements* [online]. Available from: https://arstechnica.com/gadgets/20 17/06/youtubes-vr180-format-makes-vr-video-more-accessible/ (Accessed 10 February 2020).

Aradau, C. & Blanke, T. (2022) *Algorithmic Reason: The New Government of Self and Other*. New York: OUP Oxford. doi:10.1093/oso/9780192859624.001.0001.

Arnheim, R. (1957) *Film as Art: 50th Anniversary Printing*. Los Angeles: University of California Press.

Arnold, T. (2019) 'Shot Size Extraction'. Email to Taylor Arnold, 14 August 2019.

Arnold, T. & Tilton, L. (2020) 'Distant Viewing Toolkit: A Python Package for the Analysis of Visual Culture', *Journal of Open Source Software*, 5 (45), 1800. doi:10.21105/joss.01800.

Arnold, T. & Tilton, L. (2019) 'Distant Viewing: Analyzing Large Visual Corpora', *Digital Scholarship in the Humanities*, 34 (1), pp. i3–I16. doi:10.1093/llc/fqz013.

Arnold, T., Tilton, L, & Berke, A. (2019) 'Visual Style in Two Network Era Sitcoms', *Journal of Cultural Analytics*, 4 (2). doi:10.22148/16.043.

Atkinson, S. (2018) From Film Practice to Data Process: Production Aesthetics and Representational Practices of a Film Industry in Transition. Edinburgh: Edinburgh University Press.

Auger, J. (2013) 'Speculative Design: Crafting the Speculation', *Digital Creativity*, 24 (1), pp. 11–35. doi:10.1080/14626268.2013.767276.

Badiou, A. (2012) *In Praise of Love*. London: Serpent's Tail.

Bail, C. A., Argyle, L. P., Brown, T. W., Bumpus, J. P., Chen, H., Fallin Hunzaker, M. B., Lee, J., Mann, M., Merhout, F., & Volfovsky, A. (2018) 'Exposure to Opposing Views on Social Media can Increase Political Polarization', *Proceedings of the National Academy of Sciences*, 115 (37), pp. 916–922. doi:10.1073/pnas.1804840115.

Balaz, B. (1952) *Theory of the Film*. Universal Digital Library. [online]. Available from: http://archive.org/details/theoryofthefilm000665mbp (Accessed 15 May 2019).

BARB (2018) *The Viewing Report*. [online]. Available from: https://www.barb.co.uk/ (Accessed 19 September 2019).

Barthes, R. (1993) [1957] *Mythologies*. London: Vintage.

Baxter, M. (2014a) *Cinemetrics – a Bibliography*. Available from: http://www.mikemetrics.com/ (Accessed 8 November 2017).

Baxter, M. (2014b) *Notes on Cinemetric Data Analysis*. Available from: http://www.cinemetrics.lv/dev/Cinemetrics_Book_Baxter.pdf (Accessed 8 November 2019).

Bazin, A. (2010 [1958]) 'The Evolution of the Language of Cinema', in Marc Furstenau (ed.) *The Film Theory Reader: Debates and Arguments*. Routledge. pp. 23–40.

BBC (2016) *Royal Charter for the continuance of the British Broadcasting Corporation*. [online]. Available from: http://downloads.bbc.co.uk/bbctrust/assets/files/pdf/about/how_we_govern/2016/charter.pdf (Accessed 22 October 2018).

BBC (2016) *An Agreement Between Her Majesty's Secretary of State for Culture, Media and Sport and the British Broadcasting Corporation*. [online]. Available from: http://downloads.bbc.co.uk/bbctrust/assets/files/pdf/about/how_we_govern/2016/agreement.pdf (Accessed 21 July 2020).

BBC (2020) First Experimental BBC TV Programme [online]. Available from: https://www.bbc.com/historyofthebbc/anniversaries/august (Accessed 4 May 2019).

BBC R&D (2017a) *AI in Production* [online]. Available from: https://www.bbc.co.uk/rd/projects/ai-production (Accessed 28 September 2018).

BBC R&D (2017b) *Data Science Research Partnership* [online]. Available from: https://www.bbc.co.uk/rd/projects/data-science-research-partnership (Accessed 28 September 2018).

Belton, J. (1990) 'Historical Paper: The Origins of 35mm Film as a Standard', *SMPTE Journal*, 99 (8), pp. 652–661. doi:10.5594/J02613.

Bender, E. M. et al (2021) 'On the Dangers of Stochastic Parrots: Can Language Models Be Too Big? 🦜', in *Proceedings of the 2021 ACM Conference on Fairness, Accountability, and Transparency. FAccT '21* [online]. 1 March 2021, New York, NY, USA: Association for Computing Machinery, pp. 610–623. Available from: https://dl.acm.org/doi/10.1145/3442188.3445922 (Accessed 1 May 2023).

Benjamin, W. (1969) [1935] 'The Work of Art in the Age of Mechanical Reproduction', in *Illuminations: Essays and Reflections*. New York: Schocken Books, pp. 217–252.

REFERENCES   185

Bense, M. (1982) [1965] *Aesthetica: Einführung in die neue Aesthetik*. Baden-Baden: Agis-Verlag.

Bergson, H. (2004) [1896] *Matter and Memory*. New York: Dover Publications.

Bergson, H. (1998 [1907]) *Creative Evolution*. New York: Dover Publications.

BFI (2018) *Key Archives and What They Do* [online]. Available from: https://www.bfi.org.uk/archive-collections/archive-projects/artist-archive/key-arch ives-what-they-do (Accessed 15 October 2018).

Bhargav, S. et al (2019) 'Deep Learning as a Tool for Early Cinema Analysis', in *Proceedings of the 1st Workshop on Structuring and Understanding of Multimedia heritAge Contents*, SUMAC '19, New York: Association for Computing Machinery, pp. 61–68. doi:10.1145/3347317.3357240.

Birkhoff, G. D. (1932) 'A Mathematical Theory of Aesthetics', *The Rice Institute Pamphlet*, 19 (3).

Blackwell, A. (2010) 'When Systemizers Meet Empathizers: Universalism and the Prosthetic Imagination', *Interdisciplinary Science Reviews*. 35 (3–4), pp. 387–403. doi:10.1179/030801810X12772143410485.

Blackwell, A. (2015) 'Interacting with an Inferred World: The Challenge of Machine Learning for Humane Computer Interaction', *Aarhus Series on Human Centered Computing*, 1 (1). doi:10.7146/aahcc.v1i1.21197.

Blumenthal-Barby, M (2015) 'Cinematography of Devices: Harun Farocki's Eye/Machine Trilogy', *German Studies Review*, 38 (2), pp. 329–351.

Blyth, A. (2019) '"Mary Queen Of Scots": Margot Robbie & Saoirse Ronan On Separation, Smallpox & The Power Behind The Female Throne', *Deadline* [online]. Available from: https://deadline.com/2019/01/mary-queen-of-s cots-margot-robbie-saoirse-ronan-interview-female-throne-1202529307/ (Accessed 1 April 2020).

Bogers, L. & Chiappini, L. (eds.) (2019) *The Critical Makers Reader: (un) Learning Technology*. Institute of Network Cultures. doi:10.25969/mediarep/19278.

Bogost, I. (2019) 'The AI-Art Gold Rush Is Here', *The Atlantic* [online]. Available from: https://www.theatlantic.com/technology/archive/2019/03/ai-created -art-invades-chelsea-gallery-scene/584134/ (Accessed 17 July 2020).

Bordwell, D. (1985) *Narration in the Fiction Film*. Madison: University of Wisconsin Press.

Bordwell, D. (1989) 'Historical Poetics of Cinema', in *Palmer*, R. B. *The Cinematic Text: Methods and Approaches*. New York: AMS Press.

Bordwell, D. (2006) *The Way Hollywood Tells it: Story and Style in Modern Movies*. Berkeley: University of California Press.

Bordwell, D. (2008) *Poetics of Cinema*. New York: Routledge.

Bordwell, D. (2012) *A Video Essay on Constructive Editing* [online]. Available from: http://www.davidbordwell.net/blog/2012/10/28/news-a-video-essay -on-constructive-editing/ (Accessed 3 April 2017).

Bordwell, D. & Carroll, N. (1996) *Post-theory: Reconstructing Film Studies*. Madison: University of Wisconsin Press.

Bordwell, D. & Thompson, K. (2017) [2008] *Film Art: An Introduction*. McGraw-Hill Education: New York.

Bordwell, D. & Thompson, K. (2019) *Christopher Nolan: A Labyrinth of Linkages*. Second Edition. Madison: Irvington Way Institute Press.

Borges, J. L. (1998) [1941] 'The Library of Babel', in *Collected Fictions*. New York: Viking, pp. 112–118.

Box, G. E. P. (1976) 'Science and Statistics', *Journal of the American Statistical Association*, 71 (356), pp. 791–799. doi:10.2307/2286841.

Bradshaw, P. (2006) '*Grizzly Man* Review – Werner Herzog retraces Timothy Treadwell's Steps', *The Guardian*. 3 February. [online]. Available from: https://www.theguardian.com/culture/2006/feb/03/1 (Accessed 2 April 2020).

Bradshaw, P. (2013) '*Upstream Color* – Review', *The Guardian*. 29 August. [online]. Available from: https://www.theguardian.com/film/2013/aug/29/upstream-color-review (Accessed 6 July 2018).

Braun, M. (1994) Picturing Time: The Work of Etienne-Jules Marey (1830–1904). Chicago: University of Chicago Press.

Buolamwini, J. & Gebru, T. (2018) 'Gender Shades: Intersectional Accuracy Disparities in Commercial Gender Classification' [online], *Proceedings of the 1st Conference on Fairness, Accountability and Transparency*, Proceedings of Machine Learning Research, 81, pp. 77–91. Available from: http://proceedings.mlr.press/v81/buolamwini18a.html (Accessed 4 June 2019).

Burch, N. (1981) *Theory of Film Practice*. Princeton: Princeton University Press. doi:10.1515/9781400853366.

Burch, N. (2002) *Interview mit Noël Burch* [online]. Available from: https://www.haussite.net/haus.0/PROGRAM/02/redirect/E/burch_inter_E.html (Accessed 13 April 2020).

Buskirk, E. V. (2009) 'How the Netflix Prize Was Won', *Wired* [online]. Available from: https://www.wired.com/2009/09/how-the-netflix-prize-was-won/ (Accessed 4 December 2018).

Bunz, M. Chavez Heras, D., et al (2023) *Towards a C5 Model in Creative AI*. [online]. Available from: https://d37zoqglehb9o7.cloudfront.net/uploads/2020/07/Toward-a-C5-model-in-Creative-AI.pdf (Accessed 13 April 2023).

Butterworth, B. (2008) *History of the 'BBC Redux' Project* [online]. Available from: http://www.bbc.co.uk/blogs/bbcinternet/2008/10/history_of_the_bbc_redux_proje.html (Accessed 15 October 2018).

Cardon, D., Cointet, J.-P., & Mazieres, A. (2018) 'Neurons Spike Back. The Invention of Inductive Machines and the Artificial Intelligence Controversy', *Réseaux*, 211 (5), pp. 173–220.

Carroll, N. (1984) 'Hume's Standard of Taste', *The Journal of Aesthetics and Art Criticism*, 43 (2), pp. 181–194. doi:10.2307/429992.

Carroll, N. (1988) *Philosophical Problems of Classical Film Theory*. Princeton: Princeton University Press.

Carroll, N. (2009) *On Criticism*. New York: Routledge.

Castellano, B. (2020) *Breakthrough / PySceneDetect* [online]. Available from: https://github.com/Breakthrough/PySceneDetect (Accessed 13 April 2020).

REFERENCES

187

Cave, S. et al (2018) *Portrayals and Perceptions of AI and Why They Matter*. Apollo – University of Cambridge Repository. doi:10.17863/CAM.34502.

Cavell, S. (1979) The World Viewed: Reflections on the Ontology of Film. Cambridge: Harvard University Press.

Chávez Heras, D. (2012) 'The Malleable Computer: Software and the Study of the Moving Image', *Frames Cinema Journal*, 1 (1). Available from: https://framescinemajournal.com/article/the-malleable-computer/ (Accessed 26 March 2021).

Chávez Heras, D. (2019) 'Spectacular Machinery and Encrypted Spectatorship', *APRJA* 8 (1), pp. 170–182. doi:10.7146/aprja.v8i1.115423.

Chávez Heras, D. (2023) 'Creanalytics: Automating the Supercut as a form of Critical Technical Practice', *Convergence* [forthcoming].

Chen, M., Radford, A., Child, R., Wu, J., Jun, H., Luan, D. & Sutskever, I. (2020) 'Generative Pretraining from Pixels', in *International Conference on Machine Learning*, 21 November, pp. 1691–1703. PMLR.

Christie's (2018) *Is Artificial Intelligence Set to Become Art's Next Medium?* [online]. Available from: https://www.christies.com/features/A-collaboration-between-two-artists-one-human-one-a-machine-9332-1.aspx (Accessed 27 February 2019).

CIPA (2019) *Camera & Imaging Products Association: Statistical Data Report*. [online]. Available from: http://www.cipa.jp/stats/dc_e.html (Accessed 27 February 2020).

CISCO (2019) *Visual Networking Index: Forecast and Trends* [online]. Available from: https://www.cisco.com/c/en/us/solutions/service-provider/visual-networking-index-vni/index.html (Accessed 26 March 2021).

CISCO (2020) *Annual Internet Report* [online]. Available from: https://www.cisco.com/c/en/us/solutions/executive-perspectives/annual-internet-report/index.html (Accessed 27 July 2023).

Civjans, G. (2011) *Cinemetrics Database*. Personal communication with Gunars Civjans, 19 July 2011.

Clarkson, E., Levi-Setti, R., & Horváth. G. (2006) 'The Eyes of Trilobites: The Oldest Preserved Visual System', *Arthropod Structure & Development*, 35 (4), pp. 247–259. doi:10.1016/j.asd.2006.08.002.

Cohen, J. & Meskin, A. (2004) 'On the Epistemic Value of Photographs', *The Journal of Aesthetics and Art Criticism*, 62 (2), pp. 197–210. doi:10.1111/j.1540-594X.2004.00152.x.

Colangelo, D. (2017) 'Hitchcock, Film Studies, and New Media: The Impact of Technology on the Analysis of Film', in Santiago Hidalgo & André Gaudreault (eds.) *Technology and Film Scholarship: Experience, Study, Theory*. Amsterdam: Amsterdam University Press., pp. 127–148 [online]. Available from: https://doi.org/10.2307/j.ctt1zqrmrh.10.

Collins, A. F. (Archie F.) (c1932) Experimental television; a series of simple experiments with television apparatus; also how to make a complete home television transmitter and television receiver. Boston: Lothrop. [online]. Available from:

http://archive.org/details/experimentaltele00collrich (Accessed 10 August 2020).

Collins, H. M. & Kusch, M. (1998) *The Shape of Actions: What Humans and Machines Can Do.* Cambridge & London: MIT Press.

Colton, S. Charnley, J., & Pease, A. (2011) 'Computational Creativity Theory: The FACE and IDEA Descriptive Models', *Proceedings of the 2nd International Conference on Computational Creativity*, Mexico City, pp. 90–95.

Colton, S. & Wiggins, G. A. (2012) 'Computational Creativity: The Final Frontier?', *ECAI'12: Proceedings of the 20th European Conference on Artificial Intelligence*, Montpelier, pp. 21–26.

Coppola, F. F. (1994) *Academy of Achievement.* [online]. Available from: https://achievement.org/achiever/francis-ford-coppola/ (Accessed 16 April 2020).

Copyright, Designs and Patents Act 1988 [online]. Available from: https://www.legislation.gov.uk/ukpga/1988/48/contents (Accessed 25 September 2023).

Cortez, P., Cerdeira, A., Almeida. F., Matos, T., & Reis, J. (2009) 'Modeling Wine Preferences by Data Mining from Physicochemical Properties', *Decision Support Systems*, 47 (4), pp. 547–553. doi:10.1016/j.dss.2009.05.016.

Costello, D. (2017) *On Photography: A Philosophical Inquiry.* New York: Routledge.

Cowlishaw, T. (2018) *Using Artificial Intelligence to Search the Archive* [online]. Available from: https://www.bbc.co.uk/rd/blog/2018-10-artificial-intelligence-archive-television-bbc4 (Accessed 28 September 2018).

Cronin, P. (2002) *Herzog on Herzog.* London: Faber and Faber.

Cumberbatch, G., Bailey, A., Lyne, V., & Gauntlett, S. (2018) *On-screen Diversity Monitoring BBC One and BBC Two.* [online]. Available from: https://www.ofcom.org.uk/__data/assets/pdf_file/0019/124255/bbc1-bbc2-diversity-monitoring.pdf (Accessed 10 October 2019).

Currie, G. (1999) 'Visible Traces: Documentary and the Contents of Photographs', *The Journal of Aesthetics and Art Criticism*, 57 (3), pp. 285–297. doi:10.2307/432195.

Cutting, J. E. et al (2011) 'Quicker, Faster, Darker: Changes in Hollywood Film over 75 Years', *i-Perception*, 2 (6), pp. 569–576. doi:10.1068/i0441aap.

Daigle, A. (2018) *How the 50-mm Lens Became 'Normal'* [online]. Available from: https://www.theatlantic.com/technology/archive/2018/05/how-the-50-mm-lens-became-normal/560276/ (Accessed 23 May 2019).

Dargis, M. (2003) *The '70s: Get Over It* [online]. Available from: https://www.latimes.com/archives/la-xpm-2003-aug-17-ca-dargis17-story.html (Accessed 19 May 2019).

Debruge, P. (2017) 'Film Review: "*Dunkirk*"', *Variety* [online]. Available from: https://variety.com/2017/film/reviews/dunkirk-review-christopher-nolan-1202495701/ (Accessed 1 April 2020).

Deleuze, G. (1986) *Cinema 1. The Movement-Image.* Minneapolis: University of Minnesota.

Delpeut, P. & Klerk, N. (2018) 'Bits & Pieces: The Limits of the Film Archive',

REFERENCES

Medium [online]. Available from: https://medium.com/janbot/the-limits-of -film-archive-76ae5d338eae (Accessed 29 June 2020).

Deng, J., Dong, W., Socher, R., Li, L.-J., Li, K., & Li, F.-F. (2009) 'Imagenet: A Large-scale Hierarchical Image Database', *IEEE Conference on Computer Vision and Pattern Recognition*, Miami, pp. 248–255. doi:10 .1109/CVPR.2009.5206848.

Denson, S. (2020) *Discorrelated Images*. Durham: Duke University Press Books. doi:10.1215/9781478012412.Dewdney, A. (2021) *Forget Photography*. Cambridge & London: MIT Press.

Difallah, D. et al (2018) 'Demographics and Dynamics of Mechanical Turk Workers', in *Proceedings of the Eleventh ACM International Conference on Web Search and Data Mining*. WSDM '18. [Online]. 2018 New York, NY, USA: ACM. pp. 135–143. doi:10.1145/3159652.3159661.

van Dijck, J. (2014) 'Datafication, Dataism and Dataveillance: Big Data Between Scientific Paradigm and Ideology', *Surveillance & Society*, 12 (2), pp. 197–208. doi:doi.org/10.24908/ss.v12i2.4776.

Doane, M. A. (2002) *The Emergence of Cinematic Time: Modernity, Contingency, the Archive*. Cambridge: Harvard University Press. doi:10.2307/j.ctv1pnc1jq.

Doane, M. A. (2003) 'The Close-up: Scale and Detail in the Cinema', *Differences: A Journal of Feminist Cultural Studies*, 14 (3), pp. 89–111. doi:10.1215/10407391-14-3-89.

Dosovitskiy, A. et al (2021) An Image is Worth 16x16 Words: Transformers for Image Recognition at Scale. doi:10.48550/arXiv.2010.11929.

Dreyfus, H. L. & Hubert, L. (1992) What Computers Still Can't Do: A Critique of Artificial Reason. Cambridge: MIT Press.

Eagleton, T. (2005 [1996]) *The Function of Criticism*. New York: Verso.

Elsaesser, T. (2005) 'Cinephilia: The Uses of Disenchantment', in Marijke de Valck & Malte Hagener (eds.) *Cinephilia: Movies, Love and Memory*. Amsterdam: Amsterdam University Press. pp. 27–44. doi:10.25969/mediarep/11988.

Enns, C. (2012) 'Navigating Algorithmic Editing: Algorithmic Editing as an Alternative Approach to Database Cinema', *Millennium Film Journal*, pp. 66–72.

EPIC GAMES (2020) *A First Look at Unreal Engine 5*. Available from: https://www.unrealengine.com/en-US/blog/a-first-look-at-unreal-engine-5 (Accessed 19 May 2020).

Espeland, W. N. (1997) 'Authority by the Numbers: Porter on Quantification, Discretion, and the Legitimation of Expertise', *Law & Social Inquiry*, 22 (4), pp. 1107–1133. doi:10.1111/j.1747-4469.1997.tb01100.x.

Everingham, M. Van Gool, L., Williams, C.K.I., Winn, J., & Zisserman, A. (2010) 'The Pascal Visual Object Classes (VOC) Challenge', *International Journal of Computer Vision*, 88 (2), pp. 303–338. doi:10.1007/s11263-009-0275-4.

Ewerth, R. et al (2009) 'Videana: A Software Toolkit for Scientific Film Studies', in Michael Ross, et al (eds) *Digital Tools in Media Studies. Analysis and Research. An Overview*, Bielefeld: transcript, pp. 101–116. doi:10.25969/mediarep/2559.

Farocki, H. (2004) 'Phantom Images', in: *Public* 29, p. 17.

Floridi, L. (2018) 'Artificial Intelligence, Deepfakes and a Future of Ectypes', *Philosophy & Technology*, 31 (3), pp. 317–321. doi:10.1007/s13347-018-0325-3.

Flueckiger, B. (2012) '*Material Properties of Historical Film in the Digital Age*', *NECSUS. European Journal of Media Studies*, 1(2), pp. 135–153. doi:10.25969/mediarep/15053.

Flueckiger, B. & Halter, G. (2018) 'Building a Crowdsourcing Platform for the Analysis of Film Colors', *The Moving Image: The Journal of the Association of Moving Image Archivists*, 18 (1), pp. 80–83. doi:10.5749/movingimage.18.1.0080.

Foster, H. (2004). 'The Cinema of Harun Farocki', *Artforum International*, 43 (3), p. 160.

Frampton, H. (2009 [1971]) 'For a Metahistory of Film: Commonplace Notes and Hypotheses', in B. Jenkins (ed.) *On the Camera Arts and Consecutive Matters: The Writings of Hollis Frampton*, pp. 131–139. Cambridge: MIT Press. doi:10.7551/mitpress/7851.003.0021.

Francisco, C. (1980) *You Must Remember This: The Filming of Casablanca*. First edition. New Jersey: Prentice-Hall.

Frey, M. & Sayad, C. (2015) *Film Criticism in the Digital Age*. New Brunswick: Rutgers University Press.

Frierson, M. (2018) Film and Video Editing Theory: How Editing Creates Meaning. New York: Routledge.

Frizot, M. (2001) *Étienne-Jules Marey: chronophotographe*. Paris: Nathan Delpire.

Fukushima, K. (1980) 'Neocognitron: A Self-organizing Neural Network Model for a Mechanism of Pattern Recognition Unaffected by Shift in Position', *Biological Cybernetics*, 36 (4), pp. 193–202. doi:10.1007/BF00344251.

Gaboury, J. (2021) Image Objects: An Archaeology of Computer Graphics. Cambridge: MIT Press.

Giardina, C. (2011) 'Christopher Nolan Credits Editor Lee Smith with Helping Viewers Understand "*Inception*"', *The Hollywood Reporter* [online]. Available from: https://www.hollywoodreporter.com/news/christopher-nolan-credits-editor-lee-159655 (Accessed 16 April 2020).

Gidal, P. (1985) 'Interview with Hollis Frampton', *October*, 32, pp. 93–117. doi:10.2307/778288.

Girvan, M. & Newman, M. E. (2002) 'Community Structure in Social and Biological Networks' *Proceedings of the National Academy of Sciences*, 99 (12), 7821–7826.

Gitelman, L. (ed.). (2013) '*Raw Data' is an Oxymoron*. Cambridge: MIT Press.

Goodfellow, I., Pouget-Abadie, J., Mirza, M., Xu., B., Warde-Farley, D., Ozair, S., Courville, A., & Bengio, Y. (2014) 'Generative Adversarial Nets', in *Advances in Neural Information Processing Systems*, pp. 2672–2680.

Grant, C. (2014) 'The Shudder of a Cinephiliac Idea? Videographic Film Studies

REFERENCES 191

Practice as Material Thinking', *ANIKI: Portuguese Journal of the Moving Image*, 1 (1), pp. 49–62. doi:doi.org/10.14591/aniki.v1n1.59.

Grant, C. (2015) 'Film Studies in the Groove? Rhythmising Perception in Carnal Locomotive', *NECSUS. European Journal of Media Studies*, 4 (1), pp. 85–90. doi:10.5117/NECSUS2015.1.GRAN.

Grant, C. (2016) 'The Audiovisual Essay as Performative Research', *NECSUS. European Journal of Media Studies*, 5 (2), pp. 255–265. doi:10 .25969/mediarep/3370.

Gray, F. (1998) 'Smith the Showman: The Early Years of George Albert Smith', *Film History*, 10 (1), pp. 8–20.

Greenfield, G. R. (2005) 'Computational Aesthetics as a Tool for Creativity', *Proceedings of the 5th Conference on Creativity & Cognition*, pp. 232–235. doi:10.1145/1056224.1056259.

Grba, D. (2017) 'Avoid Setup: Insights and Implications of Generative Cinema', *Technoetic Arts*, 15 (3), pp. 247–260. doi:10.1386/tear.15.3.247_1.

Grobar, M. (2018) '"*The Favourite*" DP Robbie Ryan Brings Fisheye Lenses & Fluid, Roving Camera to Yorgos Lanthimos' Madcap Period Piece', *Deadline* [online]. Available from: https://deadline.com/2018/11/the-favourite-robbie -ryan-yorgos-lanthimos-cinematography-interview-1202494103/ (Accessed 7 February 2020).

Guerlac, S. (2006) *Thinking in Time: An Introduction to Henri Bergson*. Ithaca: Cornell University Press. Available from: http://www.jstor.org/stable/10.75 91/j.ctt1t89kd4 (Accessed 5 May 2020).

Gunning, T. (1990) 'The Cinema of Attraction[s]: Early Film, Its Spectator and the Avant-Garde', in W. Strauven (ed.) *The Cinema of Attractions Reloaded*. 2006 edition. Amsterdam: Amsterdam University Press, pp. 381–388.

Han, B. C. (2017a) *Saving Beauty*. Cambridge: Polity.

Han, B. C. (2017b) The Scent of Time: A Philosophical Essay on the Art of Lingering. Cambridge: Polity.

Han, B. C. (2020) *The Disappearance of Rituals: A Topology of the Present*. First Edition. Cambridge: Polity.

Hanjalic, A. (2002) 'Shot-boundary Detection: Unraveled and Resolved?' *IEEE Transactions on Circuits and Systems for Video Technology*, 12 (2), pp. 90–105. doi:10.1109/76.988656.

Harrison, C. (2018) *Production Meeting*. Personal communication with Gunars Civjans, 6 June 2018.

Harvey, A. & LaPlace, J. (2019) *MegaPixels: Origins, Ethics, and Privacy Implications of Publicly Available Face Recognition Image Datasets* [online]. Available from: https://megapixels.cc/ (Accessed 8 October 2019).

Haugeland, J. (1989) *Artificial Intelligence: The Very Idea*. MIT Press. doi:10.7551/mitpress/1170.001.0001.

Hayles, N. K. (2012) 'How We Think: Transforming Power and Digital Technologies', in David M. Berry (ed.), *Understanding Digital Humanities*. London: Palgrave Macmillan, pp. 42–66. doi:10.1057/9780230371934_3.

He, K., Zhang, X., Ren, S., & Sun, J. (2015) 'Deep Residual Learning for Image Recognition', doi:10.48550/arXiv.1512.03385.

Heffernan. J. A. W. (2004) *Museum of Words: The Poetics of Ekphrasis from Homer to Ashbery*. Chicago: University of Chicago Press.

Heffernan, J. A. W. (1991) 'Ekphrasis and Representation', *New Literary History*, 22 (2), pp. 297–316. doi:10.2307/469040.

Heftberger, A. (2018) 'Introduction', in *Digital Humanities and Film Studies: Quantitative Methods in the Humanities and Social Sciences*. Cham: Springer International Publishing, pp. 1–5. doi:10.1007/978-3-030-02864-0_1.

Herrman, J. (2018) 'It's Almost 2019. Do You Know Where Your Photos Are?', *The New York Times*. 29 November. [online]. Available from: https://www.nytimes.com/2018/11/29/style/digital-photo-storage-purge.html (Accessed 27 February 2020).

Hill, R. (1924) 'A Lens for Whole Sky Photographs', *Quarterly Journal of the Royal Meteorological Society*, 50 (211), 227–235. doi:10.1002/qj.49705021110.

Hoel, A. S. (2018) 'Operative Images. Inroads to a New Paradigm of Media Theory', in *Operative Images: Inroads to a New Paradigm of Media Theory* [Online]. De Gruyter, pp. 11–28. Available from: https://www.degruyter.com/document/doi/10.1515/9783110464979-002/html (Accessed 28 April 2023).

Hoening, F. (2005) 'Defining Computational Aesthetics', in L. Neumann, M. Sbert, B. Gooch, & W. Purgathofer (eds) *Proceedings of the First Eurographics Conference on Computational Aesthetics in Graphics, Visualization and Imaging*, Goslar: Eurographics Association, pp. 13–18. doi:10.2312/COMPAESTH/COMPAESTH05/013-018.

Hong, L. & Yap-Peng, T. (2005) 'An Effective Post-refinement Method for Shot Boundary Detection', *IEEE Transactions on Circuits and Systems for Video Technology* (11), pp. 1407–1421. doi:10.1109/TCSVT.2005.856927.

Horton, A. (2023) 'John Oliver on New AI Programs: "The Potential and the Peril Here Are Huge"'. *The Guardian*, 27 February [online]. Available from: https://www.theguardian.com/tv-and-radio/2023/feb/27/john-oliver-new-ai-programs-potential-peril (Accessed 1 May 2023).

Hubel, D. H. & Wiesel, T. N. (1959) 'Receptive Fields of Single Neurones in the Cat's Striate Cortex', *The Journal of Physiology*, 148 (3), pp. 574–591. doi:10.1113/jphysiol.1959.sp006308.

Huff, C. & Tingley, D. (2015) '"Who Are These People?" Evaluating the Demographic Characteristics and Political Preferences of MTurk Survey Respondents', *Research & Politics*, 2 (3). doi:10.1177/2053168015604648.

Hume, D. (1910) [1757] 'Of the Standard of Taste', in C. W. Eliot (ed.) *English Essays from Sir Philip Sidney to Macaulay*, New York: P. F. Colier & Son, pp. 215–236.

Ignatov, A., Kobyshev, N., Timofte, R., Vanhoey, K., & Van Gool, L. (2017) *DSLR-Quality Photos on Mobile Devices with Deep Convolutional Networks*. doi:10.48550/arXiv.1704.02470.

Ipeirotis, P. G. (2010) 'Analyzing the Amazon Mechanical Turk Marketplace'

REFERENCES

193

[online], *XRDS: Crossroads, The ACM Magazine for Students*. Available from SSRN: https://ssrn.com/abstract=1688194.

Jockers, M. L. (2013) *Macroanalysis: Digital Methods and Literary History*. Urbana: University of Illinois Press.

Johnson, J., Karpati, A. & Li, F.-F. (2015) *DenseCap: Fully Convolutional Localization Networks for Dense Captioning*. doi:10.48550/arXiv.1511.07571.

Jones, J. M. (2009) *The Annotated Godfather*. New York: Black Dog & Leventhal.

Jones, S. E. (2016) 'The Emergence of the Digital Humanities', in Matthew K. Gold & Lauren F. Klein (eds) *Debates in the Digital Humanities 2016*. Minneapolis: University of Minnesota Press.

Jordanous, A. (2014) 'What is Computational Creativity?', *The Creativity Post* [online]. Available from: https://www.creativitypost.com/article/what_is _computational_creativity (Accessed 7 March 2020).

Joyce, R. A. & Bede, L. (2006) 'Temporal Segmentation of Video using Frame and Histogram Space', *IEEE Transactions on Multimedia*, 8 (1), pp. 130–140. doi:10.1109/ICIP.2000.899612.

Jung, E. A. (2019) 'Bong Joon-ho's Dystopia is Already Here', *Vulture* [online]. Available from: https://www.vulture.com/2019/10/bong-joon-ho-parasite .html (Accessed 1 April 2020).

Kermode, M. (2012) *My Cronenberg Top Five.* [online]. Available from: https:// www.bbc.co.uk/blogs/markkermode/entries/a38718f5-ab47-377f-ab0f-9128 3be8a7d7 (Accessed 16 August 2019).

Kingslake, R. (1989) *A History of the Photographic Lens*. Cambridge: Academic Press.

Klare, B. F., Burge, M. J., Klontz, J. C., Vorder Bruegge, R. W., & Jain, A. K. (2012) 'Face Recognition Performance: Role of Demographic Information', *IEEE Transactions on Information Forensics and Security*, 7 (6), pp. 1789–1801. doi:10.1109/TIFS.2012.2214212.

Krishna, R., Zhu, Y., Groth, O., Johnson, J., Hata, K., Kravitz, J., Chen, S., Kalantidis, Y., Li, L.-J., Shamma, D. A., Bernstein, M. S., & Li, F.-. (2017) 'Visual Genome: Connecting Language and Vision Using Crowdsourced Dense Image Annotations', *International Journal of Computer Vision*, 123 (1), pp. 32–73. doi:10.48550/arXiv.1602.07332.

Krizhevsky, A., Sutskever, I. & Hinton, G. E. (2012) 'ImageNet Classification with Deep Convolutional Neural Networks', in F. Pereira, C. J. C. Burges, L. Bottou. & K. Q. Weinberger (eds) *Advances in Neural Information Processing Systems 25*, pp. 1097–1105. [online]. Available from: http://papers.nips.cc /paper/4824-imagenet-classification-with-deep-convolutional-neural-networ ks.pdf (Accessed 8 July 2019).

Kuhn, V. (2018) 'Images on the Move: Analytics for a Mixed Methods Approach', J. Sayers (ed.) *The Routledge Companion to Media Studies and Digital Humanities*. New York & Abingdon: Routledge. pp. 300–309.

Kuhn, V., Craig, A., Simeone, M., Puthanveetil Satheesan, S., & Marini, L. (2015) 'The VAT: Enhanced Video Analysis', *Proceedings of the 2015 XSEDE*

Conference: Scientific Advancements Enabled by Enhanced Cyberinfrastructure. doi:10.1145/2792745.2792756.

Laskin, N. (2015) 'Watch: Video Essay Explores the Impact Of Different Aspect Ratios in Film', *IndieWire* [online]. Available from: https://www.indiewire.com/2015/09/watch-video-essay-explores-the-impact-of-different-aspect-ratios-in-film-260072/ (Accessed 18 May 2020).

Last, M. & Usyskin, A. (2015) 'Listen to the Sound of Data', in A. K. Baughman, J. Gao, J.-Y. Pan, & V. A. Petrushin (eds.) *Multimedia Data Mining and Analytics: Disruptive Innovation*, pp. 419–446, doi:10.1007/978-3-319-14998-1_19.

Lebo, H. (1997) *The Godfather Legacy*. New York: Simon & Schuster.

LeCun, Y. et al (1989) 'Backpropagation Applied to Handwritten Zip Code Recognition', *Neural Computation*, 1 (4), pp. 541–551. doi:10.1162/neco.1989.1.4.541.

LeCun, Y. et al (2015) 'Deep Learning', *Nature*, 521 (7553), pp. 436–444. doi:10.1038/nature14539.

Lee, A. (2014) *An Interview with Adam Lee, BBC Archive Expert* [online]. Available from: http://www.bbc.co.uk/archive/tv_archive.shtml (Accessed 15 October 2018).

Lee, C. (2018) 'Extreme Close-ups Are Defining the Current Movie Moment', *Vulture* [online]. Available from: https://www.vulture.com/2018/11/extreme-close-ups-are-defining-the-current-movie-moment.html (Accessed 27 April 2020).

Lessig, L. (2003) 'The Creative Commons', *Florida Law Review* [online], 55 (3), pp. 763–777. Available from: https://scholarship.law.ufl.edu/flr/vol55/iss3/1.

Li, F. (2019) *Where Did ImageNet Come From?*, The Photographers Gallery: Unthinking Photography [online]. Available from: https://unthinking.photography/articles/where-did-imagenet-come-from (Accessed 4 February 2020).

Li, F. (2010) '*ImageNet: Crowdsourcing, Benchmarking & Other Cool Things*' [online]. Available from: http://image-net.org/papers/ImageNet_2010.pdf, pp. 18–25. (Accessed 17 May 2019).

Lin, T.-Y., Maire, M., Belongie, S., Hays, J., Perona, P., Ramanan, D., Dollár, P., & Zitnick, C. L. (2014) 'Microsoft Coco: Common Objects in Context', in D. Fleet, T. Pajdla, B. Schiele, & T. Tuytelaars (eds) *ECCV 2014. Lecture Notes in Computer Science*. Springer: Cham, pp. 740–755. [online] Available from: https://doi.org/10.1007/978-3-319-10602-1_48.

Litman, B. R. (1983) 'Predicting Success of Theatrical Movies: An Empirical Study', *Journal of Popular Culture*, 16 (4), pp. 159–175. doi:10.1111/j.0022-3840.1983.1604_159.x.

Lohr, S. (2009) 'A $1 Million Research Bargain for Netflix, and Maybe a Model for Others', *The New York Times*. 21 September. [online]. Available from: https://www.nytimes.com/2009/09/22/technology/internet/22netflix.html (Accessed 4 December 2018).

Lopes, D. M. (2016) Four Arts of Photography: An Essay in Philosophy. New York: John Wiley & Sons.

REFERENCES

Maaten, L. van der & Hinton, G. (2008) 'Visualizing Data using t-SNE', *Journal of Machine Learning Research*, 9 (Nov), pp. 2579–2605.

Machado, P. & Cardoso, A. (1998) 'Computing Aesthetics', in: F. M. de Oliveira (ed.) *Advances in Artificial Intelligence. SBIA 1998. Lecture Notes in Computer Science*, vol 1515, Berlin: Springer, pp. 219–228. doi:10.1007/10692710_23.

Machado, P., Romero, J., & Manaris, B. (2008) 'Experiments in Computational Aesthetics', in J. Romero & P. Machado (eds) *The Art of Artificial Evolution: A Handbook on Evolutionary Art and Music*, Berlin: Springer, pp. 381–415. doi:10.1007/978-3-540-72877-1_18.

Manovich, L. (1999) 'Database as Symbolic Form', *Convergence*, 5 (2), pp. 80–99. doi:10.1177/135485659900500206.

Manovich, L. (2007) 'Deep Remixability', *Artifact: Journal of Design Practice*, 1 (2), pp. 76–84. doi:10.1080/17493460701206751.

Manovich, L. (2009) 'Cultural Analytics: Visualising Cultural Patterns in the Era of "More Media"' [online]. Available from: http://manovich.net/content/04-projects/063-cultural-analytics-visualizing-cultural-patterns/60_article_2009.pdf. (Accessed 3 March 2021).

Manovich, L. (2013) Visualizing Vertov. *Russian Journal of Communication*, 5 (1), pp. 44–55. doi:10.1080/19409419.2013.775546.

Manovich, L. (2016) 'The Science of Culture? Social Computing, Digital Humanities and Cultural Analytics', *Journal of Cultural Analytics*. doi:10.22148/16.004.

Manovich, L. & Kratky, A. (2005) *Soft Cinema: Navigating the Database.* Cambridge: MIT Press.

Maynard, P. (1997) *The Engine of Visualization: Thinking through Photography.* Ithaca & London: Cornell University Press.

McCarty, W. (2014 [2005]) *Humanities Computing.* London: Palgrave Macmillan.

McInnes, L. et al (2020) UMAP: Uniform Manifold Approximation and Projection for Dimension Reduction. doi:10.48550/arXiv.1802.03426.

Metawelle, C. (2009) *Analysis of 100M CC-Licensed Images on Flickr. Creative Commons* [online]. Available from: https://creativecommons.org/2009/03/25/analysis-of-100m-cc-licensed-images-on-flickr/ (Accessed 16 October 2019).

Mitchell, W. J. T. (1995) *Picture Theory: Essays on Verbal and Visual Representation.* Chicago: University of Chicago Press.

Mittell, J. (2019) 'Videographic Criticism as a Digital Humanities Method', in Matthew K. Gold & Lauren F. Klein (eds) *Debates in the Digital Humanities 2019.* Minneapolis: University of Minnesota Press, pp. 224–242. doi:10.5749/j.ctvg251hk.23.

Moretti, F. (2013) *Distant Reading.* London: Verso.

Moretti, F. (2007) Graphs, Maps, Trees: Abstract Models for a Literary History. London: Verso.

Moretti, F. (2000) 'Conjectures on World Literature', *New Left Review* (1), pp. 54–68. Available from: https://newleftreview.org/issues/ii1/articles/franco-moretti-conjectures-on-world-literature (Accessed 2 January 2019).

Narayan, A. et al (2021) Assessing Single-cell Transcriptomic Variability

Through Density-preserving Data Visualization', *Nature Biotechnology*, 39 (6), pp. 765–774. doi:10.1038/s41587-020-00801-7.

Narayanan, A. & Shmatikov, V. (2006) *How to Break Anonymity of the Netflix Prize Dataset*. doi:10.48550/arXiv.cs/0610105.

Nazeri, K. et al (2019) 'EdgeConnect: Generative Image Inpainting with Adversarial Edge Learning', doi:10.48550/arXiv.1901.00212.

Nicolaescu, L. I. (2007) *Lectures on the Geometry of Manifolds*. Singapore: World Scientific.

Noble, S. U. (2018) Algorithms of Oppression: How Search Engines Reinforce Racism. New York: NYU Press.

NVIDIA (2020) *Ampere Architecture: The Heart of the Modern Data Center* [online]. Available from: https://www.nvidia.com/en-gb/data-center/nvidia-ampere-gpu-architecture/ (Accessed 19 May 2020).

OFCOM. (2017) *Annual Report on the BBC*. [online]. Available from: https://www.ofcom.org.uk/__data/assets/pdf_file/0013/124420/BBC-annex-2-performance.pdf (Accessed 17 May 2019).

OFCOM (2018) *Media Nations UK Report 2018*. [online]. Available from: https://www.ofcom.org.uk/research-and-data/tv-radio-and-on-demand/media-nations (Accessed 18 May 2019).

Pang, B. & Lee, L. (2005) Seeing Stars: Exploiting Class Relationships for Sentiment Categorization with Respect to Rating Scales. doi:10.48550/arXiv.cs/0506075.

Pantenburg, V. (2016) 'Working Images: Harun Farocki and the Operational Image', in Jens Eder & Charlotte Klonk (eds) *Image Operations: Visual Media and Political Conflict* [online]. Manchester: Manchester University Press, p. 0. Available from: https://doi.org/10.7228/manchester/9781526107213.003.0004 (Accessed 28 April 2023).

Papert, S. A. (1966) *The Summer Vision Project* [online]. Available from: https://dspace.mit.edu/handle/1721.1/6125 (Accessed 31 July 2020).

Parikka, J. (2023) *Operational Images: From the Visual to the Invisual*. Minneapolis: University of Minnesota Press.

Pariser, E. (2011) The Filter Bubble: How the New Personalized Web is Changing What we Read and How we Think. London: Penguin.

Pasquinelli, M. (2015) 'Italian Operaismo and the Information Machine', *Theory, Culture & Society*, 32 (3), pp. 49–68.

Pearlman, K. (2015) *Cutting Rhythms: Intuitive Film Editing*. New York: CRC Press.

Peres, M. R. (2007) The Focal Encyclopedia of Photography: Digital Imaging, Theory and Applications, History, and Science. Waltham: Focal Press.

Petric, V. (1978) 'Dziga Vertov as Theorist', *Cinema Journal*, 18 (1), pp. 29–44.

Pfeiffer, S. et al (1998) 'The MoCA Project', in Jürgen Dassow & Rudolf Kruse (eds) *Informatik '98*. Informatik aktuell. Berlin, Heidelberg: Springer, pp. 329–338. doi:10.1007/978-3-642-72283-7_33.

Phillips, D. M. (2009) 'Photography and Causation: Responding to Scruton's Scepticism', *The British Journal of Aesthetics*, 49 (4), pp. 327–340.

REFERENCES

Piotte, M. & Chabbert, M. (2009) The Pragmatic Theory Solution to the Netflix Grand Prize. *Netflix Prize Documentation.*

Porter, T. M. (1996) Trust in Numbers: The Pursuit of Objectivity in Science and Public Life. Princeton: Princeton University Press.

Ramesh, A. et al (2021) *Zero-Shot Text-to-Image Generation.* doi:10.48550/arXiv.2102.12092.

Ramesh, A. et al (2022) Hierarchical Text-Conditional Image Generation with CLIP Latents. doi:10.48550/arXiv.2204.06125.

Rappaz, J., Catasta, M., West, R., & Aberer, K. (2018) 'Latent Structure in Collaboration: The Case of Reddit r/place', doi:10.48550/arXiv.1804.05962.

Ray, R. B. (2001) How a Film Theory Got Lost and Other Mysteries in Cultural Studies. Bloomington & Indianapolis: Indiana University Press.

Redfern, N. (2012) 'The Log-normal Distribution is not an Appropriate Parametric Model for Shot Length Distributions of Hollywood Films', *Digital Scholarship in the Humanities*, 30 (1), pp. 137–151. doi:10.1093/llc/fqs066.

Redfern, N. (2013) 'Film Studies and Statistical Literacy', *Media Education Research Journal*, 4 (1), pp. 58–71.

Redfern, N. (2014) Quantitative Methods and the Study of Film [Invited lecture], University of Glasgow, 14 May.

Roberts, L. G. (1963) *Machine Perception of Three-dimensional Solids.* Unpublished PhD thesis. Massachusetts Institute of Technology. Available from: https://dspace.mit.edu/bitstream/handle/1721.1/11589/33959125-MIT.pdf (Accessed 5 May 2017).

Rodowick, D. N. (2007) *The Virtual Life of Film.* Cambridge: Harvard University Press.

Rodriguez, H. (2019) *ERRANT: The Kinetic Propensity of Images.* [online]. Available from: http://concept-script.com/Errant/ (Accessed 24 April 2020).

Rombach, R. et al (2021) High-Resolution Image Synthesis with Latent Diffusion Models. doi:10.48550/arXiv.2112.10752

Rosenblatt, F. (1957) *The Perceptron, a Perceiving and Recognizing Automaton* (Project PARA). Cornell Aeronautical Laboratory Report No. 85–460–1.

Rytz, R. (2019) *Northern Mexican Territory* [online]. Available from: https://draemm.li/various/place-atlas/?id=628 (Accessed 18 May 2020).

Saharia, C. et al (2022) Photorealistic Text-to-Image Diffusion Models with Deep Language Understanding. doi:10.48550/arXiv.2205.11487

Salt, B. (1974) 'Statistical Style Analysis of Motion Pictures', *Film Quarterly*, 28 (1), pp. 13–22. doi:10.2307/1211438.

Salt, B. (1992) Film Style and Technology: History and Analysis. London: Starword.

Salt, B. (2006) Moving into Pictures: More on Film History, Style, and Analysis. London: Starword.

Schäfer, M. T. & Es, K. van (eds) (2017) *The Datafied Society: Studying Culture through Data.* Amsterdam: Amsterdam University Press. doi:10.5117/978904 8531011.

Schnapp, J. & Presner, T. (2009) *The Digital Humanities Manifesto 2.0* [online]. Available from: https://jeffreyschnapp.com/wp-content/uploads/2011/10/Manifesto_V2.pdf (Accessed 1 May 2018).

Shih, M.-L. et al (2020) '3D Photography using Context-aware Layered Depth Inpainting', doi:10.48550/arXiv.2004.04727.

Shon, J.-H. et al (2014) 'Classifying Movies Based on Audience Perceptions: MTI Framework and Box Office Performance', *Journal of Media Economics*, 27 (2), pp. 79–106. doi:10.1080/08997764.2014.903959.

Siegel, T. (2019) 'Making of "*1917*": How Sam Mendes Filmed a "Ticking Clock Thriller"', *The Hollywood Reporter* [online]. Available from: https://www.hollywoodreporter.com/features/making-1917-how-sam-mendes-filmed-a-ticking-clock-thriller-1263469 (Accessed 18 May 2020).

Singel, R. (2009) 'Netflix Spilled Your *Brokeback Mountain* Secret, Lawsuit Claims', *Wired* [online]. Available from: https://www.wired.com/2009/12/netflix-privacy-lawsuit/ (Accessed 24 January 2019).

Simondon, G. (2017) [1958] *On the Mode of Existence of Technical Objects*. Minneapolis: University of Minnesota Press.

Smith, A. R. (2021) *A Biography of the Pixel*. Cambridge: MIT Press.

Sotheby's (2019) *Artificial Intelligence and the Art of Mario Klingemann* [online]. Available from: https://www.sothebys.com/en/articles/artificial-intelligence-and-the-art-of-mario-klingemann (Accessed 6 March 2019).

Stability AI (2022) 'Stable Diffusion Launch Announcement', *Stability AI* [online]. Available from: https://stability.ai/blog/stable-diffusion-announcement (Accessed 1 May 2023).

Stiny, G. & Gips, J. (1971) 'Shape Grammars and the Algorithmic Specification of Painting and Sculpture', *IFIP Congress*, pp. 1460–1465.

Szegedy, C. et al (2014) 'Going Deeper with Convolutions', doi: 10.48550/arXiv.1409.4842.

Tarkovsky, A. (1989) *Sculpting in Time: Reflections on the Cinema*. Austin: University of Texas Press.

Thein, M. (2013) *Review: The 2013 Ricoh GR* [online]. Available from: https://blog.mingthein.com/2013/05/06/review-2013-ricoh-gr-digital-v/ (Accessed 17 February 2020).

Thomee, B., Shamma, D. A., Friedland, G., Elizalde, B., Ni, K., Poland, D., Bordth, D., & Li, J.-A. (2016) 'YFCC100M: The New Data in Multimedia Research', *Communications of the ACM*, 59 (2), pp. 64–73.

Thompson, A. (2018) 'Inside the Obsessive World of Alfonso Cuaron and His "Roma" Production Design', *IndieWire* [online]. Available from: https://www.indiewire.com/2018/12/roma-behind-the-scenes-production-design-alfonso-cuaron-exclusive-video-1202029407/ (Accessed 18 May 2020).

Thompson, K. (1988) *Breaking the Glass Armor: Neoformalist Film Analysis*. Princeton: Princeton University Press.

Thompson, K. (2005) Herr Lubitsch Goes to Hollywood: German and American Film after World War I. Amsterdam: Amsterdam University Press.

REFERENCES

Tode, T. & Wurm, B. (2006 [1947]) *Dziga Vertov: The Vertov Collection at the Austrian Film Museum*. Austrian Film Museum/SYNEMA.

Tohline, M. (2021) 'A Supercut of Supercuts: Aesthetics, Histories, Databases'. *Open Screens* 4 (1), p. 8.

Tronti, M. (1962) 'La fabbrica e la società'. *Quaderni Rossi*, pp. 21–31.

Tsivian, Y. (2009) 'Cinemetrics, Part of the Humanities' Cyberinfrastructure', in Michael Ross et al (eds) *Digital Tools in Media Studies: Analysis and Research. An Overview*. Bielefeld: transcript Verlag, pp. 93–102. doi:10 .1515/9783839410233-007.

Tukey, J. W. (1962) 'The Future of Data Analysis', *The Annals of Mathematical Statistics*. 33 (1), pp. 1–67.

Turvey, M. (2014) 'Vertov, the View from Nowhere, and the Expanding Circle', *October*. 148, pp. 79–102.

Udden, J. (2009) Child of the Long Take: Alfonso Cuaron's Film Aesthetics in the Shadow of Globalization. *Style*, 43 (1), pp. 26–44. doi:10.5325/style.43.1.0026.

Vallance, C. (2023) 'AI Image Creator Faces UK and US Legal Challenges', *BBC News*, 18 January [online]. Available from: https://www.bbc.com/news/tech nology-64285227 (Accessed 1 May 2023).

Van Leeuwen, T. (1985) 'Rhythmic Structure of the Film Text', in Teun A. Van Dijk (ed.) *Discourse and Communication: New Approaches to the Analysis of Mass Media Discourse and Communication*. Berlin: W. de Gruyter, pp. 216–232. doi:10.1515/9783110852141.216.

Vaswani, A. et al (2017) 'Attention is All You Need', in I. Guyon et al (eds) Advances in Neural Information Processing Systems 30: Annual Conference on Neural Information Processing Systems 2017 (December 4–9), Long Beach, CA.

Vertov, D. (1984 [1922]) *Kino-Eye: The Writings of Dziga Vertov*. A. Michelson (ed.). Berkeley, Los Angeles & London: University of California Press.

Virilio, P. (1994) *The Vision Machine*. Bloomington: Indiana University Press.

Walden, S. (2005) 'Objectivity in Photography', *The British Journal of Aesthetics*, 45 (3), pp. 258–272.

Weizenbaum, J. (1976) Computer Power and Human Reason: From Judgment to Calculation. San Francisco: W. H. Freeman.

Wickman, F. (2015) 'What Wes Anderson and P.T. Anderson have Taken from Jonathan Demme', *Slate Magazine* [online]. Available from: https://slate.com /culture/2015/04/jonathan-demme-close-up-supercut-shows-what-pt-and erson-and-wes-anderson-have-taken-from-the-director-video.html (Accessed 27 April 2020).

Wieczorek, M. (2019) 'What I Think About When I Think About Focal Lengths', *Medium* [online]. Available from: https://medium.com/ice-cream-geometry /focal-lengths-1a281a3509ed (Accessed 17 February 2020).

Wold, S., Esbensen, K., & Geladi, P. (1987) 'Principal Component Analysis', *Chemometrics and Intelligent Laboratory Systems*, 2 (1–3), pp. 37–52.

Wright, R. (2010) *The Value of Everything* [online]. Available from: https://www

.bbc.co.uk/rd/blog/2010-06-the-value-of-everything (Accessed 22 October 2018).

Yang, Y., Lin, H., Yu, Z., Paris, S., & Yu, J. (2016) 'Virtual DSLR: High Quality Dynamic Depth-of-Field Synthesis on Mobile Platforms', *Electronic Imaging*, pp. 181–189.

Young, P. (2010) 'Media on Display: A Telegraphic History of Early American Cinema', in L. Gitelman (ed.) *New Media, 1740–1915*. Cambridge: MIT Press.

Youngblood, G. (2020) *Expanded Cinema: Fiftieth Anniversary Edition*. New York: Fordham University Press.

Zylinska, J. (2017) *Nonhuman Photography*. Cambridge & London: MIT Press.

Films and Television

Anderson, W. (2014) *The Grand Budapest Hotel*

BBC (2018) *Made by Machine: When AI Met the Archive*

Carruth, S. (2013) *Upstream Color*

Coppola, F. (1972) *The Godfather*

Cuarón, A. (2018) *Roma*

Demme, J. (1991) *The Silence of the Lambs*

Demme, J. (1993) *Philadelphia*

Demme, J. (1998) *Beloved*

Frampton, H. (1970) *Zorns Lemma*

Goldberg, R. (2010) *Jaws: The Inside Story*

Kon, S. (2006) *Paprika*

Lanthimos, Y. (2018) *The Favourite*

Nolan, C. (2017) *Dunkirk*

On Story: 414 (2018) *Jonathan Demme in Conversation with Paul Thomas Anderson*

Ozu, Y. (1953) *Tokyo Story*

Slade, D. (2005) *Hard Candy*

Spielberg, S. (1975) *Jaws*

Spielberg, S. (1993) *Jurassic Park*

Tarkovsky, A. (1975) *Mirror*

Villeneuve, D (2017) *Blade Runner 2049*

Art and Design

Maigret, N. (2014) *Pirate Cinema* [online]. Available from: http://thepirate cinema.com/

Marclay, C. (2010) *The Clock*

Marclay, C. (1995) *Telephones*

Wardle, J. (2017) *r/place* [online]. Available from: https://www.reddit.com /r/place

REFERENCES   201

Tools and Datasets

Arnold, Taylor, T. (2019) *Distant Viewing Toolkit.* [online]. Available from: https://distant-viewing.github.io/dvt/

Castellano, B. (2014) *PyScene Detect* [online] Available from http://scenedetect.com/

ChatGPT (2023) [online] Available from: https://openai.com/blog/chatgpt

COCO (2015) [online] Available from: https://cocodataset.org/

Densecap (2016) [online] Available from https://cs.stanford.edu/people/karpathy/densecap/

Flickr 1024 (2019). [online]. Available from: https://yingqianwang.github.io/Flickr1024/.

ImageNet. (2009) [online]. Available from: http://www.image-net.org/.

Kaggle (2019) *Wine Quality Dataset* [online]. Available from: https://www.kaggle.com/danielpanizzo/wine-quality

movie2vec. (2017) [online]. Available from: https://github.com/leaprovenzano/movie2vec

Rogers & Cairo (2020) *TwoTone* [online] Available from: https://github.com/datavized/twotone

Stable Diffusion 1.5 (2022) [online] Available from: https://stability.ai/

Tsivian, Y. & Civjans, G. (2005) *Cinemetrics* [online]. Available from: http://cinemetrics.lv/index.php

Visual Genome (2017) [online]. Available from: https://visualgenome.org/.

Index

Note: *Italics* denote a figure.

'3D photography', 124
5 × 3 relational matrix, *103*, 104
50mm 'normal' lenses, 69–70
1917 (2019), 118

Academy awards, 111
Adobe Photoshop, 127
aesthetic judgement, theories of, 13, 149
aesthetic preferences
  and digital traces, 30
  recommender systems *see* recommender
    systems
  subjectivity, 149
aggregators (algorithms), 89
Agre, Philip, 12–13, 14, 145, 146–7, 157
AI: More than Human (2019), 162
algorithmic films, 141–3, 159
algorithms
  and the 'infinite film', 135
  SVMs, 132
Alquati, Romano, 56
Amazon Mechanical Turk (AMT), 45,
    48–50, 52
analogue photography, 83
analytical editing, Hollywood classics, 102,
    106
Anderson, Paul Thomas, 92
Anderson, Wes
  big close-ups (BCU), 92
  Grand Budapest Hotel, The, 95
animals, non-human, visual perception,
    70, 71
animation, 118, 124
annotation, digital tools for, 9
annotators (algorithms), 89
anthropocentrism, 71, 142
Apple, 67–8, 75

applied visionics, 11–12
archives, 25, 26, 28
  see also BBC; MbM (*Made by Machine*)
Arnheim, Rudolf, 84
Arnold, Taylor, 88–9, 90–1, 97, 115
Artificial Intelligence (AI)
  cinema in the age of, 2–3
  computer vision *see* computer vision
  corporate, 133
  creative applications of, 161–2
  'Good Old-Fashioned', 132
  public perceptions of, 145, 147
  and re-encoding of cultural artefacts,
    137
  see also critical technical practice; Deep
    Learning; inductive computing;
    language; MbM (*Made by Machine*)
assemblages, 49
Atkinson, S., 10
Attenborough, David, 92–3
attention mechanisms, 121
automatic segmentation, 35
average shot lengths (ASLs), 8–9

back propagation algorithm, 7
Balaz, B., 94
Barthes, Roland, 111
Bazin, André, 60, 63
BBC, 46–7
  2006 Framework Agreement, 32
  commitment to public interest, 31–2
  first experimental TV programme, 15
  gender bias, 47
  iPlayer, 26–7
  nature documentaries, 92–3
  Television Archive, 17; *see also* MbM
    (*Made by Machine*); object detection

INDEX

203

BBC Four, 26
  MbM, 16–17
  viewership, 49
BBC R&D
  Content Analysis Toolkit, 35
  MbM *see* MbM (*Made by Machine*)
BBC4.1 AI-TV, 16
BellKor's Pragmatic Chaos, 28–9, 30
Beloved (1998), 93
Bender, E. M., 166, 167
Bense, M., 13, 149
Bergson, Henri, 115–16
bias *see* demographic bias; gender
  representation
Big Chaos, 29
big close-ups (BCU), 91, 92–3, 95
Birkoff, G. D., 13, 149
Blackwell, Alan, 137–8
Blade Runner 2049 (2017), 170–1
Bong Joon-Ho, 100
Bordwell, D., 97, 102, 103, 106, 110, 133
Borges, J. L., *The Library of Babel*, 133–4,
  138
Bradshaw, Peter, 154–6
Brakhage, Stan, 85
brand packaging, 36
Bresson, Robert, 102
Burch, Noël, 101–2, 110
  continuity matrix, 103–4, 106–9, 112

camera motion, and DenseCap, 41–2
cameras, photographic
  lenses and focusing *see* lenses,
    photographic
  see also DSLR cameras
candidate shots, 95
Canon (cameras), 74–7
Carroll, N., 133, 151–2, 155, 157
Carruth, Shane, *Upstream Color*, 154–6
Casablanca (1942), 99
ChatGPT, 164–6
Chevalier Meniscus, 65
chromatic aberration, 65
chronophotography, 123
Cinematheque of Babel, 134, 138
cinematic time, 83–5, 115–16, 122–3; *see
  also* continuity editing
cinematographers, 99–100

Cinemetrics, 9, 103, 115
Civjans, Gunars, 9
classical analytical approach, 114
CLIP Interrogator, 170
close-ups (CU), 88, 91, 93–4; *see also* big
  close-ups (BCU)
Colangelo, D., 163–4
Collins, H. M., 166–7
colour analysis, 90
colours
  chromatic aberration, 65
  see also pixel colour values
community detection, 30
computational aesthetics, 13–14; *see also*
  critical technical practice
computational chronographs, 124–5
computational critics, film criticism, 156–7
computational gaze, 4–5
computational poetics of film, 98
computer graphics market, 126
computer programs, 121
computer vision, 6, 38
  critical view of, 63
  inductive photography, 72
  mind-independence mechanical process,
    61
  symbolic abstraction, 89
  see also critical technical practice;
    Distant Viewing Toolkit (DVT);
    inductive computing; machine vision
constructive editing, 102
continuity editing, computational analysis,
  99–113
contrastive learning, 126
Coppola, F. F., *The Godfather*, 104–9, 111
copyright, 35–6, 148, 168
corporate AI, and cultural data, 133
Costello, D., 62
'Creative AI', 148
Creative Commons initiative, 46
Creative Commons licences, 51, 52
creative industries, AI editing tools, 127
critical technical practice, 11–15
critics/criticism
  component operations, 155, 157–8
  computational, 132, 156–7
  individual, 131–2; *see also* Bradshaw,
    Peter; Kael, Pauline; Kermode, Mark

204 CINEMA AND MACHINE VISION

critics/criticism (*cont.*)
recommender systems, 149, 151
social dimension of, 151–3
see also ChatGPT; film criticism
crowdsourcing, 148
AMT, 48–50
Cuarón, Alfonso, 118
cultural analytics, 163
cultural production, datafication of, 132–3
Currie, Gregory, 61

Daguerre, Louis, 65
Daigle, Allain, 69–70
datafication of cultural production, 132–3
datamatic time, 122–3, 124, 126–7
datasets, 25, 26, 33, 38, 50; *see also* gender
representation; ImageNet; MbM
(*Made by Machine*); Netflix
découpage, 101–2
Deep Learning, 7, 8, 45, 51, 121–2, 126–7,
132
deepfakes, 122
Delhomme, Benoit, 92
Demme, Jonathan, 93–4, 95
demographic bias in datasets, 50, 51; *see
also* gender representation
DenseCap, 38–44, 52–5
misdetections, 40–4
and Visual Genome, 47–8
Dewdney, Andrew, 71
digital cameras, and EXIF metadata, 73
digital humanities, 7–9, 10, 91; *see also*
critical technical practice
digital photography, 83
Digital Single Lens Reflex (DSLR) *see*
DSLR cameras
digital traces, aesthetic preferences, 30
digital video, recent trends, 2
dimensionality reduction, 139
directors, temporal structuring of films,
100–1
dissolves, 104
distant reading, 114–15
distant viewing, 87–8, 139
Distant Viewing Toolkit (DVT), 88–9,
90–8, 115
Doane, Mary Anne, 91, 94, 97, 116,
123–4

documentaries
continuity editing, 100
nature, 92–3
dolly zooms, simulations, 124, 125–6
Dreyfus, Hubert, 133
DSLR cameras, 74–8
focal length classifier, 79–80
Dunkirk (2017), 99
parallel editing, 110
sonification, 109–11
duration, 115–16

Eagleton, Terry, 152–3
ectocinema, 126
editors/editing, 100, 111
continuity editing, 99–113
ekphrasis, 170
elision, 110
ellipsis, 88
embeddings
film criticism, 156
historical overview, 140
Entangled Realities (2020), 162
Epic Games, 126
Es, K. van, 8
EXIF metadata, 72
analysis, 73–8
experts, 131–2, 133
exposure times, 80
Eye/Machine (2000–2002), 141–2

face detection, 88, 90, 91
face identification, 89
faces, images of, and GAN, 122
Farocki, Harun, *Eye/Machine*, 141–2
Favourite, The (2018), 69
film analysis
critics, 89
see also Distant Viewing Toolkit
(DVT)
film archives, and datasets, 26
film criticism
Bradshaw on *Upstream Color*, 154–6
component operations, 155, 157–8, 159
sentiment analysis, 154, 155
social dimension of, 152–3
'wet embeddings', 156
see also critics/criticism

INDEX

205

film editors, 99–100; *see also* continuity editing
film poetics *see* distant viewing
film scholarship/studies, 4, 8–10, 91
Flickr, 44, 46, 51, 54, 72, 73
Floridi, L., 122
focal length *see* lenses, photographic; MbM (*Made by Machine*)
forensics, 61
formalism in film scholarship, 87, 88, 124–7
frames, 116, 120–1; *see also* synthetic imagery
framing/frame
and DenseCap, 41–2
shape of, 94–5
Frampton, Hollis, *Zorns Lemma*, 135–6
French New Wave, 102
Frierson, M., 5 × 3 relational matrix, 103–4
Frizot, M., 123
Fukushima, Kunihiko, 6–7

gaming, 126
gender representation
BBC archive, 47
BBC Four, 49
in datasets, 46–8, 50
DenseCap, 40–3
generative adversarial networks (GANs), 122, 127
generative revisionist approaches, 114
Gitelman, Lisa, 112
Godfather, The (1972), 102, 104–9, 110
Grand Budapest Hotel, The (2014), 95, *96*
Grant, C., 10
Griffith, D. W., 91
Grizzly Man (2005), 100

Hello, Robot (2019), 161–2
Herzog, Werner, 100
Hill, Robin, 68
Hitchcock, Alfred
Rope, 118
Vertigo, 125
Hollywood cinema, 70, 92, 101, 102
Huawei P series, 67
Huff, C., 49–50

Hume, David, *Of the Standard of Taste*, 149–51
hyper archive, 133–4, 137–8

image captioning *see* DenseCap; Flickr; ImageNet; MS-COCO; Visual Genome
image generation, 127; *see also* operational images
image in-painting, 127
ImageNet, 44–6, 60
Inception (2010), 138
inductive computing, 158
early AI art market, 161–2
interactive data practices, 139–40
processing of films and television, 138
inductive photography, 72
inductive vision, 55
information aesthetics, 13, 149
Instagram, 67, 95
interactionist approach to AI, 157
iPlayer, 26–7

Jahrer, Michael, 29
JanBot, 148
Jaws (1975), 100–1, 124–5
Jockers, Matthew, 88, 115
Jones, S. E., 8

Kael, Pauline, 165–6
Kermode, Mark, 165
Kon, Satoshi, 118
Krizhevsky, A., 45
Kusch, M., 166–7

labour, in the digital economy, 55–6
language, in AI, 146–7
large language models (LLMs), 164–8
Large Scale Visual Recognition Challenge (ILSVRC), 45
Lee, Spike, 92
lenses, photographic, 63–8
50mm 'normal', 69–70
focal length, 67
mobile phones, 67–8
refashioning of normal, 71
ultra-wide, 68–9
Li, Fei-Fei, 45–6, 60

long shots (LS), 88, 91
Lynch, David, 85

machine learning
  embeddings *see* embeddings
  see also MbM (*Made by Machine*)
machine vision
  and image synthesis and generation, 126
  see also computer vision
macroscope, 172–3
Made by Machine see MbM
Malick, Terence, 156
Manovich, Lev, 4, 8
Marclay, Christian, 'The Clock', 39
Marey, Étienne-Jules, 123–4
MbM (*Made by Machine*), 15–18, 26,
  32–7, 44, 46–7, 72–4
  focal length classifier, 79–80
  four sections, 33–4
  functions of critic or editor, 145–6, 148
  project breakdown, 35
  see also Visual Genome
Mendes, Sam, 118
metadata, 56; *see also* EXIF metadata
Microsoft, 165
mind-independence mechanical process,
  61
mobile phones
  cameras, 67–8
  shape of frame, 95
MoCA project, 9
Moretti, Franco, 4, 88, 114–15, 116
motion, scientific study of, 123
motion estimation, 89, 90
motion photographs, 127
Movie Database, 148
MovieLens, 148
MS-COCO, 51, 52
Mulholland Drive (2001), 85
museum exhibitions, 161–2

narrative continuity, 114, 115
Nazeri, K., 124
neocognitron, 6–7
neoformalism, 87, 97
Netflix, 28–30
network analysis, 30
neural networks, 6–7, 132

New Theory of photography, 62, 71
Nikon (cameras), 73, 74–6
Nokia, 67–8
Nolan, Christopher, *Dunkirk*, 109–11
NVIDIA (chipset manufacturer), 126

object detection, 38–40, 88; *see also*
  DenseCap
OFCOM, 27
Open AI, 164–5
operaistas, 55–6
operational images, 141–2
optics, chromatic aberration, 65
Ozu, Y., *Tokyo Story*, 1

Papert, Seymour, 6
parallel editing, 102, 110
Parasite (2019), 100
PASCAL VOC, 52
Pasquinelli, Matteo, 56
perceptron, 6
personalisation, 151
Petzval, Joseph, 65
Petzval Portrait, 65, 67
Philadelphia (1993), 93
photographers
  and machine vision, 53–5, 56–7
  see also lenses, photographic
photography
  'aboutness', 78
  deepfakes, 122
  epistemic advantage, 61–3, 71
  forensic uses, 61
  metadata, 56, 73
  New Theory, 62, 71
  as 'non-canonical images', 55
  and realism, 60, 61
photography platform *see* Flickr; Runway
  ML
Pirate Cinema, The (2014), 148
pixel colour values, 35, 117, 119–20
pixels, 124
  flow of, 117–18
  plotting of, 124
point of view shots, 100–1
post-humanists, 141, 142
post-production editing, big close-ups
  (BCU), 92

INDEX

Pragmatic Chaos, 28–9, 30
pre-editing, 100
Presner, T., 7–8
Principal Component Analysis (PCA), 139

quantification, 131, 133
quantitative analysis of film, 9–10

realism, and photographs, 60, 61
recommender systems, 29, 148–52, 154; *see also* film criticism
Reddit, 118–19
Redfern, Nick, 9–10
Repair Attribution and all That (R.A.T.), 166–7
Roberts, Lawrence G., 6
Rodowick, David, 10
Rope (1948), 118
r/place (PLACE, 2017), 118–20
Runway ML, 127
Ryan, Robbie, 69

Salt, Barry, 8–9, 112
Schäfer, M. T., 8
Schnapp, J., 7–8
sCrAmBlEd?HaCkZ! (2006), 148
scripts, 100
selective focusing, and DenseCap, 41–2
sentiment analysis, 154, 155
shot boundaries, BBC R&D's scene detection algorithm, 35
shot boundary detection, *The Godfather*, 104–9
shot detection, 90, 91
shot scale, 90, 91
'shot-reverse-shot' technique, 102
shots
   as basic units of film analysis, 115, 116
   conceptual redefinition, 117
   digital composition, 118
   see also close-ups (CU); dolly zooms, simulations; long shots (LS)
Silence of the Lambs, The (1991), 93–4, 102
Simondon, G., 49, 78, 129, 174
slow motion, 127

Smith, George Albert, 91, 92
Smith, Lee, 111
social computing, 8
social media platforms, 44
sonification, 111–12
   Dunkirk, 109–11
Soviet montage theorists, 101
space-time *see* cinematic time; continuity editing
Spielberg, Steven, *Jaws*, 100–1
Stability AI, 168
Stable Diffusion, 168–70
Stanford Literary Lab, 88
statistical analysis of film *see* quantitative analysis of film
statistics, consensus/transparency and, 131–2
storyboards, 100
streaming services, 26–30, 148
style transfer, 127
subscription video-on-demand *see* SVoD services
supercuts, 142
support vector machines (SVMs), 132
SVoD services, 27
synthetic animation, 124
synthetic imagery, growth of, 127

Tarkovsky, Andrei, 120
taste, paradox of, 149–50
taste communities, 30
T-distributed Stochastic Neighbour Embedding (t-SNE), 139, 140, 143
television
   decline in viewership, 27
   experimental, 15–16
tensors, 121, 124
text-to-video, 127
text-to-image models, 168–70
Thompson, K., 87, 97, 102
TikTok, 95
Tilton, L., 88–9, 90–1, 97
time-space *see* cinematic time
Tingley, D., 49–50
Tohline, M., 142–3
Tokyo Story (1953), 1
Toscher, Andreas, 29
trailers, 36

Treadwell, Timothy, 100
Tsivian, Yuri, 9
t-SNE, 139, 140, 143
Tukey, John, 97

ultra-wide lenses, 68–9
UMAP, 139, 140, 143
Uncanny Valley (2020), 162
Uniform Manifold Approximation and Projection for Dimension Reduction (UMAP), 139, 140, 143
Unreal 5 game engine, 126
Upstream Color (2013), 154–6
US Motion Picture Patents, 70
user-centred design approach, 151

Vertigo (1958), 125
Vertov, Dziga, 22, 141, 162–3
video erasure, 127
video essays, computational form of, 142

video-on-demand streaming services, 26–30
Virilio, Paul, *Vision Machine*, 5–6
Visual Genome, 47–8, 51, 52
  EXIF metadata, 72–8
  Flickr images, 72, 73
  human labour, 49
VoD systems, 26–30

Weizenbaum, J., 166, 167
Williams, John, 100–1
WordNet, 45

YFCC100M, 51, 52
YouTube, 27

Zeno, 115, 121
Zorns Lemma (1970), 135–6
Zylinska, Joanna, *Nonhuman Photography*, 70–1